FLY FISHING

the Tidewaters of
MARYLAND'S CHESAPEAKE BAY

A Calendar Year of
Stories, Spots, and Recipes

BRETT GABA

Woodcarvings by Danielle Spradley
Photos by A. Aubrey Bodine

4880 Lower Valley Road • Atglen, PA 19310

Library of Congress Control Number: 2015942758

Type set in Adobe Jenson Pro/Minion Pro/Frutiger LT Std

ISBN: 978-0-7643-4884-6
Printed in China

Published by Schiffer Publishing, Ltd.
4880 Lower Valley Road
Atglen, PA 19310
Phone: (610) 593-1777; Fax: (610) 593-2002
E-mail: Info@schifferbooks.com

For our complete selection of fine books on this and related subjects, please visit our website at www.schifferbooks.com. You may also write for a free catalog.

This book may be purchased from the publisher.
Please try your bookstore first.

We are always looking for people to write books on new and related subjects. If you have an idea for a book, please contact us at proposals@schifferbooks.com.

Schiffer Publishing's titles are available at special discounts for bulk purchases for sales promotions or premiums. Special editions, including personalized covers, corporate imprints, and excerpts can be created in large quantities for special needs. For more information, contact the publisher.

DEDICATION

For Hannah,
who neither shares nor understands
my appreciation for old trucks and fine tackle
but lets me own them anyway.

CONTENTS

AUTHOR'S NOTE

COMPASS

I think we need a few dreams, old wives' tales told under the guttering candles of aboriginal belief. If we know better, good for us, but there is argument for fey acceptance of romantic notions shattered by smart scientists.

—Frank Woolner
"When Grouse Catch the Crazies"

Each of the twelve chapters in this book is a story about fly fishing on the tidewaters of Maryland's Chesapeake Bay. Some are set on the open water of the bay itself while others are set at various points within the tidal creeks and rivers that feed into the bay. With nearly 12,000 miles of shoreline and over 100,000 tributaries that make up its total watershed, the Chesapeake Bay is an incredibly diverse body of water that ranges from vast open water, sheltered bays and coves to tidal freshwater creeks edged with forests and salt marsh.

By extension, just as the Chesapeake Bay works its way north from the Atlantic Ocean and spreads its arms into both sides of Maryland and Virginia, the subject of the Chesapeake Bay as a fishery branches and forks as well. Within the main part of the Chesapeake there are bluefish, seatrout, red drum, flounder, and croaker. Farther inland, bay tributaries hold freshwater gamefish like largemouth bass, chain pickerel, crappie, and perch. And above all there are the striped bass, for which the bay is known, living throughout the watershed in high and low salinity alike, delighting anglers with their numbers, natural aggression, and excellent table quality.

In the early stages of writing, as I tried to begin a book about the fish and waters of the Chesapeake Bay, I found myself intimidated by the enormity of what I had come to love as an angler. The diversity of the fishery prompted questions:

- Where did the waters of the Chesapeake Bay realistically begin and end?
- Which waters and fish told the best stories for fly fishermen?
- And how, as a lifelong Maryland resident and fisherman, could I legitimately approach writing a book about fly fishing on the Chesapeake Bay?

The first step in taking any journey is to get your bearings, so the subject of fly fishing on the Chesapeake Bay, broad as it might be, was firmly fixed as my north.

Structurally speaking, I felt like I had two options with my approach. There was the formulaic and geographic breakdown that guidebooks took to large bodies of water that, in my opinion, tended to sound the same after a few sections: the rivers, fly recommendations, and local guide plug all sometimes blend into the same chapter redone and recycled over and over again. Grab your 8 weight and a handful of clousers, the fish will be right off your bow.

On the other end of the spectrum there was something more personal and story-based, the narrative approach that other fly fishing authors, like John Gierach and Tom McGuane, had taken in the past—stories that were meant to entertain first and inform second.

There were strong cases for the first option: guidebooks sell, after all. But I ended up leaning into the second option because, for as long as I've fished with a fly rod, I've looked up to John Gierach: his personal approach, his lack of pomp in an exceedingly pompous sport, and his outward love of fish and fishing—all these things inspired me to write about saltwater fly fishing on the Chesapeake Bay as he might: as a storyteller that's present within the book as a whole. And if Gierach's voice could own and address the cold water fisheries of the American West, then perhaps mine could speak to the Chesapeake Bay in similar fashion.

In this way, John Gierach gave me hope and a beginning: an east.

Between the Chesapeake Bay and John Gierach, I was closing in something, but I wasn't dead-center on a concept yet. My writing struggled to take root or gain momentum. So I continued to stew, to ruminate, to search for a way into this book that I wanted very badly to write.

Looking back now, I'm glad that my writing never really took root in the beginning, because if it had, I would've written Gierach's story of the Chesapeake Bay, not my own. But through this gradual beginning, two things eventually happened: one slowly and quietly, the other loudly and suddenly.

Listening to Merle Haggard one summer, it hit me like a punch to the stomach. I had heard him before and liked him well enough, but on a windy, coastal road in Northern Ireland, between Portaferry and Newtonards, I heard "It's Not Love, But It's Not Bad" through the tinny, blown-out speakers of a small two-door Peugeot. I was drunk (a good daytime whiskey and cider drunk) and on my way back from an afternoon wedding.

My Irish friends were up front, smoking cigarettes and singing along with the enthusiasm that only comes from drunk foreigners enjoying old American music, and I was in the back of the car fighting off the beginnings of motion sickness. Perhaps it was hearing Merle out of normal context, an unexpected piece of Americana played far from home, but the effect was sobering: I heard every word with clarity and felt an intense connection to this dated and rural music that stayed with me long after I came home to Maryland.

I began thinking about Haggard's music and realized that there was something refreshingly straightforward about older country music: the men were unapologetically masculine, the songs dealt squarely with important themes like booze, women, and loss, and the delivery was heartfelt, structured, and rural as a church picnic. I loved that. It felt right to me. And more to the point, I wanted that kind of straightforward country sentiment and imagery within my book about the Chesapeake Bay because I felt that it belonged there. So I embraced the imagery and latent homeyness of old trucks and aluminum johnboats, cornfields and country roads, smoky bars and bathroom graffiti, and run down hotels and pawn shops. These images belonged in fishing stories and this sentiment gave them a working-class legitimacy.

The more I listened to older country music, the braver and more confident I became with my approach. And if a man like Merle Haggard could sing "It's Not Love, But It's Not Bad," then I could write my fly fishing stories with the same sensitivity and rural drawl. If John Gierach gave me a beginning and a voice, Merle Haggard gave these stories the soul of a country music song, and a west to the east that Gierach had established.

My subject was a sprawling body of water, my approach was based on contemporary outdoor writing, and stylistically I wanted to set the folksy craft of fly fishing against the rural backdrop of Chesapeake Bay country. To bind all of this together, I wanted a natural organization to the book, because as Steinbeck says, "Everything in the world must have design or the human mind rejects it." At some point I began considering a seasonal arrangement to fly fishing on the Chesapeake Bay rather than a loose collection of stories. Calendar months became the basis for chapters within the circular construct of a year, and from there the idea of a farmer's almanac emerged.

I came to see that an annual portrait is as natural as the concentric rings in a tree trunk, that we measure our lives in yearly increments and compare them one against the next. There was a symmetry in examining a fishery like the Chesapeake within the context of a year— the understood boundaries of the four seasons, and the framework of twelve months.

Although an annual portrait certainly wasn't a new idea—among fishing writers especially—this approach felt right, and I began to scrutinize these rural and old-fashioned publications that so closely tied readers to the land and the natural world. Almanacs held gardening and fishing tips, they contained astrological information and old wives' tales, and they were dotted with recipes[1], tide tables, and strange advertisements. The more I wrote and planned within the eclectic trappings of an almanac, the more comfortable it felt, like old boots, or a broken-in Filson jacket.

Each month has its own character though, and this character can change from season to season. If you compared notes on every September over a decade in the mid-Atlantic, you'd get ten varying pictures of a month that typically defines the beginning of fall. Some of these images might be calendar-perfect harvest portraits; some might feel more like extensions of August, hot as late summer; and other Septembers might be characterized with a string of late season hurricanes with the early part of the month drenched in heavy rains and latter half spent recovering from high water.

With these natural variances in mind, I plucked the best stories from over twenty years of living and fishing on Maryland's Eastern Shore and stitched them together to form a patchwork quilt for what I saw as a complete picture of the Chesapeake Bay.

In this way, my fourth compass point emerged and the almanac became fixed as my south, that downward pull that grounded the work into the rural and old-fashioned impulse behind the work.

Along with the monthly organization of the almanac there was a reconnection with fundamental concepts that modern life had removed, a different belief system in some ways. I found stories in the facts and scientific truths that I had glanced over previously: that shad will truly run when dogwoods bloom, that the rising and falling tides are in fact waters directly connected to the ocean and pulled by the distance of the moon, and that a compass finds its needlepoint direction through an actual pull of energy running from pole to pole.

Fly fishing the Chesapeake Bay, John Gierach, Merle Haggard, and a farmer's almanac: those were my compass points as I navigated through the turbid, fog-edged, and riddled waters of writing this book. Once these compass points were fixed, the stories began to take root and grow like summer corn.

Perhaps a more straightforward approach would have been easier, but this was the route set before me: a slow, seasonal journey on country roads, through small towns and farmlands, and eventually ending at a boat ramp (hopefully empty) where the tide is just starting to fall and gamefish are beginning to feed in the strengthening current.

Brett Gaba
April 2014

ENDNOTE

[1] **A note on game recipes:**

Like any superstitious jinx, planning to prepare a meal as a result of a fishing trip can bring doom to a day on the water. What they say about the best laid schemes of mice and men—well, the same holds true for game recipes. You cook with what you bring home and nine times out of ten you have to adjust or fill in the gaps with what's laying around. Sure you can plan and portion, but real cooking is based on *methods* of cooking as opposed to *prescriptive* recipes.

The recipes at the end of each chapter are meant to match the month of the year, as well as the fish and produce available at that time. Within them, there are very few instances of exact measurements, but rather a list of ingredients and the broad steps to follow to prepare the meal. In my opinion, these are recipes in the truest sense of the word, those of a verbal tradition passed along in kitchens from cook to cook.

The goodbyes we speak and the goodbyes we hear are the goodbyes that tell us we're still alive, after all.

—Stephen King
Wolves of the Calla

FALL

SEPTEMBER

BAD WEATHER

Capricorn, the sea-goat to the north, rises slowly from the horizon as autumnal equinox and the harvests draw near. Crickets chirp louder as the weather cools, but dry wheat and brittle corn stalks whisper in growing winds. The first migratory Canada geese will begin to arrive and oyster-tongers begin their work in cooler, sheltered waters. Early in the month, look for strong storms coming from the south if leaves begin to show their silver backs.

Mackerel scales and mare's tails make lofty ships carry low sails.

There was a hurricane off the coast, aptly named for a beautiful ex-girlfriend. During the first days of the storm, Michelle's rainy fingertips reached 100 miles inland, stirring up the waters of the Chesapeake Bay and rustling the tips of the marsh grass. The breeze steadily built to an all-out wind, and after a day or so, the blue skies of late summer were gone and the clouds, wind, and rain were there with an early fall permanence. Michelle was 300 miles south, just off the Outer Banks of North Carolina, and slowly walking up the coast.

The summer wasn't quite over. The hot weather would probably hang on for a couple more weeks, but the hint of fall was there for the first time: cool early mornings and hooded sweatshirts in the evenings. Soon enough the water temperatures of the bay would start to drop and the rockfish would venture out of the deeper channels into the shallow tidal creeks to feed on silversides and blue-back herring.

By the time the storm had moved through the mid-Atlantic and into coastal New England, the rivers would be high and muddy and the bay would be full of silt and refuse from the draining tributaries. Everything would be unfishable until a few tides flushed in fresh water from the Atlantic and the runoff in the upper reaches cleared.

There was a strange comfort to the sounds of the storm: rain falling on the roof of my house, the low, cozy sound of thunder with dim lamp lights, the washer and dryer running, AM radio playing—NPR, the Orioles playing in Cleveland, winning some, losing some. With a storm blowing outside, the fishing shot to hell, and plenty of food in the kitchen, there was really no need to leave home, so I stayed in, cooked meals that were far too extravagant for one person, and relished in the sudden slowness of things.

Time. All of a sudden in the all-out sprint of summer—the frantic and fast-paced chase for breaking fish, searching the tidal rivers for largemouth bass in spot after spot, and timing night fishing with the tides—all of a sudden it was late August and I wondered how most of the summer had flown by.

Even before the hurricane, in the background of all of this summer fishing was the sound of thunder and heat lightning in the evenings. There always seemed to be the possibility of a storm, an outside chance that the sky could open up at any time with rain. Now the storm was in the foreground of the picture with Hurricane Michelle moving slowly up the coast, and me trying to wait the whole thing out. It had been raining for five days straight, shifting between mist and a steady downpour, and I prepared myself for a long silence.

* * * * * * *

Most fishermen on the Chesapeake own a waterproof book of marine charts that they bring with them on the water. Some even have large-scale charts of their home waters pinned to a wall with notes scratched here and there alongside thumbtacks. On these charts are numbers and it's easy to get lost in them.

I've never been a numbers guy, but with marine charts, they make sense to me—probably because the trick is to look for big discrepancies: a drop off or ledge that goes from twelve feet to thirty feet, a twelve-foot hole in a shallow three-foot flat, a nine-foot mound in the middle of consistent sixteen-foot depths. A discrepancy like that means that a good current rip sets up there, which means that fish are probably there too, waiting on forage and baitfish to be swept by with a moving tide.

As the storm moved north, I sat at my kitchen table in the soft, gray gloom of the morning and pored over the marine charts of the middle Chesapeake Bay like the morning paper. I'd drink coffee and look at the same page of water and numbers, searching for a clue that would lead me to new fishing, a secret in plain sight that only I was clever enough to find. Of course, no chart ever really gives up a fishing spot that easily. At best they're just loose guides that hint at good places to explore.

There's just no substitute for time on the water, especially when you're dealing with the overall size of the Chesapeake Bay, a large and complicated body of water consisting of open water, smaller bays, sounds, rivers, and creeks. Within all of these parts, even the smallest body of water still needs to be broken down into fishable pieces, and the devil is in the details.

This became plainly obvious to me one day when I fished with Captain Matt Tawes. We were in his twenty-one-foot Parker center console fishing for striped bass and seatrout out in the open water of Tangier Sound. It was late summer, and at that time, the pattern was submerged structure—humps, ledges, old ship wrecks, and rock piles held good numbers of fish in the deeper, cooler water.

We worked a couple spots and pulled in a few fish, but didn't really get into them. Matt kept working at it, and after a lot of motoring around and fiddling with his GPS Captain Matt slowed down and took his boat out of gear. "Start casting," he said.

We were in the middle of open water with very little land visible on the horizon. There were no current rips visible anywhere and the depth finder was reading a steady depth of nine feet. I thought that a channel might be nearby or some kind of mound or depression that would hold fish, but the surrounding water seemed more like a flat that you'd find near shore.

Looking on the depth finder, shapes became visible—boulders the size of cars scattered over about two acres– with rockfish holding just off them. There was no visible hint of this in the opaque and algae-rich water of late summer and none of this structure was marked on a marine chart.

We had a good day fishing 7 and 8 weight rods with sinking lines and full bodied clousers. The stripers ran between sixteen inches and twenty-three inches and we even caught a few elusive seatrout before the day was over, beautiful fish with a purple sheen over mottled, olive-gray sides and yellow fins. We had steady bites until the tide stopped running around 3 p.m.

Toward evening on our way back to the boat ramp, we caught good numbers of croaker from a deep hole on the Manokin River and kept half a dozen of the smaller ones for dinner. To me, croaker is best filleted and dusted in seasoned flour, fried past a golden-brown crisp, splashed with lemon juice, and finished with Old Bay seasoning. Croaker prepared like this are more of a fried indulgence than a Chesapeake delicacy, but it's a simple way to enjoy a plentiful panfish from Bay waters, and served with potato salad and tomato slices, it's an absolute delight.

Driving home after dinner, I thought about the water we had fished and couldn't believe that an area like that boulder field wasn't marked on a chart. It wasn't like we were fishing a structure the size of a jetty or rock pile—which are typically noted as navigation points—but this area spread over acres without any visible structure anywhere.

Of course, Matt's a licensed guide and a hell of a fisherman. He was born and raised in Crisfield, Maryland, and if anyone should know about a spot like that, it's him. My point is that even a detailed chart of that area doesn't begin to hint that structure like that is there, and that discovering a spot like that can only happen through real-life exploration.

There's just too much water, the conditions are constantly changing, and the structure you're fishing is usually smaller than a car. Even a bridge can be skipped over on a marine chart pretty easily, and think about the size and amount of structure that comes with a typical bridge—maybe 10 bridge pilings plus the remnants of whatever bridge was there before the new one was built. That's a lot of fishable structure.

There's a comfort in knowing that much of the Chesapeake has been explored and charted and that so much information is available for those who choose to do a little research. Charts might not be perfect blueprints, but the outlines are still useful. At the same time, there is something nice in knowing that some places can still remain wild and secret, and that public information still doesn't replace practical knowledge and experience.

For me, fishing is an aggregation of learned secrets: finding spots like the boulder field, beaches that drop off right to deep water, flats that fish better on rising tides than falling tides, and creeks full of bass holding structure. I was worried that the hurricane would change the face of the Bay that I had come to know over the past ten years, maybe not drastically, but enough for me to lose the edge that I had gained. I thought about this as the rain continued to fall outside and the rivers ran higher and swelled with muddy water.

* * * * * * *

Michelle stalled off the coast of Virginia, but eventually moved up through Delaware and into New Jersey. At its strongest, the wind knocked down trees and power lines while the rain saturated the ground and flooded the rivers. Even after the main body of the hurricane had passed through, there were still wispy remnants that brought occasional rain showers between the clearing skies.

I had been getting out on the water quite a bit that summer, so after nearly two weeks of being cooped up in my house, I was starting to get cagey. During those days I did what most any other fisherman would've done: I tied flies, organized fly boxes, cleaned fly lines, pored over marine charts, and thought about where I should fish once the weather cleared.

There were two different areas that I wanted to check that I thought might be good bets if I timed them right: the upper reaches of Marshyhope Creek off the Choptank River, and open water structure in upper Tangier Sound.

I was concerned about the short-term and long-term effects of the hurricane. The land on the Eastern Shore of Maryland is mainly coastal farmland. Local farming practices haven't always had the health of the Chesapeake Bay in mind, and the boom of housing developments removed much of the coastal plain forests that once filtered water draining into the rivers and then into the Bay. Because of this, an overabundance of nutrients from septic tanks and fertilizer run unimpeded into river waters under normal conditions, so part of me wondered how the hurricane would affect the overall water quality. What would that much mud and silt do to the river bottoms and aquatic vegetation? What would so much fertilizer runoff do to water quality? How would the structure of the Bay and rivers be different after the waters cleared?

Considering that the natural coping mechanisms had been removed from the landscape and even more manmade problems had been introduced to the ecosystem, the potential for a hurricane to really alter the Bay was truly there. But as far as the fish themselves were concerned, I imagined that the largemouth bass would be eager to sight feed after so much time hugging the bottom, and out on the open water of the Chesapeake, I guessed that it would take two or three surges of incoming tides from the Atlantic to bring Bay conditions back to normal, and the stripers would be on the feed again.

I hoped that the fish felt the same way I did—just plain anxious to get back to the way things were before the storm.

* * * * * * *

Marshyhope Creek was in pretty good shape, considering the amount of debris and water that Michelle had pushed through there. The edges of the creek with thick stands of lily pads and spatterdock had been pruned back from the wash of the hurricane. Trees had also been uprooted and knocked down, washing downriver to make new tangles along with the old laydowns.

The water was still pretty muddy at the put-in near Federalsburg, and I felt like I might have been a few days early. But as I headed up river against the falling tide, I could see that the water clarity was improving bit by bit. By the time I had paddled two miles upstream to the skinny upper reaches of the creek, I could see a dark fly in a foot of off-colored water.

I started fishing with a 9 weight rod rigged with a floating line and a deer hair popper for no other reason than that I love catching bass on the surface with these flies if I can. There were plenty of laydowns, new and old, where I could cast up against, along with edges of spatterdock and lily pads. But after fishing promising water for over an hour with no takes, I decided that the bass just weren't ready to come to the surface so soon after the storm.

I switched to an 8 weight rod rigged with an intermediate line and a black and olive conehead wooly bugger tied with extra long hackle and lots of marabou. The darker color stands out better in stained water and the longer hackle helps the fly suspend in the water so I can fish it slower. So much of largemouth bass fishing requires a fast and aggressive retrieve that it's easy to lose sight of delicacy. I've always found bass to be equal parts predator and brooder; they are capable of chasing a streamer back to the boat and slashing at it at the end of a retrieve without fear, or they're just as likely to hold underneath a deer hair popper, methodically examining every detail of the fly until its patience wears through.

It took me a while to figure out that the bass were in a subtle mood and that they didn't want to chase flies; they wanted to study first before they struck. I cast along structure and let the fly sink slowly, twitching it every now and then, but consciously letting the deliberate pauses in the water work for me as much as the fleeting action of the fly.

On the second half of the ebbing tide the action finally started to pick up. My first bass came from a pocket in a long stand of spatterdock. One moment I was slowly twitching the fly along, giving it time for its hackle to sway and pulse in the current, and then some time during a pause in my retrieve I found that I was connected to a fish. This kind of slow fishing makes actually connecting with a fish seem more like a miracle than usual. One moment you're holding a rod in your hand, barely doing much else then maintaining contact with the fly, and then all of a sudden there's a fish pulsing on the end of your line. The fish ran and sloshed at the surface before I could hand-line it into the boat. I lipped it and dropped it back in the water.

To me, the first fish is always the most satisfying, sometimes even more so than the occasional hog. Although I certainly feel awed and grateful when I'm lucky enough to catch a big fish, I know that I am always thankful when I catch the first fish of the day. Under normal circumstances I can go out and catch a few fish, although there are certainly times when I won't catch a thing, but the difference between each of these results always leads back to that first fish, the fish that tells you that the day holds possibility and that other fish might be willing as well.

I caught other fish like the first of that day, almost carbon copies of each other: stocky two and three pounders, olive green with a single thick dark band along their flanks and pale undersides. Bass from tidal rivers always seem to put up a stronger fight than the same fish from a pond or lake and I'm always surprised by it; there just seems to be something about the current, tide, and brackish water that make for stronger fish.

Near the end of the hurricane, while I was planning my next outing at my kitchen table with marine charts spread out in front of me, I had thought that the bass would be frantic to hit anything resembling food after such a long time of rain and high water. But what I found was that the fish were still hunkered down from the storm, and that they had to be coaxed with a suspended fly to get a strike. I wasn't 100 percent right about the whole thing, but I wasn't 100 percent wrong either, which on any day fishing is really all you can ask for.

* * * * * * *

There's an intimacy that comes with fishing the small upper reaches of tidal creeks and rivers in a kayak or small boat. As a fisherman, you are a tangible part of the environment in scale to your surroundings. I've just preferred fishing this kind of water because small water is beautiful to me.

Of the Outer Banks striped bass fishery, Captain Brian Horsely once said, "One from the beach is worth ten from the boat." The point being that of the two, fishing from the surf is the more accessible, but the more challenging. I find fishing the inshore waters of the Chesapeake comparable to that: most people can do it, but it's hard to really get a handle on it, so one sixteen-inch fish from a tidal creek holds more challenge than a twenty-inch fish from a school of breakers. There's just something in my outdoorsman's personality that finds value in doing things the hard way.

That being said, there is an excitement that comes with fishing the open water of the Chesapeake—slowly motoring out of a boat ramp or marina, pushing down the throttle, and blasting to the next marker two miles out—that you simply don't get with small water fishing.

As I headed out from the Dames Quarter boat ramp, I planned on fishing a series of rock piles from the Nanticoke River on out through Hooper Strait to the main stem of the Bay. Along the way, there were visible and submerged piles at Great Shoal, Sharkfin Shoal, Hooper Strait, and the Holland Island Bar and I thought that fishing spots like this—

from river mouth, to sound, and out into the main Bay stem—would give me a good idea of the water quality after the storm.

Over the years, I've had mixed luck at each of these spots—some fished better on rising or falling tides, while others fished better in the morning or evening hours. Smarter men might have found the science behind all of this, but lately I've honestly come full circle: I think that it ultimately comes back to luck. Sometimes the fish are where you're fishing and sometimes they're not. And sometimes the fish are there, but they're just not feeding.

Either way, as an angler you don't have any control over it, but at worst, you spend the day on the water. Even the best poker players have runs of good and bad luck and they have to play the cards they're dealt no matter what their skill level is. With the right mindset, fishing can be a win-win proposition.

The Great Shoals rip is all that remains of the base that held a nineteenth century lighthouse at the mouth of the Wicomico River. Now it's just a submerged rock pile that serves as navigation aid for boats and barges heading upriver to Salisbury. This structure also holds striped bass on falling tides. I had a feeling that Great Shoals would be the dirtiest water I'd see all day so I wasn't too surprised when I saw that the water was still pretty muddy.

As I motored up next to the rock pile and drifted past the markers, I saw that the water was still pretty dirty and that there were still signs of debris—the occasional log or Styrofoam cooler—drifting with the current. The current was just starting to ebb at that point, but after ten casts, a snagged fly, and not even a look or nibble, I decided to move on to Sharkfin Shoal.

The water was much cleaner at Sharkfin Shoal and the tide was running at a good pace. This rock pile is actually visible above water and, over the years, I've caught most of my fish from the eddy that forms behind the rocks, so I usually start fishing that area first. Without anchoring, I just drifted into position, made a cast, and began my retrieve, and within a few strips I was connected to a fish. I landed a young seventeen-inch striper, an inch short from being a keeper, and dropped it back into the water. This short fish turned out to be the big fish of the day.

I had drifted out of position at that point so I had to motor back to the rocks and anchor into position. The fishing was pretty steady for the next hour and a half, but the fish got smaller and smaller. At one point I was catching fourteen-inch bluefish and stripers that eventually turned into hefty white perch. With the fish still biting, I decided to pick up and move on to the Hooper Strait rock pile.

The next two spots didn't yield any fish at all. The Hooper Strait rock pile was usually one of my go-to spots in the summer that gave up stripers, along with the occasional seatrout and bluefish, but as I motored around I wasn't even marking any fish on my fish finder. I stayed and worked it pretty thoroughly, changing rods and flies a few times, but I eventually bagged it and headed south to the Holland Island Bar. It was the same story there: cleaner water, a dying tide, but no willing fish.

I felt like I had itched whatever it was that needed scratching. Like a few days before on the Marshyhope, I had been half right and half wrong about what the conditions and fishing would be like, but I had still managed to catch a few fish.

One thing you get from being holed up for over two weeks in the middle of fishing season is a sense of perspective. After all the gloom and rain and inaction, it was honestly good to be out of the house and on the water again. By late afternoon the wind started to pick up, the first signs of another tropical depression, Nadine. So I packed up, pulled up the anchor, and headed north for the long bumpy ride back to Deal Island.

Smoked Bluefish
with Potato Salad and Arugula

Smoking bluefish is a nice way to take advantage of a firm, oily meat from a plentiful Chesapeake Bay gamefish and the beginning of fall just feels like a right time to smoke something. When blues are running in the 2–3 pound range, I like to keep a few for the smoker because the meat from younger fish of this size seems to be flakier than larger, older fish. Once caught, I bleed the fish immediately, and then put them on ice.

Ingredients
- · Filets from 2–3 pound bluefish

Ingredients for Brine
- · Water
- · Equal parts salt and sugar
- · Peppercorns
- · Bay leaves

Wood chips
- · Mix of maple, cherry, and hickory

Ingredients for Potato Salad
- · Small red potatoes
- · Bacon, cooked crisp and crumbled
- · Green onions
- · Fresh tarragon
- · Mayonnaise
- · Dijon mustard

- · Arugula bed for each serving

Directions:

Back home I fillet them and remove the skin and brine them overnight. Nothing too extravagant here, just water, salt, sugar, peppercorns, and bay leaves. The next day, I'll set them out to dry for a few hours on wire racks. (My wife's cookie cooling racks work incredibly well here, but it drives her crazy when I use them for this.) It's a little unnerving setting raw fish out to dry like this, but this step really helps the smoking process.

Depending on my patience, appetite, and the fish itself, I might smoke the fish with a mix of maple, cherry, and hickory chips for anywhere between three to five hours. The fillets that I use aren't typically too thick, so they cook fairly quickly, and it's really a matter of taste that dictates how long I smoke them. Unlike the brighter pink of salmon, smoked bluefish has a woody brown exterior while the inside stays fairly white.

To make the potato salad, I chop the red potatoes and boil in salted water. While they boil, I dice celery, chop green onions and tarragon, and crumble bacon. I add all of these to a bowl along with mayonnaise and mustard. Once potatoes are cooked, I strain them and cool them down with cold water before adding them to the bowl with the rest of the ingredients. Toss and let chill in a refrigerator.

On a plate, add a bed or arugula, top with a generous scoop of potato salad and smoked bluefish.

OCTOBER

JANES ISLAND RITUAL

Neat cords of firewood are tucked beneath the dry eaves of sheds, stacked and ordered like books on shelves, while Aquarius in the northern sky pours water from a bottomless vase. Emboldened by the reds and golds of maple and oak, squirrels gather acorns for the encroaching winter and busy themselves in the rafters and joists of the forest. Wait to harvest the unexpected purples of kale until after a few frosts: this will sweeten them. A lowering Saturn and waning moon at the beginning of the month keep an Indian summer at bay.

There are no ugly loves,
nor handsome prisons.

Loblolly Pines, c. 1970. Chesapeake Bay from Kent Point. Loblolly pines frame Jefferson and Poplar Islands.

CRISFIELD

To get to there, you follow Maryland State Route 413 heading south from Westover, and it's a good, straight road and newly paved. Or it was new the day we drove down it. You look down the highway and it's straight for miles, with fresh black asphalt and a school bus yellow band down the center. All around there are golden-brown tracts of corn and soy stretching on for acres and the weedy remains of the Pennsylvania Railroad train tracks flanking one side of the road.

It was mid-October and I was driving ten miles over the speed limit in the buttery sunlight, every now and then passing produce stands piled high with bumpy gourds, Indian corn, and festive, orange pumpkins, caught in the autumn delirium on a direct, never-ending road. After a few hours on the road, the 1,000-yard stares had settled in, and if I had zoned out completely, I would have ended up in town—in Crisfield—where the road stops dead at the docks and, all of a sudden, you're nose to nose with Tangier Sound and the moored work boats and the seafood packing plants on Somers Cove. But I snapped to at the last moment and eased my brakes, just as I saw the truck ahead of me start to make the right turn to Janes Island.

There were three of us headed into the marshes to fish: me and the two Propper brothers, David and Matt, who I had befriended years before when I was living in Salisbury. David and his brother were hauling a twenty-four-foot Palomino camper with his Ford F350, while I followed behind towing a sixteen-foot Polar Kraft johnboat with my small Toyota™ truck.

It had become an annual event, evolving over the past six or seven years from an exploratory day trip to a well-planned excursion that lasted for close to a week. Between the three of us, we had the johnboat and camper, three kayaks, and enough food, fishing, and camping gear to outfit ten guys for a month. It was probably overkill, but I think it amounted to how three grown men quietly express their excitement for a greatly anticipated trip: with over-packing, over-planning, and unbridled consumerism.

The Janes Island State Park campground is set in a stand of tall pines. It's quiet and orderly, and, in late October, effectively devoid of campers. By the time we checked in, got settled, and built a fire, it was getting late in the afternoon. The sunlight was beginning to slant, which brought a slight chill that felt comfortable and seasonally appropriate. The air smelled of dry pine needles and a number of wood fires. Off in the distance we could hear the occasional rifle shot, someone either sighting in their 30-06 or poaching.

We weren't exactly roughing it. David's camper and our ample supplies aside, the campsite was close to the boat ramp, there were hot showers and clean bathrooms just a few feet away, and the camp store sold snacks, firewood, and pretty much everything else we might need while we were there. On top of that, Crisfield was just a few miles to the south if we really needed something—like a night out in a small-town bar, or dinner at a local seafood restaurant.

I got some sausages and pasta salad out of one of our coolers and handed out beers to Matt and David. Before we'd even cast a fly or hooked a fish, we all felt downright victorious. There's always an excitement to the first night in camp, but that first dinner felt distinctly celebratory, although none of us could put a finger on what exactly we were celebrating—besides just being there. We were in camp, the weather was beautiful, and, for the first time in our years of making this trip, it felt like we had really timed it right.

While the sausages grilled over the fire and there was still some daylight left, we started organizing rods and gear for a quick departure in the morning. It was mainly just busy work though—I knew we'd each tied and retied leaders half a dozen times over the past week. Our fly boxes were full and organized. Tide tables were printed out and memorized. The water conditions were perfect, the tides looked good, and if the shallow water bite was on, it'd be now.

Sometime between my third beer and second sausage, it started getting dark. We talked before heading to bed and decided to try fishing the skinny water from our kayaks first thing in the morning. If that didn't pan out, we'd take the boat out into the open water of Tangier Sound to look for breakers.

With the mild weather, I opted to sleep in my tent while the brothers snored happily inside the camper. I could still hear them from outside and wondered what it was that made them impervious to each other's snoring. Shared blood maybe, or years of sharing a room in a small farmhouse.

* * * * *

The protected tidal creeks surrounding Janes Island State Park are uniquely set up for exploration by small boat or kayak. Locals call this "the guts and ditches," and in October they provide ideal conditions for saltwater fly fishermen when falling water temperatures bring striped bass from the deeper waters of the rivers and bay into the shallows to feed before winter drives them south.

Janes Island itself is surrounded by small tidal creeks with pockets of deep water. There's one main channel on the island's east side that separates it from the mainland. It leads to the larger water of the Annemessex River to the north and Tangier Sound to the south. Within the maze of tidal creeks are shallow bays and ponds that open up and spread out. One moment you're paddling in the tight quarters of a water trail no more than ten feet wide and three feet deep, hedged in by tall marsh grass and the occasional tough coastal pine, and then you turn a corner to find herons and egrets stepping quietly through the open water of a salt pond that's inches deep. Much of this water is very shallow, but woven throughout are deeper channels where fish will hold to feed on baitfish and blue crabs and grass shrimp as they're swept by with the tide.

The campground has a wide boat ramp with a small pier and bulkhead. It's nicer and less crowded than your standard Chesapeake Bay boat ramp, and there's also a low, floating dock complete with rollers that make launching a canoe or kayak extremely easy.

Fishing from a small boat in these undeveloped marsh creeks is a nice change of pace from the late summer open water and structure fishing that tend to dominate things mid-season. You get the intimacy of smaller water along with larger-than-typical stripers. The top water bite is consistent, the water is clear, and the fish are aggressive. Plus, if the shallow water bite isn't on, getting out into Tangier Sound is easy enough. The typical fall pattern of schools of breaking fish in open water is there for the taking.

All this brought us to Janes Island again and again. Get the timing just right, and the weather would be crisp and lovely, the baitfish would still be around, and the stripers would be feeding aggressively in clear, shallow water. It's the perfect combination of events for fly fishing, but like any natural occurrence, the balance is fragile and not necessarily tied to a specific month or date. All things being equal though, mid-to-late October is a fair target and a good enough guess.

* * * * *

These trips to Janes Island rank among my favorites. The destination is close enough to home where the fishery feels familiar, but far enough away from my usual haunts that there's a slightly foreign quality to the fish and surroundings. Little differences, really: coastal scrub pines just a little more common, pelicans sighted more often, and less of the steep bluffs and mountain laurel that you see farther north. A trip to Janes Island is right in between serious business, natural curiosity, and casual ease—a good place for a fishing trip to be.

Over the years, each of our trips to Janes Island brought varying combinations of suffering and good fortune. One year the stars seemed like they had aligned. The reports of a solid shallow water bite the week before sounded promising, the weather was predicted to be overcast and mild, and it was looking like we had timed our trip perfectly. But two nights before we got there, a bitter cold front moved in unexpectedly, a stiff wind picked up, and the fishing basically shut down for four days as we shivered in our tents and out on the water.

That year, we stayed inside the water trails because the wind never stopped howling and Tangier Sound was a choppy, frothy mess. There was a small craft advisory on the marine radio, but we already had all the signs we needed in the trees and marsh grass bent to the wind. So we stuck inside the creeks casting at shoreline drop-offs and the deeper ditches from my johnboat.

Every day that week it felt like the water was empty, but we worked it anyway. Each of us went through the motions: cast in the wind, retrieve with numb fingers, repeat. I think we all lost any hope of connecting with a fish by the second day, but none of us wanted to quit. So we doggedly stuck it out in the windy gloom, layered up and sipping coffee from a thermos for warmth, hoping for a break in the wind that never came, and casting into the constant wind. For a few days we launched the boat and worked one side of a tide for a few hours. It was an unspoken relief each time we saw that the tide was dying and the thermos was empty—and that it was time to head in.

Once we loaded the boat onto the trailer, we'd drive straight into town for a bowl of crab bisque or oyster stew, taking our time with second and third cups of coffee before heading back to the campground. We'd get the fire going again and sit around it, watching it like television, before returning to the chilly seclusion of our tents.

I remember the discouragement of the poor fishing and the weather, but I don't recall having a bad time. We were doing what we wanted after all, and there was a strange satisfaction to enduring conditions like that. And, on the bright side, it wasn't like we'd paid thousands of dollars for a guided trip and out-of-state fishing licenses halfway across the country.

I'm sure at one point each of us thought, "What the hell are we doing out here?" but at least we were giving it a shot. You never really know how these things will turn out. And so you stick it out, find the good in the bad, even if one week earlier the temperatures would've been in the 50s and our thumbs would've been raw from the number of fish we'd lipped.

Then there was the year that fall never really materialized and an Indian summer lasted well into November. The fishing was decent but slow, with far more seatrout in shallow water than typical. We'd fish in shorts from our kayaks during the day, and in the evenings we'd head out into Tangier Sound in my johnboat to look for breaking fish at dusk.

If the tide was moving, each night there would be schoolie stripers mixed with two- or three-pound bluefish breaking under flocks of birds. We'd motor out into Tangier Sound, just past one of the first green markers, and there they'd be—gulls and terns diving under a pink-blue sky, stripers and bluefish slashing through the chop, and doomed baitfish caught between them. It was fast fishing for around an hour: cast, connect, unhook, cast again. Sometimes I'd just stay at the wheel to keep us with the moving school as David and his brother cast into the chaos, and after a while we'd switch off.

As the tide stopped running and daylight weakened, the action slowed and the adrenaline wore off. We'd look down to see the deck of the boat cluttered with hastily discarded flies, pliers, and a few half-eaten baitfish that had been spit up by bluefish as we were unhooking them. It was cooler on the water with a moderate breeze, and we knew once we got back to the campground we'd be prisoners to its still, muggy heat enclosed within the pines.

We'd eat a quick dinner and sometimes get ice cream sandwiches from the camp store. Then we'd try to sleep in our tents on top of our sleeping bags, with a chorus of katydids and crickets singing late into the night. Sometime before dawn I would wake up shivering and climb inside my sleeping bag for a few more hours of rest.

The days and nights were hot, but in the early mornings it was absolutely beautiful out on the water. We'd launch with mist hanging over the creek and, as we paddled out into the marsh, we could see signs of baitfish being pushed against shorelines by stripers and seatrout. It was tricky fishing, and it took us a day or so to get a handle on just how spooky the fish were. We used intermediate lines, and small weightless flies like mushmouths and deceivers cast to one side of the action. The water was very shallow—two or three feet usually—and the fish were touchy as hell. But if we found them actively feeding and we stopped paddling well off the shore, we could drift in to make a cast or two before the spot was blown.

Nearly all of the seatrout that year were around the same size, stout fifteen and sixteen inchers with mottled, olive-gray sides, yellow-edged fins, and the telltale canine teeth at the front of their mouths. David caught a solid nineteen-inch monster one morning from an undercut marsh bank. He didn't see any baitfish activity, but he made the cast on a hunch and thought he was snagged before he realized it was the weight of a heavy fish. I tried to help by netting it, but between two kayaks, a nine-foot fly rod, and a heavy fish, it started getting ugly, so I backed off.

David finally boot-landed it after the fish was tired enough. He tried to revive the exhausted fish; its gills were still moving, but it was starting to roll on its side. Somewhat guiltily, he said that we might have to keep it for dinner—and as if on cue, the fish understood the gravity of the situation and finally kicked its tail and swam away. We had a good laugh over that.

Each day on Janes Island that year was hotter than the next. I remember our last night being particularly uncomfortable. I'd taken a cold shower before turning in and removed the fly off my tent. Not a breath of air came through the mesh windows, and I could hear the sibilant cadence of the Propper brothers snoring from inside their tent. Just a few moments before drifting off, I considered checking into a hotel in town for a good night's sleep in air conditioning. It was October 22 and a few weeks later it actually snowed.

The next year it rained the entire time. This was the first year David had his camper, so it was an absolute luxury. Instead of grilling hot dogs in the rain and roughing it in damp tents, we ate and played chess in the dry comfort of the camper. And once the presto tempo of the rain on the roof slowed to a spotty largo, we would put on our damp waders and head outside.

We actually did pretty well during the first few days before the waters muddied up. We didn't know how much time we'd have between downpours, so we'd motor through the creeks from one ditch to another and take turns casting into the deeper water to see if anyone was home. Each hole would give up a few decent stripers, typical Tangier Sound fish that just seemed a bit stouter than fish we'd catch in the upper Chesapeake around the Bay Bridge and Kent Island. The fish were active and fearless, following flies back to the boat, slashing at poppers a few times before actually taking them, and schooled up on the flats where we could sometimes see them tailing like bonefish.

On the fourth day it rained all night and all morning, and when we went down to the boat ramp we didn't even launch. The water was a muddy mess and there was no point in heading out. It was time to pack up, grab a big breakfast in town, and head home.

* * * * *

So often while we planned and prepared for these October trips to Janes Island, I'd let myself imagine the marsh and the fishing. It wasn't drizzly rain, constant wind, or muggy heat that I envisioned, it was calendar-perfect harvest pageantry combined with the excitement of the fall fishing pattern of the Chesapeake Bay. And although we had gotten to the edges of this vision, we had never really hit it head on.

I think that's what we were celebrating that first night: the realization of the fantasy. We were each pleased to finally experience a true autumn camping trip in Janes Island. We'd caught fish there and soldiered through the heat and cold and rain with varying levels of success, but this year, the initial signs felt auspicious.

The Propper brothers are Eastern Shore natives, born and raised outside Salisbury, Maryland. They're active sportsmen, and they have a casual, lifetime knowledge of many of the rivers and waters I love. They both drive big Ford trucks, they're both comfortable around farms, and they both own dogs. And although they're active fishermen, they both detest waking up early.

After years of friendship, I knew that it took a subtle hand to rouse them, and that a head-on approach would just drive them deeper into their beds. I've found that merely making coffee or frying up some bacon usually gets their attention without having to push too hard.

So once I was up and dressed that first morning, I considered getting a fire going in the fire pit and cooking there. The morning had a frost to it, and there's nothing quite like coffee percolating over a wood fire on a fall morning, with bacon frying in a cast iron skillet. But knowing that David and Matt were comfortably entrenched in the camper, I let myself inside and started cooking breakfast in the small, efficient kitchen. They were up and moving by the time I had some breakfast sandwiches made and I was drinking my second cup of coffee.

We launched our kayaks at the boat ramp and right off the bat Matt caught the big fish of the trip, a beautiful twenty-six-inch striper, while David and I were still in the process of launching. He caught it on light tackle, within sight of the camper, just casting to the shoreline opposite the boat ramp. I remember pushing off from the floating dock and looking up to see Matt's rod bent over. I started digging for my camera as I drifted closer to him.

"I've worked that point almost every year we've come here, just messing around while I waited for you guys, and this is the first fish I've ever pulled off it," he said after I took a picture and he let the fish go. With trophy fish swimming right next to camp, things looked promising.

Our original plan was to head south out of the campground and then take the blue water trail up into the marsh to see how things went. But since we had found willing fish close to camp, we took it as a sign and started fishing right away. We split up as much as we could in the narrow channel. I took one side and the brothers took another, leapfrogging each other as they cast at the shorelines while we worked our way south.

There wasn't a lot of visible activity, but the fish were there and they were more than cooperative. David said he had a few follows and soon he was hooked up. I paddled until I saw a water depth I liked—five feet with a sharp shoreline drop-off—and only had to make a few casts until I connected. My first fish was around seventeen inches, just under keeper size.

I think we were all surprised that it was easier than expected. We hadn't even paddled that far or been on the water for that long, and without much work or hardship, we would cast and connect with fair regularity. It wasn't nonstop action, but it was steady fishing. And more than all that, it had never been this good—mid-size schoolie stripers caught in shallow water with relative frequency.

Matt had said he could feel that first fish swiping at his jig as he reeled it back, so on a hunch, he just stopped working the lure and let it dive until the fish finally committed. I took the same approach with the clouser minnow I was fishing—I'd cast out, retrieve for a few strips, and then let the lead dumbbell eyes do their work, making the fly dive for the bottom as I stopped retrieving. Sometimes the fish would hit right away, other times they'd wait until the fly was diving down. More than a few times, like Matt reported, I could feel the fish short-striking. It took a little getting used to—having the patience to essentially stop my retrieve around the same moment I felt that a fish was interested.

I alternated between two rods: a 6 weight with an intermediate line and a 7 weight with a 175 grain sinking line both tied with black and orange clouser minnows. Most of the fish came off the 6 weight, but I'd switch over to the 7 after I had made a few casts to some of the deeper holes when I wanted to work some of the deeper water. A few times it made a difference.

David stubbornly fished poppers and gurglers on an 8 weight and floating line. I don't think he fished a subsurface fly the entire trip that year. He didn't catch as many fish as Matt or I, but I admired his dedication. It's not often that you get perfect conditions to fish topwater flies, and he wasn't going to squander the clear, calm water, the willing fish, and the mild weather. David also has that predatory patience that a lot of big game hunters have. He'd rather focus on catching a single big fish his way than mess around with smaller fish some other way. I'm unapologetically on the other side of that school of thought, happily preferring quantity over quality.

Matt fished light tackle and caught a ton of fish. Fishing light jig heads with four- to six-inch plastics, he could effectively cover more water and make quicker casts than David and I with our fly rods. He'd get in five or six casts per drift before needing to paddle or reposition, where David and I would only get in two or three. That might have bothered me any other time, but since we were all catching fish with regularity I didn't hold it against him.

The fishing was steady, but there was a time limit on it. Without fail, each day once the tide stopped moving, the fishing would shut down. As the week progressed and we got a better handle on the water pattern, we started exploring some of the shallower inner creeks and ponds that we hadn't gotten to before. We'd start out at slack tide, using the down time as paddle time. By the time we got to where we wanted to fish, the tide was beginning to rise or fall. And the deeper we went into the marsh, the more aggressive the fish got. It was almost like largemouth bass fishing, where fishing pressure had a direct impact on fish activity, and with the marshes so empty and the fish so aggressive, it felt like no one had paddled there in weeks.

Most days we headed south out of the campground from our kayaks to fish the main channel, and then we'd poke up into the yellow and blue water trails for the small marsh creeks. In the evenings we'd head north to the open water of Acre Creek in my boat. Most of the time we stayed out in the main stem, sometimes working our way to some of the main waterway intersections with nice ditches that always held a few fish. We did most of this with my trolling motor down, so we could quietly move through the shallow water with the outboard trimmed up. In a lifetime of fishing the Chesapeake, it was the first time I ever thought a push pole would be handy. The water was shallow and glassy calm.

The only boats we saw that week were heading past us to the bigger open water: the fishermen looking at us like we were crazy to be fooling around in such skinny water with fly rods, the Propper brothers and I looking at them, wondering if they knew they were wasting a ton of gas to pass up splendidly willing fish.

THE SEAFOOD CAPITAL
OF THE WORLD

It's impossible to talk about Janes Island without mentioning Crisfield. On one hand, you have the marshland and the waters of Tangier Sound and the Chesapeake Bay, but on the other are the people and their heritage. Much how Janes Island is iconic of the Chesapeake's fall fishery, Crisfield is a small town whose prosperity, past and present, is directly tied to the health of the bay.

In the early 1900s, Crisfield was the second largest town in Maryland, with a population of more than 25,000 dedicated to exporting the Chesapeake Bay's seafood all over the world. As the self-proclaimed Seafood Capital of the World, it goes without saying that the town was built upon the business of crab and oyster—literally. When it came time for Crisfield to expand, the industry's soot and discarded oyster shells were used to fill in the marshland in the town's southwest corner, making it stable enough to support new construction.

By the 1920s, there was even a baseball team, the Crisfield Crabbers. But as the health of the Chesapeake Bay declined and catches diminished, so too did the town's economy. By the 1940s, the Eastern Shore Baseball League folded, and by the '70s, the railway stopped service into town. Stores began closing, people moved on, and watermen who had plied the waters of the bay for generations began urging sons and daughters to look for another line of work.

Nowadays, the population of Crisfield is around 2,000. Many of the residents still work as watermen or within the two or three remaining seafood plants, and the connection to the bay is still prevalent with annual festivals complete with crab races and oyster shucking contests.

After a few days of steady and impossibly good fishing, the frenzied need to spend so much time on the water had waned. We were sated, pleased, and consciously thankful. So on our fourth day there, we got off the water early and headed into town for a seafood dinner.

A meal at Waterman's Inn had become a steady part of our Janes Island trips. Their jumbo lump crab cakes are a first-rate extravagance, but my favorite combination has become a cup of their crab bisque with a shot of sherry, along with a fried oyster sandwich on a potato roll. You get all the shellfish the Chesapeake has to offer, and you still have room for a piece of Smith Island cake. David and Matt both prefer Waterman's fish and chips—usually fresh rockfish, but sometimes locally caught flounder.

I remember the drive into town that year: the dated architecture of the empty buildings and storefronts downtown, the low, gray clouds with traces of a pink dusk poking through, the Halloween decorations and kids riding bikes, and the waterfront condos being built within sight of crab shacks on stilts out in Somers Cove. Yes, it was a town that was a shadow of its early success, but there was also progress—and the decided feeling that this was home.

I looked over a real estate magazine as we waited for our food, fantasizing about the cheap housing costs and the proximity to so much good water. As a fisherman, it's easy to consider relocating when you are faced with the possibility of so many wild gamefish: seatrout from the skinny water around Janes Island, stripers from the open water of Tangier and Pocomoke Sounds, croaker from the Manokin and Annemessex Rivers, even flounder from Chincoteague and Wachapreague were just a short drive to the coast. It might be hard to get by in Crisfield, but living was cheap, and the fishing would be fantastic year-round.

When I look at the life I've built in a city far from a fishery like this, in terms of happiness, time, and money left over, I wonder if I'm any further ahead than I'd be if I had chosen a simpler life on the Eastern Shore. A modest place to come to in Crisfield might eventually be in the cards, but for now, David's camper once a year would do just fine.

* * * * *

The brothers left the next morning to head home for something nauseatingly wholesome—either a church picnic or a nephew's birthday party—and I stayed on Janes Island for one more night. Although the laughs and camaraderie of the past few days had been welcome, it was nice to have some solitude and quiet. I had planned on just staying at the campsite and using the rest of the firewood, but on a whim, I walked to the campground office and asked about the back-country campsites on the marsh islands.

The ranger said that both were open, but fires weren't permitted. They weren't real popular in the summer when the horseflies were a nuisance, but after the first few frosts, it got pretty nice for the right kind of person. He said that last bit rather pointedly, and gave me an appraising look as if he were trying to decide if I were the right kind of person.

"The nicest one is about two miles from the boat launch in the Flatcap Basin. I'm actually heading out to do a round through the water trails if you want to come with me and check it out," he said.

It was a nice offer, and with just a handful of other campers there, I figured the ranger must have been pretty bored to ask. I accepted and we headed out in his Carolina Skiff.

We motored quietly through the marsh, and it felt mildly liberating to be without a fishing rod. Although I had been intently studying the water for the past few days, I had not noticed much of the marsh. The marsh grass and phragmites had begun to dry and it had the same golden-brown color of the roadside soy and corn. I saw the occasional redwing blackbird clinging to a stem of marsh grass while its trilled whistle saluted us. Above us an osprey perched on a dead limb on a pine tree. Every now and then there was a small splash on the surface of the water—perch, spot, or baby stripers.

Between two shorelines of marsh grass was a natural sand beach with a boat landing that extended into the water. The park ranger pulled the throttle out of gear well off shore and let the boat drift with the light wind up against the wooden landing. I jumped out and he motored off, saying he'd be back in twenty minutes.

I walked up a path through some small dunes, and at the end was a small copse of scraggly pine with the campsite up against it. Another path lead down to another beach, this one much larger. That was the western edge of Janes Island facing the open water of Tangier Sound and Smith Island off in the distance. Part of me wished that David and Matt were there, while another part of me was glad that I was on my own.

For years I had looked at the Janes Island map and wondered what camping at one of these sites would be like. Coming out here with the park ranger had just been out of politeness, probably much like the invitation, but my mind had been made up the moment I went in to ask about the back country sites, maybe even before that.

Once the ranger picked me up, we headed back in and I filled out the back country permit. Within half an hour, I broke camp and loaded up my truck, packing just the basics in my kayak: one fly rod (my 6 weight with an intermediate line) and one box of flies, my tent and sleeping bag, a soft side cooler with food and a gallon of water, and a change of clothes. It was only for one night and one morning, but after the relative safety of friends, and the comfort of electricity and plumbing, it felt a little intimidating to be heading off into the marsh alone.

When compared to the bed of my truck filled with food and gear, I thought I had been Spartan when I loaded up my kayak, but once I was under way I saw that my boat was riding noticeably lower in the water. I had considered trying to fish as I paddled out, but decided to paddle the two miles or so to the site first. I'd try fishing once I set up camp for the night.

This was my first time paddling a heavily loaded kayak and like many maiden voyages, it wasn't exactly perfect. I hadn't thought to balance the load, so I was listing to port, and over-correcting with stronger starboard paddles against the wind and tide the entire time. By the time I had covered the two miles out from the campground out through Flatcap Basin, I was fairly tired, but I felt relieved once I saw the shape of the boat landing in the distance. I beached my kayak and began unloading and setting up camp.

Once I set up my tent and carried everything up from the beach, I saw that I had an ethical dilemma. There was a fire pit at the campsite and it had clearly been used recently. But the ranger had been nice as hell and he had clearly told me that fires weren't permitted. Although I hadn't brought any of the seasoned firewood with me, there was plenty of moderately dry driftwood on the beach to make a small fire. So, I had a decision to make. On one hand was respect for park rules, but on the other was Machiavellian enjoyment of the moment. I decided to stew on it while I spent my last evening on the water.

I fished that evening from my kayak, heading north out of the marshes into an area known as the Rock Hole that opened up into Tangier Sound. There was a falling tide, and I knew that fish might be stacked up outside the mouth of the tidal creek, waiting for baitfish and other forage to be swept out of the marsh with the tide. I positioned myself well above a current rip and began casting into a modest breeze. I could see small slashes through the rip occasionally—nothing too sizable or violent, but clear feeding activity.

My first few casts yielded some small schoolie stripers, but soon the rip and the feeding stripers were out of my initial casting range. By then, the water was moving at a good clip and I was anchored in less than a foot of it. I decided to get out and wade. As the tide continued to fall, the position of the rip changed and I could adjust to it much easier on foot. The bottom was hard sand.

I fished and followed the rip off shore, and after a while I looked back to see my kayak sitting in wet sand. Once I was finished, I'd have to drag it a few yards to water, and then again to the deeper water of the channel until it was serviceably afloat. Where I was fishing, it looked as though the water at the mouth of the Rock Hole had yielded to the substantially deeper water of the sound. I was basically standing on the ever-shifting sand bar just inside the creek mouth and casting to where the waters of Tangier Sound began. The wind had picked up and there were some grayish clouds scuttling by as the dry marsh grass rustled and pulsed. I noticed that while the evening had a distinctly autumnal feeling to it, it wasn't the welcoming harvest fall that I had felt up until then. For the first time that season, it felt like winter was approaching.

As the tide continued to pick up, a nice school of fish had set up in the Rock Hole rip. Most of the fish I caught were on the smallish side, between a foot and fourteen inches, but near the end of the evening I had a take that was incredibly solid and jarring. One moment I was stripping my fly through the strike size of the tidal rip; the next, my rod was pulsing and my line was heading west toward Smith Island.

I found myself wishing that I had chosen my heavier 8 weight instead of my six, but I fought the fish with the butt of the rod and tried to slow it down with my lighter saltwater rod. And for a moment, I felt like I might turn it, but just like that, the fish shook its head and the fly came unbuttoned, and there was that sudden heartbreaking stillness at the end of the line. It wasn't a bad knot or a bent hook, just an unlucky failed connection, and then silence.

That was the sign to head back in, and the crucible of the trip. I was alone in the marsh, and although I was disappointed by not landing or even seeing the fish, I was still fundamentally thankful to have had the days in Janes Island that I was given. We had caught a ton of fish, more than we had expected or deserved. Part of me still wonders what that big fish was. A large striper? A late season redfish? Maybe one of those doormat flounder that were occasionally caught by bait fishermen? I know that it doesn't matter, but of the many fish that have gotten away, the memory of this one still rings bittersweet.

Paddling back to the campsite was tougher than I anticipated. The tide was still falling and I was working against it, but by then the water was much shallower, and a few times I had to get out and drag my kayak behind me to find the deeper channel that would lead me back to Flatcap Basin. It was nearing dark as I got back to camp, and I pulled my kayak well up the beach and even threw the anchor out for good measure to ensure that it would be there in the morning.

The wind had died down and after the sun had mostly set, a frosty chill settled into the marsh. My fleece and waders were damp with sweat and bay water from the effort of the hike and paddle back in, and once I was finally still I noticed that I felt cold for the first time. I decided to keep moving and before I changed into drier clothes, I walked down to the beach to gather some driftwood for a fire. The decision for a campfire was at least backed by a need other than aesthetics.

After carrying back a few armfuls of branches and driftwood in the weakening light, I waited for full dark before I lit the fire. At the western horizon the sky was the dark blue of old glass bottles but above in the darkening sky there were early stars and a low half moon. To the south I could see the faint glow of Crisfield, Aquarius just above it.

Others before me had done it, I told myself as the fire began to take, and the ranger or anyone else who might see the fire had left the park hours ago. The smaller bits and pieces of driftwood caught easily, but it took some time for the larger logs to finally take. Once a few of the bigger pieces had caught, the fire started kicking out some real warmth.

I changed into my dry clothes and as I sat near my illicit fire, the chill in my body finally started to drift upwards with the woodsmoke. I had never fully understood the genius of a Whelen tent until that moment; the clever gift of being sheltered, yet open to nature, while still being close to a fire.

Fried Oysters with Old Bay Whipped Butternut Squash and Jalapeño Creamed Corn

There's something about harvest vegetables and fried oysters in autumn. As squash and oysters come into season and sweet corn is getting scarce, this recipe bridges the gap between fall and winter nicely.

Ingredients
- Oysters
- Vegetable oil or shortening
- Garlic salt and pepper
- Evaporated milk
- 1 egg
- Flour
- Old Bay Seasoning, to taste

Ingredients for Butternut Squash
- Butternut squash
- Olive oil
- Old Bay Place seasoning, to taste
- Chicken stock
- Heavy cream

Ingredients for Jalapeño Creamed Corn
- Ears of corn shucked and washed
- Jalapeño, diced
- Red pepper, diced
- Onion, diced
- Garlic, minced
- Butter
- Heavy cream

Directions:

Preheat oven to 375°

   Peel, de-seed, and cube butternut squash. Spread on baking tray, coat with olive oil, season with Old Bay Place on lower rack in oven.

   While butternut squash roasts begin grating corn. A large cheese grater will work fine, if you don't have a corn grater. Grate corn into large glass bowl catching the milk and tops of kernels down to the cob.

   Dice jalapeño, red pepper, onion, and mince garlic. Mix with shucked corn along with butter and heavy cream. Spread corn mixture into pie dish. Top with a few pats of butter and place on the top rack of the oven.

   Heat vegetable oil or shortening in dutch oven on medium-high heat. Remove oysters from liquor and pat dry. Season with garlic salt and pepper. Whisk evaporated milk and egg together.

   Dredge oyster in flower, dip in evaporated milk mixture, and dredge oysters for a second time in flour.

   Fry until golden brown. Set aside to dry and season immediately with Old Bay.

   When corn has golden brown edges and squash is fork tender, remove from the oven to cool. Turn off oven, but place plate of fried oysters into oven to keep warm.

   Empty squash into the bowl of a standup mixer. Add chicken stock and heavy cream and begin mixing until thoroughly blended into the consistency of mashed potatoes.

   Place a large serving spoonful of whipped butternut squash on the plate and top with a smaller spoonful of creamed corn. Finish with an arrangement of fried oysters.

NOVEMBER

THE BIG HAPPY GOODBYE

Early in the month, Sadie Hawkins stands forgotten against a busy wall of holiday decorations and grocery store sales. Pisces chases the summer in the night sky, heading south for warmer days while Venus and Jupiter reach their heights. Crab apples ripen in the autumn mornings, their tartness broken with bright foliage and a sudden flush of grouse. An Indian summer at the end of the month prolongs the fall harvests, but cannot keep the holidays at bay.

If a woolly worm has a longer middle brown band, the coming winter will be short and mild; the shorter the brown band, the longer and more severe winter will be.

Oyster Tonger, c. 1948. THE MOST DIFFICULT JOB IN THE WORLD—Tonging oysters by hand from the bay bottom is tough, cold, rugged work. Men go out in small boats with rakes on the ends of handles that sometimes measure twenty-four feet in length. Most of the tonging is done in the cold weather when ice frequently forms on the handles. The teeth of the rake scrape the oysters off the bottom. Special areas are set aside for the hand tongers; dredgers are not allowed there. If either finds the other infringing, an argument ensues. This photograph appeared in a January 1949 *Sun Magazine* article that identified the setting as Tilghman Island, Maryland.

I t had been a drawn-out fall, which let the baitfish to linger, but by early November in southern Maryland, the oaks and maples were still a golden-yellow canopy of gold and burnt-orange edges. The corn was tall and dry, the soybeans were a brittle brown that rustled low to the ground, and, out in the fields, there were a few combines at harvest with dust clouds floating above them.

I was heading through St. Mary's County to meet Captain Pete Dahlberg for a day of fishing out on the middle Chesapeake Bay. Pete had a mixed bag planned: first we'd look for breaking fish in the open water of the Bay as we crossed over to the Eastern Shore, and once across we'd fish the shallow water around the islands through the falling tide, then later in the afternoon we'd start heading back to port where we'd mess around with more breakers and fish some middle-bay structure as we worked our way home.

Although fall had taken its time this year and the temps were still fairly mild, a stiff wind had picked up the day before, and Pete had reached out to say that we didn't need to launch too early as the winds looked to die down later in the day. Driving down from the city into that beautiful stretch of land between the Potomac and Patuxent Rivers was an absolute pleasure that morning. I had a full cup of coffee, I was on time, and that perfect golden sunlight that comes with clear fall mornings in the country lit the world in an optimism that couldn't be at all clouded.

We met at Buzz's Marina off St. Jerome's Creek near Point Lookout. Out on the dock there was the working-class odor of gasoline and oil from the outboard motor coupled with the light baitfishy smell of organic decay in brackish water. The wind wasn't too bad in the protected cove we were in, but looking up at the swaying trees on a hill above the marina, it promised to be fairly choppy with a falling tide and a wind blowing from the south against it.

While we loaded our gear, there were quick introductions and handshakes with the other guys fishing with our charter that day, and in short order we were motoring out of the protected creek into open water to begin the bumpy ride across the bay to fish the shallow waters around Bloodworth Island.

* * * * *

Captain Dahlberg is a retired Air Force captain with the leftover timbre of military authority in his voice. Being both a New Yorker and ex-military, he's a world class ball-buster who loves nothing more than airing good stories about the anglers he knows on the boat and ribbing guys for every little thing. It wouldn't come off as charming if he wasn't such a nice guy.

Pete's built his reputation as one of the most hardworking guides on the Chesapeake Bay. He knows the fishery like most captains and has his share of spots up his sleeve that seem impossible to sniff out from a chart. But there's also an energy and enthusiasm when you're on his boat that you can't help but notice and catch. It's clear that he guides because he loves fishing the bay and knows what he's doing. And even though he's been guiding full time for over fourteen years, I swear he still gets excited to see people catch fish on his boat.

Pete isn't known as a fly fishing guide, but he lets them on the boat anyway. He's mostly a light tackle guy and knows the middle Chesapeake Bay fishery very well: if the fish were there, he'd put us on them, and then the ball would be in my court as a fly fisherman. For years, I'd honestly just been dying to fish with him because I knew he'd get us into good fish, so I decided to call him up one day to see how he'd feel about guiding a fly fisherman.

He was extremely open to having me aboard, and for shallow water fishing, he wasn't at all concerned, for the breaking fish he saw the advantage, and for the mid-bay structure, he was willing to let me give it a shot if I was.

Sometimes Pete sends word out to his email list when a scheduled trip starts to unravel, and a group of guys can fill the open spots. This is a pretty cost-effective way of getting out for a full day of guided fishing if you don't mind fishing with strangers. Pete has a network of decent anglers who like fishing with him, so they tend to be pretty nice guys, and the system seems to work for the right kind of angler— frugal, easy going, and anxious to get into the kind of fishing that a guide like Pete typically experiences.

This trip specifically had a nice mix of anglers with a retired Smithsonian butterfly scientist, a dry-waller, and a mutual friend and fly angler, Joe Cap. Joe's a custom rod maker at Shore Tackle on Kent Island, and he brought a few rods for me to try out. It was a diverse group—socially, economically, and generationally—and throughout the day we talked between casts and in the brief moments as we motored between spots over the roar of the Honda outboard.

I think it's a good thing to go on trips like this and to get out of the routine of fishing your typical haunts with people you know. It's also nice to be the only guy fly fishing sometimes, fielding the typical questions and good-natured ribbing that can come from light-tackle anglers.

On this trip specifically, it was just a great group of guys with easy conversation and polite curiosity about writing and fly fishing. We talked about spots we'd fished in the area, the forgotten superiority of fall apples, and the unique and masculine satisfaction that comes with building a house.

The ride across the bay was quick and comfortable. Pete's boat is a twenty-seven-foot Judge Chesapeake with a generous cabin and a broad deck where four anglers can fish comfortably. We were nearly across to the islands when we stopped and cast to a school of breaking fish in the choppy open water. There were gulls, terns, and pelicans working a small school, and after two casts I was hooked up with a decent fish.

The fresh, conditioned fight of these November rockfish was simply incredible. As we worked the school of breaking fish, I could feel the smaller fish jab at the fly, just testing it out until one of them finally committed and punched it with fully committed force. The fights were short-lived and violent. After I played the fish to the boat, I'd lip it, unhook it, and cast again in to the school, and after a few aggressive strips, it was the same thing all over again.

* * * * *

Anyone who thinks that a guided fishing trip is a guarantee for success is probably disappointed with life in general. Sure, there are moments of overall superiority out on the water, and having a guide who knows what they're doing can provide a distinct advantage. New waters, coaching, and the benefit of having an expert introduce you to a known or unknown fishery all improves your effectiveness on the water. The range of a larger boat can also open up more options, and more fish can be caught, larger fish even.

What I've found over the years is that you basically pay for a guide's gas and knowledge, everything else is still dependent on the overall conditions and your ability as an angler. When I head out with a guide, I'm hopeful for fish, but understand that the conditions are out of everyone's control, and my skill as an angler is what ultimately accounts for fish in the boat.

By this point in my life, I can say with confidence that I know how to fish the way I like to fish, and I've been around the Chesapeake Bay enough to know the what's, where's, and how's of most of it. I know and understand angling tactics, reading water, seasonal changes, and fish behavior, but the reality is that we all get into ruts and we go and do what typically comes natural, whether that's the best decision or not. Sometimes it takes another angler's perspective to give you a new way of looking at water that you think you know intimately and that's the kind of clarity that I don't mind paying for occasionally.

From a tactical standpoint, what I learned that day was that with that sudden change in conditions Pete was constantly looking for clean water. The strong wind had worked up the bay into a frothy mess, but inland in the protected waters, it was possible to see the darkly colored clean water (dark because it was clear and you could see through the weed beds below) in contrast to the chalky, muddy light water.

Once we found clean water, we'd work the shorelines and points, even the edges where the dirty water met the clean, sometimes connecting with good fish, but with increasing regularity after the tide began to rise again. One of the best fish of the day came in the skinny water: a twenty-eight-inch fish that the butterfly scientist pulled off a point.

We were fishing in the creeks of South Marsh Island, in water that I hadn't fished before. I had fished the channel edges around these islands mostly in the spring and summer, never in the fall, and certainly not up in the small creeks that weave throughout them. As we motored through, I saw that there were shockingly deep holes through many of these creeks and guts. We'd move though these small waterways and, all of a sudden, the water would drop down to twelve feet and the fish finder would be stacked with fish. Each one of us remarked that we'd never known to even look for these ditches, and I'm not sure I could find them again if I tried.

* * * * *

It was good spending some time on the boat with Joe Cap. I've known him for about fifteen years now, and because he's always been a few steps ahead of me in the fly fishing business, I've always looked up to him. When I met him, he was already writing articles about fly fishing before I had begun to take writing seriously, and he had already devised a few clever fly patterns of his own design before I even bought my first vise. He had all of the glamour of a rod company pro-staffer to someone who could barely afford the reel on his rod, and even more than all that, we saw eye-to-eye on things, like the importance of fly fishing for perch and other panfish in a world dominated by largemouth and striped bass.

I like fishing with Joe because he's an expert caster and it's like having an instructor alongside you as you fish. He knows about all of the technical and instructional corrections, he's incredibly patient, and also possesses the rare gift of knowing when to back off and just let a guy fish. Like Pete, he has an innate love of the Chesapeake Bay and the outbound desire to share this joy with others.

I think it's always helpful just to watch someone who really knows how to cast. Watching Joe, it was clear how little physical effort he put into casting, and just how much work the rod could do to propel the fly line out. We were fishing in a decent breeze, nothing unmanageable, but something you had to consider as you picked the line off the water and began your back cast. I think it's common practice to try to muscle a fly line into the wind, to cast quickly and overcome the breeze with a sharp double haul in an effort to punch through the resistance. Joe's casting technique in comparison looked like the wind wasn't at all a factor. The line shot out in perfect, effortless loops over the water, with just a few false casts to work out line.

Seated on the cabin roof with a cigarette in his mouth, Joe could make a better backhand cast than any of my best forward casts when I was standing. His casting style was very much his own, a natural sidearm cast where much of the line is up in the air and casting as a fly line is meant to be cast with a powerful loop fueled by a deep bend in the rod.

Watching him was a double-edged sword. On one hand, it was incredible to see someone cast so far with such little effort and it was beautiful to watch. But on the other hand, it was a little unnerving to be casting in front of someone so talented.

It was refreshing to see someone cast a fly line the way it was meant to be cast, and by extension, it was illuminating to cast a rod that was mean to be powered by a deep bending, slowly developing back cast. The rods that Joe had built at Shore Tackle's weren't spiritless production rods—they had old souls and a craftsman's sentiment. They were meant to bring the beginnings of fly fishing back into saltwater fly fishing, nodding to a time before fast-action rods were the only game in town.

So many of the saltwater fly rods that I had owned over the years had fast, punchy actions that it felt strange to feel the power of a rod load so progressively. It took a little getting used to, but once I forgot the hurried casting rhythm I was so used to, I finally felt the rod working for me happily.

Joe had tied a few flies specifically for the trip, reverse clousers that used about one-quarter of the hair of a standard clouser, but still had the thick, pulsing profile that would get a fish's attention. Because the flies were fairly sparse, they cast easily, and sank quickly in the water, even though the eyes he tied them with were fairly light.

Pete took his twenty-five-foot boat into the creeks and guts of the island and we worked the shallow water that afternoon with good results. Later, we worked our way out of the small waterways and cast at the island shorelines, pulling good fish out of the stump fields and main points as the wind settled down.

* * * * *

The day went by fairly quickly. We'd snack as we moved from spot to spot, talking quickly over the roar of the outboard, drinking water when we remembered that we were thirsty. We finished the day out in the open water of the bay, messing around with a few schools of breaking fish out near the Target Ship, an old World War II destroyer that the US Navy sank in eighteen feet of water to use as target practice. It's a huge, rusted-out, and battered vessel, and every once in a while the Coast Guard will come out and chase off anglers casting at the rusty structure when the Navy flies over to drop duds onto the deck.

Once Pete got tired of chasing the breaking schools of fish, he motored over to the Middle Grounds and we worked the deeper water structure where a huge school of fish was holding. He'd motor above the humps and we'd cast out, letting our jigs and flies sink down into the deeper water. Once we were at least fifteen feet deep, we'd start retrieving, and after two to three strips, I'd feel the familiar weight of a good striper.

Throughout the entire day, Pete was always looking to put us onto more and better fish. The guys on the boat were experienced fishermen, and he'd fished with them a few times and knew what they were about. He'd let us make a few casts at each spot and, if the action was steady, we'd stay, but if it didn't produce, he'd start the engine and move on to the next spot.

He takes a largemouth bass fisherman's mentality to his bay fishing, working a spot and then quickly moving on if it didn't pan out.

"There's a ton of water and structure out here, and only so much time in a given day to fish it. No point in wasting time with water that's not producing when there are so many options," he said as we gunned between spots.

* * * * *

Breaking fish are one of the iconic fishing scenes of fall on the Chesapeake Bay. It's possible to see breaking schools throughout the year, but fall is when this pattern emerges as a steady fixture. Often out in the open water of the Bay stem, or in the big water of river mouths or secondary bays and sounds, schools of striped bass will blitz on schools of baitfish. They'll push these small fish to the surface, slashing and jumping after them with energized fury. Birds will see this action in the water and will fly in to investigate, hovering over the water and diving into the chaos to feed on the baitfish on the surface.

The flock of working birds is usually proportionate to the size of the school of baitfish and gamefish. I've seen small, fast moving schools that were more trouble to cast to than they were worth, and I've seen countless terns and gulls diving, wheeling, and working over acres of breaking fish. Sometimes the fish have been so thick that I've foul hooked them as I retrieved my fly back to the boat.

The size of the fish can be variable. Most often there are skinny schoolie stripers in the fourteen-inch class, scrappy and voracious eaters that can be impossible to keep off a small clouser fished in the first five feet of the water column. Larger fish are usually found in the deeper water beneath the school. I will often fool around with the smaller fish in the surface first, and once I've scratched my breaking fish itch, I'll wait until my fly has sunk ten to fifteen feet below the surface before beginning my retrieve.

Sometimes a smaller fish will still hit a fly as it drops through the school, but other times the waiting can pay off with a larger grade of fish. I've even caught other species, like red drum and seatrout, hanging beneath the schools to pick off wounded baitfish as they fall from the chaos near the surface. In the fall, one of the hardest parts of fishing to breaking fish on the Chesapeake Bay for me is ignoring the school of small willing wish at the surface in an effort to find a larger grade of fish.

Of course, the nirvana of breaking fish is to find that fabled school of twenty- to thirty-inch fish simply going crazy at the surface. It honestly happens—later in the season especially—and anyone who's ever left a school of small schoolies for another pod of breaking fish in the distance has had this potential in mind.

There have been a few times when I've experienced this kind of fishing, although I tend to hear about it more than I actually see it firsthand. And to be honest, I have a soft spot for small schoolies, and on a given day I'm happy to stick with one school through a tide until the action peters out, messing with the smaller fish in the upper water column, and working the deeper water for larger fish. Nine times out of ten, the largest fish I'll catch will be a stout seventeen-inch, a lucky undersized fish just one inch short of being table fare, and that will honestly be enough for me.

Regardless of the grade of fish, wind, current, and the direction that the school is moving are all working against a drifting boat. It's rare for all four factors to align on an effortless drift. Sometimes we'd motor above the breaking school and get in a few casts in before we drifted in one direction, and the school went off in another. Other times we'd drift along with the school for a while, making casts into the school and its edges as the fish and birds worked within easy casting range. But once the school moved off, Pete would tell us to reel up, and he'd work to get us up current of the moving school again.

There's a realistic social component to this kind of fishing, of marine radio code, and boat traffic, and having to share water with other boats and anglers. Sometimes it works out fine, other times you have to stomach some idiocy.

I can remember one fall day when three other boats and I were near the mouth of the Chester River, just north of Love Point, and we were working a small school of breakers. The water was calm and the frenzied activity of the early morning was starting to die down a little, but the school of fish was still feeding with regularity. A few other boats and I drifted along with it, occasionally motoring back into position when we drifted out of casting distance.

From the west, a boat came tearing into the school of fish and pulled right into the middle of our group of boats, in the exact piece of water that the school of fish had been working. The anglers from the ignorant boat made a few casts, didn't catch anything, and then just motored off. One of the guys in a Parker center console swore loudly. Another boat agreed and then left shortly after. I waited a bit to see if the fish would come back to the surface, but after a while, we all knew that the tide was about done running anyway and that the party was over, blockheads aside.

* * * * *

The fishing that day with Captain Pete had been steady, not the wide open action of common thirty-inch that he was accustomed to late in the season, but decent by any standards. The 14 knot wind from the night before had churned up the waters significantly, and throughout the day he was openly apologetic about the conditions. I told him that bit about only really paying for gas and knowledge and he seemed to appreciate it, but the guy's sincerity was still shining through—he really wanted to put us onto better fish.

As we were wrapping things up at the Middle Grounds, there was the bittersweet feeling that the action had built to a crescendo and that it would eventually end. That feeling comes with every moving tide, but in the fall it's compounded. The drawn-out fall had sustained the pattern, and the fish had been on the feed since late September. We'd been enjoying shallow water fishing, breaking fish, and an all-out orgy of aggressive fish in mild weather for weeks now, but there on the deck of Pete's boat, it felt like we were finally and inexorably on the downside of the bite. The current had been pulling us steadily southward for most of the evening, and it felt like the fish were heading in that direction as well.

As we made our final casts of the day, the moon began rising over Smith Island, low and full on the horizon. The sun was setting in the west and the sky was done up in a soft, pink-blue that five tired and quiet men couldn't help but notice and comment on. Along with the knowledge of the stripers' migration, we could see the impeding sentence of daylight savings time and the desolate feeling of early sunsets. The weakening sun that had felt like such a gift that morning suddenly had the first hint of a pale December afternoon.

After a full day of working breaking fish, my thumbs were rough and torn from lipping fish, my fingers had scrapes and cuts from fins and hooks, and there was the chalky feeling of sweat and saltwater on my face, hands, and forearms.

In the wind-blocked warmth of the cabin, Pete started pushing buttons on his electronics and pointed the bow of his boat to the northeast, and we started heading back to port. Back at the marina, Pete cleaned and filleted a decent mess of keeper rockfish with one red drum thrown in for good measure. We had fished hard all day and barely eaten lunch or dinner without so much as a pee break.

On shore there was that open water post-fishing daze: still running off the adrenaline of an exciting day, a little wobbly from an equilibrium adjusting to being back on dry land, tired from rising early that morning, and starving for a decent meal. The goodbyes between me, Pete, Joe, and the other anglers were quick, and soon I was back on the road heading north, back through St. Mary's County where every other road and body of water is named after a saint, and the deer eyes glowed eerily in the fields besides the road lit by my headlights.

* * * * *

Parents always say that it's impossible to choose a favorite, that love spread across children is distributed evenly. I think there are truths and lies to this position and that the same can be said of the full range of Chesapeake Bay gamefish; that their broad variety holds no favorites amongst anglers, and that the swarming tenacity of white perch, the rarity of red drum, and the predatory perfection of bluefish all hold equal shares of most sportsmen's hearts.

When it's all said and done though, I know deep down that striped bass are my favorites. Their handsome profiles, their uncontrollable aggression, and the fundamental fragility all create a likable character, but their versatility is what sells them through: to catch the same species of fish from the beaches of small tidal creeks, to submerged lower-river points and rock piles, and all the way out into the open water of the bay where schools of stripers feed beneath gulls and terns—all of this characterizes a fish that clearly knows where its home is throughout the watershed, and despite the downward trends in their stocks, the poor water quality, pollution, and overfishing, Chesapeake Bay striped bass are fighting to keep their place in their part of the world. If we had a fraction of their toughness, adaptability, and perseverance, it'd be hard not to see ourselves in them.

Each fall brings their year in the bay to a crescendo. They arrive with a flourish in the spring to spawn, settle into the summer pattern, and then cool weather triggers the big feed and eventual exit. And once November comes, we say goodbye to the fish, just as much as we say goodbye to the season, and there's a point in late fall when you know that the trip will tell you that the season is over. You layer up, launch the boat, and head out anyway, hoping for some late fish, but knowing deep down that most of the fish you caught a week ago are in Virginia. And despite the grim outlook, you play out the losing hand anyway and hold onto the outside chance of bluffing a few fish into the boat. This is what you do to close the chapter on November and say goodbye to the fish.

About a week after that trip with Captain Dahlberg, the southward pull of November was impossible to deny on the waters closer to home. The tinny smell of snow and wood fires was in the air along with a pale gray sky above that had winter at its edges.

I launched my boat at Little Creek Landing on Kent Island and, as soon as I motored out from the launch at full throttle, I felt the undeniable chill of winter cutting through my jacket that I hadn't felt before. It was a gray and bitterly cold day, but with light winds and a good tide, the day looked promising on paper. My plan was to do a circuit of Kent Island: first I'd check Eastern Bay to see if there were any breakers left, and if I didn't see any birds working, I'd head out into the main stem of the bay to see if any visible action was there. From there I'd work the pilings of the Bay Bridge, and finally hit the Love Point rip to see if anything was home there. To wrap the day up, I'd head back to Eastern Bay by way of the mouth of the Chester and Kent Narrows.

All in all, the full trip around Kent Island was around thirty-six miles, during which I'd be able to fish everything from breakers, structure, and current rips. Diversity aside, this was a circuit that I hadn't completed once that fall, since the breakers had been so consistent in Eastern Bay. I'd only taken a handful of trips that fall, but without fail, on a moving tide, there would be large schools of breaking fish off Tilghman Point and inside the Miles River that would occupy me indefinitely.

A few times I had made it as far as the Bay Bridge where I could always depend on pulling a few fish from the structure and eddies of the pilings, but for the most part that fall, the small breaking fish kept me happily occupied. Most fish tended to be schools in the twelve- to fourteen-inch class with the occasional keeper thrown in. There was the odd bluefish in the mix at the beginning of the month, but they had grown scarcer and scarcer as the weeks went by.

Other times I had put in at Kent Narrows and fished there, before heading out to the mouth of the Chester and eventually Love Point where I found the same class of breakers—small stripers from twelve- to sixteen-inches with larger fish beneath the school. In both the mouth of the Chester and Eastern Bay, the steady action had conveniently slowed my progress around the island, and the small fish were too fun to pass up with the knowledge that they'd soon be gone. On a few days I fished only my 7 weight with my 8 and 9 weights remaining strung up and un-cast in the rod holders.

So, on that day in November I had a feeling that if anything, I'd be burning some gas and that the boat would get one last good run before I put it away for the winter, and that if anything, this was a November ritual in putting another fall season to rest and saying goodbye to home waters until the following spring.

As expected, Eastern Bay was empty of boats and birds as I headed out of Crab Alley and, after a few fruitless casts over the humps near Long Marsh Island, I pointed the boat south and headed out into the main stem of the bay off the western shore of Kent Island. The wind was starting to pick up by then, but even with a mild chop and moving tide there didn't seem to be much surface activity there, either.

Weeks before, where I had seen acres of breaking fish, countless gulls, and dozens of fishing boats, were now just a few workboats rumbling along the Brick House Bar and a big freighter off in the shipping channel headed north to Baltimore. The water had the silence and solitude of the Ocean City boardwalk before dawn, a strangely empty place so typically full of life.

The Bay Bridge dominated the view as I headed north. Over four miles long, almost 200 feet tall at its highest point, and supported by over 400 pilings from the floor of the Chesapeake Bay, it was impossible not to notice. In the face of so much fishable structure I had a hard time deciding where I should start; knowing that nearly all of the gamefish in the region had left the area compounded my indecision further.

Off in the distance I saw a few birds hardheartedly working in the wash behind the Eastern Shore island. I headed there and in the giant eddy that formed behind the island that supported the huge eastern span of the bridge I cast down into the current where fish seemed to be holding. After counting the fly down to ten feet, I started my retrieve and within three strips, I was connected to a strong fish.

Late fall seemed to have pushed the smaller grade of fish south and what was left were heartier more mature fish who weren't quite ready to leave Maryland. After working the Easter Shore rock pile for a bit, I motored east and started casting to the small eddies behind the bridge pilings and pulled in a few fish. In about an hour and a half of fishing I might've caught four to five good stripers, all pushing twenty inches with one almost twenty-five inches.

The tide was still falling and it looked like I had less than two hours until low tide, so I reeled up and continued north to Love Point to see how things looked there and work myself just a bit closer to home. Although it was only 2:30 p.m., the daylight had a weakness to it that made the day seem colder and December a few steps closer.

Nobody was home at the Love Point rip, and there were no breakers in the mouth of the Chester River as I made my way back to the boat ramp at Little Creek. It wasn't at all the fall pace and pattern that I had enjoyed for weeks through October and November, but it was a good trip to close the season where a few fish had come begrudgingly to the boat before leaving for Virginia. In a full day of fishing I had cast one rod, fished one fly, and burned nearly a full tank of gas in a full trip around Kent Island, but I had caught a few fish and said goodbye to a good fall season on the middle Chesapeake Bay.

Just a few days later, one of those wet, blustery November days came in and tore out most of the fall foliage and put all thought of fall and the Indian summer we'd experienced well out of mind. Suddenly, the first day of deer season was upon us and within the space of a few days, the trees turned the deep brown of a Thanksgiving turkey and were promptly stripped bare by the damp chilly wind, leaving only a few lonely and brightly covered leaves holding fast against December. And just like that, it felt like winter was upon us.

Fall can change that quickly here, and even though most of the fall had been mild and slow moving as honey, now that the whole thing was over and I'd said goodbye to the season, it felt like we had been rushed into winter and that we had somehow been cheated. Things came into perspective as I was driving and I heard during a radio commercial that there were three Saturdays left before Christmas. I looked out the windows and noticed that where gourds and pumpkins had once lined the roadside produce stands, Christmas trees and wreathes now stood in their place.

Broiled Crab
and Rockfish Cakes

My mother came up with this recipe after my father and I came home with less than we had promised. Between us, after a morning of fishing, we had one small keeper rockfish that I'd caught and three blue crabs that my dad had kept while bottom fishing. It's basically a Maryland crab cake with flaked rockfish along with crabmeat to help stretch out portions.

Ingredients
- Fillets from 1 keeper rockfish
- 3 blue crabs
- Water
- 1 bay leaf
- Lemon
- Celery
- Carrots
- Shallot finely diced
- Yellow pepper
- Ritz crackers crushed
  (one half to one whole tube as preferred)
- Mayonnaise
- Eggs
- Mustard
- Worcestershire sauce
- Butter
- Old Bay Seasoning

Directions:

Start with a simple steam or boil for the crabs. Old bay can be used, but much of the flavor will come at the end. For a small number of crabs, fifteen minutes is usually plenty of time for steaming, but cook until a deep orange color and pick immediately. Save liquid and shells for a seafood stock.

Place the fillets in a shallow pan and cover with water. Add a bay leaf and poach until the meat is white and flakes easily. Remove from the pan and set into bowl with picked crabmeat to cool. Use a fork to separate meat into small flakes and chunks similar to crabmeat. Save liquid for a seafood stock.

Preheat the oven to 450°.

At this point, combine the liquid from the crab boil and the liquid from poaching the fillets into one pot. Add the fish bones, crab shells, lemon, celery, and carrots to the pot for a seafood stock. Let this simmer on low heat for an hour. (This stock makes a fantastic base for Maryland crab soup, clam chowder, or cream of crab soup.)

Add finely diced shallot and yellow pepper to meat and toss lightly until even. Add crushed Ritz crackers to mixture to suit needs—around half a tube of crackers for a meatier cake or a full tube for more filler.

In another bowl add mayonnaise, eggs, mustard, and Worcestershire sauce. Whisk until even. Add to fish and crab mixture and use hands to evenly coat and toss lightly. The goal is to bind the ingredients into a workable mixture without braking apart the meat. Use hands to pat and form into cakes and place on a buttered baking dish. Coat each cake liberally with Old Bay Seasoning and broil until deep golden brown.

Serving Suggestion

Serve with fresh succotash and stewed tomatoes.

Man ought to be able to live with himself. Idly. Without going mad.

—Andre Dubus
We Don't Live Here Anymore: Three Novellas

WINTER

DECEMBER

BETWEEN THE HOLIDAYS

Between the holidays it's best to enjoy a meal of venison and fowl with family. Mistletoe and mountain laurel maintain a hue of green within the browns and grays of bare branches, while snow may rise and fall like the tides. Jupiter shines at its brightest and Aries is most visible at this time of year. The Geminid meteor shower reaches its height near mid-month, announcing the winter solstice with a sigh.

Thunder in December presages fine weather.

She Leans, c. 1950. This picturesque ruin is on Kent Island in Queen Anne's County. It is near the former Romancoke ferry terminal and overlooks Eastern Bay. While some of the state's old structures are dilapidated and in need of repairs, there are many others whose owners have either kept them in condition over the years or have restored them to their former beauty. There is much of colonial America in Maryland.

By the end of November, the warm harvest colors of fall had been replaced by the muted brown monotones of early winter. The pumpkins were gone from the roadside produce stands, and the cornfields along the highways had been razed, leaving the soil with a rough stubble of corn stalks. As I drove on US Route 50, the fields were divided by oyster-shell driveways, stands of bare old-growth trees, and the occasional goose blind. Coursing through the Eastern Shore was the feeling that the best fishing was over until March and that it was now decidedly hunting season: deer, ducks, and geese were at the front of most outdoor sportsmen's minds and most fishing tackle had been cleaned and stored until spring.

Although I love the taste of venison and fowl, I've yet to become passionate about this kind of hunting. I respect the dog work of waterfowl hunters, and the food gathering patience of deer hunters, but it's much too sedentary for me. If I hunt at all, I'm more likely to work field or forest with a pointer for grouse, woodcock, or quail.

With limited fishing options, I decided to go to Tuckahoe Lake on the Eastern Shore for an early winter pickerel trip. It was the Wednesday before Thanksgiving and before I left home the wind was blowing close to 20 mph. A cold front had swept in a few days before, and I imagined that the fishing would be slow because of it, but I wanted to get out anyway. While I was packing up my truck, I made a last-minute decision to leave my kayak at home and to fish the shorelines of the lake and the waters of the spillway stream by foot.

Chain pickerel are the last act of the Bay tributary fly-fishing play, a slower, more pensive act punctuated by sudden bursts of action. There are other options: tailwater fisheries like the Savage or North Branch of the Potomac for trout, or a four-hour drive to the Chesapeake Bay Bridge Tunnel for stripers. But chain pickerel are the best bet at this time of year for quick trips close to home. After the stripers head south out of Chesapeake Bay waters, and the largemouth bass hunker down for winter, chain pickerel are still active in our tidal creeks, lakes, and millponds and they will hit a streamer when other fish are dormant or just plain absent.

Pickerel seem to thrive in the cold, which somehow makes sense because they look like close relatives to northern pike with their cruel eyes, green elongated bodies, and toothy beak-like mouths. In fact, they're commonly referred to as pike on the Eastern Shore. And although I have to admit that misnomer drives me a little crazy, I've never actually corrected any local anglers using that terminology. They're not exactly a handsome fish, but they're tough and active when not much else is.

Driving over the Bay Bridge, I wasn't too optimistic as I felt my truck sway in the strong crosswinds, but when I got to Tuckahoe, the winds had all but died down. The southern bank of the lake was being fished by a few other anglers—a busy day by usual standards. I fished the stream spilling from the lake, but the water was low and most of the fishy channels didn't hold any active fish. I worked my way down from the main spillway pool casting streamers against rip-rap, undercut banks, and other structure, but the best I did was a small crappie from the main spillway pool.

Farther downstream was an area that I thought would hold fish. The thick roots from an old hemlock created an undercut bank on the outside bend of the stream. It was possible to stand up-current, cast below without snagging on a tree limb, and swing a streamer through the prime water of the deeper undercut bank. During other times of the year this spot was good for a bass or two, so I figured that a pickerel might be holding there, if anywhere, on the stream. After five or six casts with nothing to show for it, I decided to take a break. I had hoped that the moving water of the stream would be a better bet than the lake, but after an hour and a half of fishing with little to show for it, things were starting to look grim.

By the time I had fished most of the stream and the northern shoreline, it was nearing 4 p.m. The sun was starting to set and I was starting to get a little cold, so I put on a pot of coffee. I keep a small pack loaded and ready for spontaneous trips like this. Inside it I have a simple camping stove, packable pots and pans, a small cutting board and fillet knife, a coffee pot with two mugs, and a kitchen bag with breading, plastic forks and spoons, a few bottles of water, and small vacuum sealed bags of coffee. Although I'm pretty bad at planning a fishing outing, I am very organized with my gear, and I love preparing for the occasional spontaneous trip like this: it gives me validation for owning a small fortune's worth of outdoor gear. And besides, it's easy enough to just have the bag ready in the closet to throw in the truck when I'm loading up.

With a warm cup of coffee in my hands, it didn't seem so foolish to have driven ninety miles to cast to fish that weren't there. For a moment I was very conscious of the present, of where I was—fishing and drinking coffee next to a piece of water that I love, with virtually no one else in sight on a day when the rest of America was stuck in traffic or waiting in line at an airport.

Looking out over the still water of the lake I could feel that the end of the year's fishing season was almost upon me. Of course the fishing is never completely over here on the Chesapeake, but the steady action of summer and fall was over and that had a final ring to it. Three or four months from now, white and yellow perch would start running up the river that the stream beside me fed into: from Tuckahoe Lake the Tuckahoe Creek runs into the Choptank River, which in turn flows into the Chesapeake Bay.

Immediately ahead of me lay a few weeks of pickerel fishing before winter set in for good. I would wait for the warmer, milder winter days to cast brightly colored streamers in the same places I would fish for largemouth bass in the summertime—undercut banks on the stream, lake flats, and shorelines whose shallow waters might warm from the sun by lunchtime, fallen trees, points, and islands. The strikes would be quick and vicious, not completely unlike a bass, but the fight would be more frenzied and erratic.

For the immediate future, at best we'd have a mild winter and the fishing would stay reasonably steady through February. At worst the lakes and rivers would freeze over with the first real cold front of consistent 20° temperatures and real snow. If that happened, I would need to start driving much farther. Either that or just wait it out.

* * * * * * *

A few weeks later and just before Christmas, I decided to take what would be my last trip of the year in my kayak before I put it away for the winter. I had only been out a few other times since my trip to

Tuckahoe and although I had caught a few fish, I hadn't actually hammered them either. As a fisherman, there's something in me that wants to figure the water out, and get it right when I'm out there—not just get by with a few fish. I had been getting by, and I was thankful for that, but there was something in me that knew that a few days after a warming trend in early winter was probably the best time to catch a few pickerel on flies. And I also knew that eventually the fishing had to end, so I had it in my head to go out and do it while I could.

I was driving up Route 213 toward Galena to fish the Sassafras River and there were still patches of snow along the shady edges of the cornfields. We had received the first snow of the year earlier that week, but the temps had risen to the high forties and had stayed there, steadily melting most of the three inches of snow on the ground—good news for me and other fishermen still trying to get out, bad news for the rest of the world hoping for a white Christmas.

One of the things I like about winter fly fishing is that there's not much of a rush to get on the water before 10 a.m. The pre-dawn sprint that I have during the summer and fall mellows to a slower pace. In winter it takes a few hours of the sun and rising temps to get things going, which makes for a slower, ambling kind of morning: coffee, breakfast, loading the truck, and stopping for gas without panic. It was just after nine o'clock when I was outside the town of Galena, and with time on my hands I decided to stop for breakfast at Vonnie's.

My father used to hunt geese in Kent County in the '70s and he met his guides here in the morning before heading out into the fields. Back then, and probably still today, Vonnie's busiest hours were from 4 to 6 a.m. (duck and goose hunters getting ready to head out) with another rush after 10 a.m. (the lucky hunters who got their bag limits early). It's no accident that Vonnie's also serves wonderfully heavy breakfasts, with the best cream-chipped beef on toast with home fries on the Eastern Shore.

Vonnie's also prints the news that the local paper won't cover. Mounted behind the bar is a poster board with the week's headlines written in marker. Some headlines over the years have been, "Mr. John got back from Las Vegas and is still an asshole," "Tom Jr. let a big snapping turtle go in big Tom's pond," "Miss Tammy says that they're still real and to stop staring." Gonzo journalism is alive and well today in Kent County, Maryland.

There's something extremely comforting about eating breakfast in a warm restaurant, knowing that the rest of the day is going to be spent outside shivering on the river. The sounds of low conversation and clinks of the spoons in coffee mugs combined with a full stomach always make me question terms like true sportsmen and real fisherman, but I grudgingly pulled myself out of the booth and paid for my meal. Few things in life give me as much satisfaction as a cheap breakfast in a small, local joint, so I felt like the day was off to a good start as I stepped back outside into the cold and headed for the launch.

* * * * * * *

The sky was a solid gray as I launched my kayak in the cold water of the Sassafras. The temperature felt like it was falling, but there was no wind at all with low, heavy clouds holding steadily above. I felt warm inside my waders and fleece and I flashed back to being young and sledding with my neighbors on a snow day, having that same bundled-up feeling. The steep banks along the river were lined with bare oak trees with stands of mountain laurel, holly trees, and small clumps of mistletoe in the treetops providing an occasional green. It felt like it was about to snow.

In winter there's a silence on the water that's absent during the other seasons of the year. During the spring, summer, and fall there's a huge collection of life and activity on the Chesapeake: insects, birds, boats, and people all create a rich collection of sounds. In winter, the silence is interrupted by singular sounds—a chickadee chirping happily on a dead branch, Canada geese honking in the distance, dry marsh grass rustling, the occasional gunshot from a hunter. Each happens one at a time and is followed by another period of silence.

I set out upriver leaving small quiet whirlpools behind me from my paddle strokes. My plan was to cover some water first and fish my way back to the boat ramp with the falling tide. Along the way I made a few casts to good-looking spots so I didn't get as far upriver as I wanted. It ended up not making much of a difference.

I started fishing with a yellow over white clouser with red flash, hoping that a little color might jar the fish into striking—the mood of the day seemed so gray and wintery that I thought that a fly with a more subdued color might slink by without being noticed. I just started casting at first, working the shorelines and along the channel edges, trying to find a pattern to the fish.

If there was a pattern, I never identified it. The first fish came halfway through my retrieve from a cast in open water near the channel. It was a younger, feisty pickerel, skinny and bright green, and only around eleven inches long, but it seemed like a good omen. My next fish, a thicker fifteen incher, came from an old dock. It hit as soon as the fly landed in the water.

I won't overdramatize landing a decently sized chain pickerel, but it can be tricky. Sometimes they roll like alligators on a short line beside the boat and break off; other times they'll come in easily, letting you net them or grab them behind the head. Regardless of their mood, when they get to the boat, they're full of teeth and simply handling them and removing a fly can take some concentration. Add cold water and numb fingers on top of all that and the potential for blood is honestly there.

By mid-afternoon, the tide had just about finished ebbing and I could drift along slowly with the current, only paddling occasionally, to cast along the banks. I had packed a few rods for the outing, but ended up only using a 6 weight with an intermediate line. Most of my fishing that fall had been primarily with sinking lines thrown on 8 and 9 weights, so it felt like a treat to be able to cast smaller streamers (well, small by striped bass standards) on an intermediate line. I was on my second yellow and white clouser—the first had been pretty mangled from the first few fish—and before I could tie a replacement on, it got snagged on a log, so I had to break it off. I've learned to take moments when simple choices are quickly and decisively made for me without much thought or discussion as gifts.

The fishing wasn't nonstop action that day, but it wasn't exactly dead either—it was all I had hoped for, and better than I had expected for a cold day in December. By mid-afternoon, I had landed around six pickerel. The nicest was over seventeen inches and it hit right at the boat. I eventually had to put it on the reel and found myself reaching for my net to land it. It was a tough, older fish with what looked like a heron scar down its side and it swam away slowly when I released it.

By then it was nearing three o'clock. There was still plenty of daylight, but it had that pale afternoon weakness that comes in winter. It seemed like the clouds had grown a shade darker and I could see the occasional snowflake begin to fall slowly in front of me.

I beached my kayak on a small sandy point that backed to a steep hill of paper birch and began making a small pot of coffee. The calm water of the Sassafras River spread out in front of me and through the light snow I could see the western point of Jacobs Creek mouth off in the distance. The next day would be the winter solstice, the most optimistic day of the year, where the days would grow progressively longer until spring and the perch arrived.

As the coffee began to boil and percolate, the snow began to fall in heavier clumps—big slow-moving flakes that stuck to the ground and the trees but disappeared in the water. It was a good moment, and one of my favorite moments on the water that year, where I had the perfect combination of luck and time. I sat beside the Sassafras River reflecting on fish caught that day and trying to remember all of the others from that year with warm coffee in my hand in the falling snow. The only thing that could have added to the scene would have been a small twig fire, but with the snow getting heavier I didn't want to risk being out too much longer. I still had a decent paddle in front of me on top of a long drive home.

By the time I got back to the boat ramp, loaded up my truck, and peeled off my waders, it was just about dark and the snow was sticking to the road. It took me another two and a half hours to get home—a trip that usually only takes just over an hour.

I walked inside and the Christmas tree was still lit up in the living room, and there were coals from the end of a fire glowing beneath the ash in the fireplace. I made a ham sandwich from the remnants of a huge family dinner earlier that week and sat at the kitchen table in the relative dark. Inside, I could hear the sound of the refrigerator compressor, while outside, I heard the occasional thundering of snowplows. The thickest part of winter was still in front of me, and even though I knew that my time on the water would be limited soon, at that moment, it felt very good to be inside.

Rosemary-Cabernet
Venison Tenderloin

I think there's a tendency for people to overcook game because they're not used to the flavor and they expect it to taste like store-bought beef or chicken. Venison tenderloin by its definition is a tender cut of meat and overcooking it actually toughens it. Cabernet and rosemary add character to the meat, while still letting the venison flavor shine through.

Ingredients
- Garlic, minced garlic
- Fresh rosemary sprigs
- Cabernet
- Sea salt
- Coarse black pepper

Directions:
Marinate the tenderloin overnight in garlic, rosemary, and cabernet.

When ready to cook, set out on cutting board. Pat dry and raise to room temperature. Coat liberally with salt and pepper.

Preheat oven to 450°.

Heat a non-stick pan on medium-high heat. Sear each side of the tenderloin to a dark brown and set on baking sheet.

Finish tenderloin in oven until medium or medium rare. Meat should be around 120°.

Set aside to rest meat before slicing into medallions.

Serving Suggestion
Serve with asparagus and mashed potatoes.

JANUARY

COWBOY HYMNS

Orion and Canis Major walk in the night sky as
Vs of geese honk beneath their feet. Jupiter
joins with a wolf moon late in the month, a
steady eye added to its pale bearing. Use flannel
sheets to warm winter beds, and the dry heat
of electric baseboards to bolster firewood stores.

If your left hand itches, you will get some
money soon, if your right hand itches,
you will shake hands with a stranger.

Someone had written the word "delicate" on the mirror of the men's bathroom in Don's Backstreet Grill. It was penned in oddly beautiful handwriting for bathroom graffiti, a balanced and masculine cursive that stood in contrast to the rest of the hurried scrawling on the walls. I could see my reflection through the word, and I thought about the mismatched context as I washed my hands. Was it the face in the mirror or the glass itself that was delicate? Or was the single word a contrived stance against standard bathroom wall pornography, or other inscrutable messages etched in the drywall there like, "This gum tastes funny," or "Diesel drives a Pinto."

Walking back into the bar from the bathroom, I could smell a blue-collar potpourri of cigarette smoke, fried food, and old carpet—a smell that's oddly comforting if you like places like this. Neon signs and gilded beer company plaques decorated the walls, along with a few painted scenes of ducks and geese in flight. The waterfowl portraits were complemented by a few fish and game mounts—whitetail antlers and mounts, as well as a few lacquered rockfish.

I'd been going to Don's long enough to have a regular spot, a seat near the end of the bar, well away from the entrance so I didn't feel the chill from outside when someone opened the front door. There was a pool table to my left, and often, in the late afternoons, I could hear the occasional sound of pool balls from two old timers playing nine ball. They shot with a light and practiced accuracy, not the over-powered bravado of youth, and after a neat diamond break there was only a light clink of pool balls that was barely audible over the light country music and quiet conversations of the other customers.

Don's was a small, local joint in Salisbury, Maryland, just a few blocks from the small house I was renting. It skewed more towards a bar than a grill, but the food there was surprisingly good, most of the younger college kids in town tended to avoid it, and the bartenders there could be generously forgetful in their final tabs.

Their generosity did not go unnoticed, and it was just one example of the complicated and necessary barter system that was an integral part of our local economy. Between Don's bartenders, my job at the pawn shop, and other bar regulars who worked at the grocery store, auto body shop, and gas station, we had an interconnected and personal micro-economy where our professional generosity was the only thing keeping our bank accounts from dipping below zero.

More specifically, I helped Casey the bartender out when she couldn't quite pay her monthly fee for the jewelry that she has pawned at the shop where I worked, and she let a few drinks slide every now and then and brought out wings or french fries for me to snack on when the kitchen was slow. Another guy, Matt, let us know when meat went on sale at the grocery store, and if something ever went wrong with one of our vehicles, a tall fellow named Steve made a few calls between his colleagues at radiator or transmission places in the area to get the best deal.

We bought and traded in favors and whatever meager professional influence we could use to improve each other's situation. This small bit of help was many times the only thing that kept our rents paid, food on the table, and our cars running. None of us were really thriving—most of us were barely getting by—and although we didn't know each other extremely well, we had the familiarity and polite willingness that came with being neighbors of a sort.

In the evenings when I went to Don's, I brought a notebook with me where I wrote...or tried to write. Most nights didn't yield much, usually a series of notes and unlinked sentences that got progressively less and less legible as my sessions there lengthened, but bringing the notebook and having it in front of me was part of the ritual. This was a time in my life when I felt that drinking alone in a bar was an important part of the process of being a man and being a writer, during winter especially. The distractions of writing at home were too great: I'd find any number of domestic things to do to avoid sitting down to work. I'd cook, I'd watch the same movies again and again, I'd do the dishes or rearrange my living room—anything to avoid the frustration of writing something tangible with a beginning, a middle, and an end.

At least at Don's my time there had a purpose, even if the purpose was shared with a small glass of bourbon. My output there wasn't significant, but there was something I loved about the solitude of it, of being alone in a room full of people with complete focus on a glass and a notebook. At the very least, I could be looked at as a writer, even though I only worked at a pawn shop and wasn't actually writing anything.

After a few months of this routine, my notebook had the watermarked circles of bar glasses as well as the grease stains from food, and contained more school and household to-do lists than actually usable content. Much of what I did manage to write were exercises for a creative non-fiction workshop I was taking, but I looked at these more as tasks than actual projects that I wanted to complete. The hardest thing I struggled with back then was the schism between what I wrote, and what I wanted to write.

"It might snow this weekend," Casey said, and I nodded back to her.

The old timers were wrapping up their game of nine ball, I was getting to the bottom of my allotted two-drink pit stop, and I had just three lines written in a half-breed list of broken poetry and sentence fragments, "delicate, the crunch of frost and loose gravel, necklaces of geese in the sky." There was nothing more written, and no clear reason behind the broad words or images, just a word dump with no action to take or ideas to explore or expand upon.

With nothing much to stay for and no unfathomable need to keep drinking, I said goodbye to Casey. I put my money on the bar, put my jacket on, and stepped out into the cold and early dark of Don's parking lot. I could see the constellation of Orion in the clear night sky. Winter had brightened the stars of his belted waist, the curve of his shield, and his arm raised to strike. Canis Major was off to the east, above the power lines and glow of the gas station across the street.

* * * * *

January wasn't good for much on the lower Eastern Shore, except for drinking bourbon and hunting waterfowl. On the best days it was still and gray with low, gray clouds and a mild threat of rain or snow. And on the clear days there was usually a mean, sharp-toothed wind that started somewhere over the cold Atlantic, punched into the coast, and sliced through the thickest winter coat thirty miles inland. If there was any snow, it wasn't the clean feathery snow of the mountains that sang of wood fires and sledding, but the thin, clingy, dirty kind that was either a muddy slush or a crunchy, slippery mess under your boots and tires. January was a time for hunting, writing, and drinking—not an easy one for fly fishing.

With the stripers gone and deer season over, most area sportsmen tended to focus on hunting geese at this time of year. Migratory and resident Canadas were nearly everywhere, and all around there was a mid-winter baritone chorus of these large birds honking and calling to each other. The heavy birds flew above in low perfect Vs, stood out in the fields, and swam in cold waters in great numbers. Their strangely unoffensive shit was everywhere.

Sportsmen traveled from all over the country to shiver in a pit or blind as they waited for geese to wheel and lock their wings as they were snared by the decoy's promise of food and company. Part of me understood the draw. The meat was certainly worth the effort and the dog work of retrievers was a joy to watch, but it just didn't take with me. The sedentary part of goose hunting didn't appeal to me, even though it was undeniably one of the main draws of this time of year. I envied those waterfowl hunters who spent all summer and fall waiting for winter to come.

Before I moved to Salisbury, I had lived on the upper Eastern Shore for nearly ten years and fished the middle Chesapeake Bay for much of that time. I'd haunted the waters north of the Bay Bridge up to the Susquehanna Flats, and south from there down as far as the Honga River. During my time there, I'd established my habitual and seasonal spots from years of living in the region and a healthy amount of time spent on the water.

Relocating to Salisbury opened a whole new world to me: the water of Tangier and Pokomoke Sounds; the isolated creeks and wrecks around Smith, Bloodsworth, and South Marsh Islands; and more creeks and rivers than I could begin to prioritize. I had done some initial exploring in the fall when I moved there, but winter had paused much of my exploration.

After the new year, I had taken to fishing the millpond spillway in Salisbury because it was close to home, the crappie fishing had been surprisingly steady, and the stream remained mostly clear of ice when many of the ponds were frozen over. Beaverdam Creek began right across the street from the Ward Museum of Wildfowl Art and ran from a spillway from Schumaker Pond and through a stretch of woods in the city park before it emptied into the upper Wicomico River. It was a small stream by any standards that had the usual warmwater species.

Back then, there was a healthy population of crappie in many of the pools, or at least there were when I fished there. The spring before I moved down there, the DNR drained Schumaker Pond to do some work on something or in an effort to fight the ample vegetation in the water. So when they drained the pond, all of the bass and bluegill and crappie from a healthy and decently sized piece of water were suddenly residents of the small stream. Throughout its length, they were thick in the pools from the spillway on down to the zoo.

That winter I mostly fished a weighted red or yellow marabou streamer because the pickerel fishing there had been fairly good and the crappie were biting fairly well too. The marabou streamer was a nice way of splitting the difference between the two species, and I found that I could catch a few fish on the same fly in a two- to three-hour session of casual fishing. The main spillway pool had the deepest hole that's good for a few fish and casts, but downstream there was a decent series of deeper pools where small pods of crappie held.

Most days the stream waters were low and clear, and when the crappie were actively feeding, it was easy to see them following behind the fly as the marabou pulsed seductively in the water. When their mouths opened, they just inhaled the fly and turned on their sides as they felt the weight of the hook. I let all of the crappie and pickerel go, although there were times when I kept a few for the pan, and they had the mild, mossy taste of the waters from where they came.

For a few weeks in January it was some easy, pleasant fishing there in the park. I went mostly in the evenings after work and class and I never once saw another fisherman there. The small stream was less than ten minutes from my front door, and ran through a thickly forested part of the city park that could've been anywhere. The action with the crappie and the occasional pickerel was steady enough to feel good about heading out into the cold, but after little variety in fish or setting, the joy my afternoons on Beaverdam Creek began wearing thin. It felt like playing the same game over and over again with the same outcome, or watching the same movie again and again until the scenes and dialogue had carved such deep channels into memory that the pleasure had been lost along with the newness.

Up until that January, winter was mostly a time of reflection and preparation, a necessary intermission between the redemptive joy of spring and the frantic pace of fall, and I always entered into it with a begrudging acceptance of the season. Much how Don's was more of a bar than a grill, January was more of a sentence than a recess.

January fishing for me back then was something I did more to define myself as a fisherman than for the actual joy I received from it. I liked having and meeting the annual goal of catching a fish during every month of the year, but I can't say that I actually looked forward to winter with its low waters, quiet woods, numb fingers, and early sunsets. But the quiet and solitude on the small stream was much more pronounced than any other time of year and the fish were there to be caught if I put in the time. It wasn't the iced guide, twig fire, and frostbite cold fishery of the mountains, but it was close and there to be endured, if not mildly enjoyed.

* * * * *

Salisbury is the largest town on Maryland's Eastern Shore with a diverse economy thanks in part to the Perdue Farms Chicken Company, a large state university, and its proximity to the summer resort town of Ocean City. Where smaller towns like Chestertown and Easton have central town squares, antique brick sidewalks, and highly pronounced historical significance, Salisbury is sprawling, suburban, and unapologetically working class. It's bisected by highways, anchored by shopping centers at its northern and southern ends, and acts as the crossroads for the lower Delmarva Peninsula.

My decision to move there was mostly to get another degree at Salisbury University, a mildly impulsive decision that turned out to be one of the best decisions I'd made in my late twenties. About the only things I had going for me at the time were that I was back in school getting another degree and I didn't have a criminal record, but my finances were in such shambles that I didn't even have a checking account, and I was afloat mostly because of my student loans. I was living off cash and paying my bills with postal money orders.

To support myself while I was in school, I found a part-time job at a neighborhood pawn shop and I worked there between classes. My working hours there were flexible, and part of my job was to research the value of items as they came in to be sold or pawned, and then in my free time, I sold the shop's choicer inventory on eBay. It was an easy job, with phone calls from the brokers at the front counter, and quiet time in a back office where I photographed and described strange and everyday items, and packed them up to be shipped.

During my first few days working there, a man brought in a shoebox full of old pocket watches and sold it for $60. These old watches are a niche part of the collectibles market with their own terms and quirks, so my boss had me spend the next few days learning about them, so I could describe them in the best possible language. I learned terms like hunter case and open face, key wind and crown wind, face and movements, coin silver and jewel. Most of the pocket watches were still in good working order, and they ticked away in their shoebox on my desk in a tiny mechanic chorus. I was a bit heartbroken a few weeks later after the auctions were over and payments were made, and I shipped them off in small padded boxes to their new owners, and the office felt quiet after the last one was gone.

The shoebox of pocket watches was just one example of treasures that washed up from the tides of need and misfortune. I worked at the pawn shop for about two years and I saw everything from small electronics to antique porcelain urns. Some things sold for a song, others sold for small fortunes. That was my daily life in my time between classes, my night's at Don's, and my winter trips to Beaverdam Creek: a professional life based on sold dreams and abandoned treasures.

If I had an appreciation for other people's junk before, working at the pawn shop cemented a love for well-worn objects that's been with me ever since. Bone handle pocket knives, old Ford pickups driving on the highway, antique goose decoys flaking paint like the Sistine Chapel: to see or hold one of these items, even for a moment, is to become part of its history, a part of that intimacy. Holding the weighty quality of old objects that are meant to span generations gives me hope that something good can last if it's cared for, and hope is essential to lasting the winter.

* * * * *

Getting things secondhand turned into a way of life in Salisbury. The Salvation Army accounted for a lot of my clothes, the pawn shop provided tools and furniture, and a few weeks after my birthday in early January, I adopted a young dog from the Humane Society. The local access channel would have a slideshow of dogs up for adoption, and over each picture, a volunteer would provide a name and a brief story. There was Jackie, the beagle mix, that loved to cuddle; Cosmo, the lab mix, looking for a running partner and a forever home; Wiggles, the older shepherd mix, who had separation anxiety, but a good heart. And Trixie.

Trixie was a young brittany whose family had moved north to Wilmington and couldn't bring her along. She was around sixteen months old then, a small dog with the orange and white coloring of her breed and bright, attentive eyes. She was described as being sporty and full of energy and being "mostly" house broken—a nice way of saying a work in progress. In the picture, they had her standing broadside to the camera and she was posed like the English pointers and setters that you see in post derby shots, poised and steady, a picture of controlled energy.

I wasn't really looking for a dog, but somehow the idea of Trixie took hold and I found myself leaving the access channel up to see her pictures. Finally, one Friday I drove out to the Humane Society's office outside of town—just to take a look at her, I told myself—but as soon as she pressed her nose through the wire fence of the kennel, I knew she was coming home with me.

As I think back to how our lives intersected, I remember that it wasn't exactly a desire to help an animal in need that motivated me to adopt her. It was a much more casual decision, and more based on companionship than anything. We had owned family dogs growing up, a collection of German shorthair pointers and labs, but I had never had one of my own.

Trixie and I got to know each other over the next few weeks, but it didn't take much adjusting on her part. Within fifteen minutes of coming home with me, she was asleep on the couch and, suddenly, I had a roommate and a reason for daily walks around the neighborhood.

My house in Salisbury had a small yard where I parked my boat, but it wasn't fenced, so we would walk to an enclosed field near an elementary school on Prince Street where she could run. I found out pretty quickly that she was great off leash, checked in willingly, and that she had a natural range of about forty yards. The walks in the field were good for getting to know and trust each other, but it was later along the train tracks in town where I really saw Trixie's promise as a sporting dog, and I found a way to trade my winters of forced fishing with something I actually wanted to do.

* * * * *

Cargo trains ran through Salisbury on tracks that were nearing the end of their careers. They were operational, but not at all busy, only running a few times during the day and never at night. Weeds, small trees, and bushes had begun to encroach on the tracks from the fenced edges, and along each side, warehouses that once used these tracks were left vacant with broken windows and locked doors.

The pawn shop where I worked was next to the railroad crossing on South Boulevard and when a train came through town, first there was the blast of the train's whistle as it warned of its approach, and then the bells at the crossing began ringing as the boom gates descended, and all around there was the weighty, ground level rumble of steel and diesel thunder that lasted for the length of the train. There was never a red caboose at the end of the string of cars, and its absence felt like a missing picture in a locket, a forgotten detail to a fading tradition.

The train tracks were just a few blocks from my house in South Salisbury, and between the gravel and fenced edges, there was a long but narrow stretch of grass where I could let Trixie run as I walked back home from getting my morning coffee. The fenced edges were thickly overgrown with the tangled remains of honeysuckle and raspberry bushes where the winter birds hid and fed. There was even a watered ditch thick with cattails and trash that backed against a junk yard and car impound that was home to a pair of ducks when the water wasn't iced over.

Trixie and I began walking along the train tracks in Salisbury as a shortcut one morning when I was running late. The gravel along the railroad tracks was dry and cold with dead Queen Anne's lace poking up through the rocks, and even in the winter morning air there was still a tarry smell of railroad ties and fast food. Up above, the sun was already over the horizon and there were power lines dripping from the tall backs of warehouses.

In the thick weedy edges along the fences, the small birds chirped happily in the warming morning light and along the gravel and a pair of pigeons walked with bobbing heads to feed. As soon as she caught site of these pigeons, Trixie lowered into a stealthy crouch and eventually locked into a point when the birds stood still. As the pigeons edged off, Trixie crept closer, intent on them, until they decided that they had had enough of the game and took off with a papery flap of wings. She looked back at me after the birds flew off, a look of excitement and disappointment, and I felt some kind of realization pass between us at that moment.

For the rest of the length of the train tracks, she worked along the fenced edges, looking for birds that were active in the mornings there. Often she could see the birds, but in the thicker cover of the dead honeysuckle, it was mostly scent that drove her as she worked her nose back and forth in the air along the winter cover.

I was a changed man when we got home that morning. It was impossible to know what kind of pedigree Trixie had in her background, if she came from hunting stock or AKC cosmetic breeding, but either way, it looked like she had plenty of drive and natural hunting instincts. In the office that day I watched videos online of bird dogs and how to train them, and after work I skipped class and drove to a bookstore to buy bird-hunting magazines: *The Pointing Dog Journal* and *The Upland Almanac*.

Suddenly, walking behind a dog had a purpose, and by extension, the idea of walking through winter woods and fields behind a dog had purpose too, along with hope. It had been twenty years since I'd last fired a shotgun, and I was over 200 miles away from the mountains of western Maryland, but coming back to bird hunting felt as natural as coming back home.

It's completely in character for me to fall in love with a sport that was just outside the bull's-eye of practicality. In high school, I was a lacrosse player in the Deep South, a region where football was a religion and lacrosse was an alien sport with sticks. Later in college I began playing rugby in lacrosse country. And later in life, I became infatuated with fly fishing on waters that were mostly worked with bait and light tackle. And now, in the middle of duck and goose country that was dominated by Labradors and Chesapeake Bay retrievers, I was drawn back to upland bird hunting with pointing dogs.

These walks along the train tracks soon became the high point of my day. Seeing Trixie work the thick cover for birds was a joy each morning and evening, and as I walked behind her, it was easy to relish the cold weather and daydream about walking behind her in a field for pheasant, or in the woods for grouse. She seemed especially fond of the starlings that weren't so easily spooked and just hopped deeper into the bushes when she got too close, and sometimes I'd have to call her off them to keep moving along the tracks.

Owning a dog means a life of ritual, and the daily walks around the neighborhood linked me with other like-minded people. Sometimes as Trixie and I finished our quarter-mile stretch of walking along the almost-abandoned train tracks, as we turned onto the railroad crossing at South Boulevard, we came across an older woman walking her black lab.

After a few friendly greetings between the dogs we began letting them off the leashes to play in a weedy lot. She and I never exchanged names, although we knew each of our dog's names. Maddie's owner was an attractive woman in her early fifties who must've been an absolute heartbreaker in her twenties. She was short, thickly buxom, with graying-brown hair that was usually hidden under a ridiculous knit hat. She had a loud genuine laugh that was contagious and disarming, and it filled the winter mornings with warmth.

One day I mentioned the strange importance my walk along the depressing train tracks had in my day and I could tell she understood the melancholy love of the ritual.

"It's enough," she said, and without verbalizing our less than ideal situations—the unspoken aspirations of a farm house outside of town, a fenced yard, or a walk in a nicer neighborhood—I saw that she was right. There was plenty that I didn't have, and lots of ground to cover before true adulthood, but the simple things I did have were small, good things. I had the promise of a young bird dog and morning walks that warmed me against the winter chill. I had a small collection of fly rods, a modest boat, and Tangier Sound to the south once I made it through the winter.

January vacillated between still-gray mornings and sharply clear days of crunchy frost and bright sunlight and my moods shifted between them equally. On my good days, the joy of watching Trixie run and point at chickadees and starlings as I walked behind her was enough to lift my spirits and start my day on a good note. The coffee on those mornings tasted richer, my job at the pawnshop was interesting, and my decision to go back to school felt tactical and forward thinking. In the evenings, when the cardinals come down from the trees to feed at the bird feeder outside my house, I watched the sun set in a calm winter flourish as dinner cooked on the stove, and my home felt simple and warm.

But there were also hard January days when the daily hopelessness of my life in Salisbury was an exacting burden. Often there was the smell of composted chicken shit in the air as farmers spread it in the fields outside of town. My days were spent between classes, a pawn shop, and sips of bourbon at a dive bar, with the best part being a walk along a stretch of littered train tracks whose best features were rusted fences clogged with dead honeysuckle. Even the bright-eyed eagerness I saw in the younger students at the university felt like fiction. Nothing felt possible. I had neither money nor the prospect of money. My reality was a pale, hairy gut boiling over old, faded jeans and late rent checks as the days alternated between a crisp winter clarity and a gray threat of light snow.

This was January on the lower Eastern Shore, and the thought of summer on Tangier Sound felt as far off and impossible as a real career after I graduated in two years. But occasionally, there'd be a gull mixed in with the crows by a parking lot dumpster and its maritime screech reminded me that the Chesapeake Bay was just thirty miles to the southwest, and that along with the promise of a young bird dog, there were waters that would soon be teeming with fish when spring came.

* * * * *

I'm not sure if a dog and a shotgun necessarily saved my life, but they certainly rescued me from the emptiness of midwinter. One morning at the pawn shop I came out onto the showroom floor from the back office to talk to the guys and saw them cleaning a few rifles and shotguns to place on the racks behind the counter.

An older woman had come in near the end of the previous day to sell a small collection of shotguns and rifles. She said that her brother had died and that she was just looking to get rid of them for a fair price to help pay for the funeral. Her brother had had nice taste in guns with a Beretta 12-gauge over and under, a pair of nice Remington rifles, a 6mm and 30-06 respectively, and a few handguns that didn't excite me too much.

The Beretta 12-gauge had some signs of wear but was still in fine condition. The wood stock was a warm polished brown with swirls of character and only lightly scratched. The barrel was clean, oiled, and unpitted, and the scrollwork detail of the receiver was still clearly visible, although some of the edges had been worn smooth. All in all, it had the look of a quality firearm that had been lovingly used but not banged up.

The owner of the pawn shop had set the policy that employees could buy anything off the floor at double off what the store paid for the item. This was a very generous offer, implemented I'm sure to discourage theft. Between the woman's acceptance of a fairly low offer for the lot of guns, and a standing line of store credit I had for exceeding sales goals, I had the opportunity to purchase the gun for a low price, so I did.

I hadn't owned a gun since my first—a 20-gauge-22 magnum over and under that my dad bought me when I was thirteen—but when I brought it home after work, some of the boyhood familiarity with shotguns came back as I put the gun together and took it apart again. Up until that moment, I had been a dog owner who was interested in revisiting bird hunting, but once I bought that shotgun, I began the journey into becoming a hunter again. I dug through an old shoebox of letters and important papers and found my hunter's safety certification card and bought my small game hunting license the next day at Walmart along with some shotgun shells.

The same rural, boyish pride came back to me as a twenty-five-year-old man at that moment: of standing at the counter of a sporting good store in Western Maryland and buying my first hunting license. My cousins and I had passed our hunter safety courses and were now old enough and legally allowed to hunt with our fathers on the first day of small game season.

* * * * *

Near the end of the month, a guy came into the pawn shop with an air compressor and some power tools that he was looking to get a loan on. He was a framing carpenter and had been out of work for a few weeks and needed some walking around money until he started his next contract in early February. Although he had a Delaware driver's license, his truck had South Dakota plates and I noticed the Pheasants Forever sticker he had on his tailgate.

We got to talking about dogs and bird hunting, and fairly casually he said that he knew of a farm up west of Seaford, Delaware, that bordered a game preserve. The game preserve had a Delaware address, but he said that his wife's brother owned a farm in Maryland that bordered it. Sometimes he helped out at the game preserve when they needed an extra hand, and a few weeks before there had been a big corporate event where some execs from the DuPont offices in Wilmington had organized a group hunt and retreat. Under the banner of corporate team building and executive leadership, dozens of quail had been released into the fields and only about half of them had been shot.

"Yeah I bet you could just walk the other side of the hedgerow between his farm and theirs and you might find some of their leftovers. They're probably still in there pretty thick unless the foxes got to them. You should head up and check it out. Let that new dog of yours stretch her legs, maybe put her on some birds."

Aside from the daily walks along the train tracks and a few trips to Pemberton Park outside of town to walk the trails, I hadn't done any actual training with Trixie, other than the standard obedience stuff. She came when I called her, sat when she wanted food, and didn't pretend to be at all interested in playing fetch when there were birds outside to be found.

Ever since our first walk along the train tracks I had been reading magazines from cover to cover on the best way to start a bird dog, and there were as many theories and training guides as there were dog breeds. I was thankful for the offer, but a little worried about diving right in.

"Does she come when you call her?" he asked.

"Yeah, she's great off the leash. We've been on some big walks outside of town and she listens really well. Doesn't run off too far either and checks back in a lot."

"Well, you can't teach that. That, or drive. If they don't love hunting, just let 'em stay home."

She looked to have plenty of drive. Each day when we turned on the train tracks, she'd take off along the fenced edges running hard and searching for birds. Ever since our first walk along the train tracks, I'd been daydreaming about getting her onto real birds, of walking a field behind her and seeing her point something other than a chickadee or a starling.

"I guess I'm just worried about ruining her. What if she's gun shy?"

"A starter pistol's usually best for introducing them to gunfire, but if you can't get your hands on one, once you get out into the field a shot up in the air works, too."

I didn't know the guy at all, a framing carpenter from Pierre, South Dakota, but he seemed comfortable talking about bird hunting, and I was warming up to his baptism-of-fire approach to dog training. The friendly offer was hanging in the air between us. I shrugged, putting concern and caution behind me, and accepted the sign that had been sent to me. Within the space of a few weeks, the secondhand tides had brought me a dog and a shotgun, and now I was faced with a generous invitation to hunt quail in a farm just north of Salisbury.

"So, if she's got it, she's got it," I said, boiling down all of the training theory I'd been reading about into one black or white statement.

South Dakota raised an eyebrow and shrugged.

"Pretty much. If you want a hunting dog, go out and actually hunt her. No fancy dog trainer will ever argue with that. She won't have all that polished steady-to-wing-and-shot stuff, but she'll get there if you work at it. And if there are birds there and she has the drive, odds are she'll find them and point them. If not, it's a beginning. Keep going and working with her and it'll come together."

The guy had the cash in his hand that he'd needed, and his compressor and power tools were on a shelf in the back room, waiting for him to buy them back next month. He had what he wanted and didn't appear to need anything more from me. It felt like two guys just talking about quail hunting in the middle of a world infatuated with geese and ducks—nothing more, nothing less. If it was a calculated play to gain some kind of favor with the brokers, or for me to keep a watchful eye out for the stuff he had pawned, it was one of the smoothest attempts I'd seen in my time at the pawn shop.

Before he left, he wrote down his name, Rick Diamond, and number and drew a little map for me that started at Route 13 in Seaford with a few turns onto smaller roads a few miles west of town. He told me where to park, and where the fields of the game preserve bordered their land.

"Head up anytime and let me know how you do. Maybe we can meet up sometime. The land's not working now so I doubt anyone will be out there, but just tell them you know me if they do."

* * * * *

Half of my time spent outdoors is spent running down rumors and lies like this, with the other half going through the well-worn motions of routine and habit. Between the dog, the gun, and the invitation from the carpenter from South Dakota, I'd have to be blind to see that winter was making me an offering. So I went.

The next Saturday I drove out to the farm west of Seaford with my new dog and shotgun. I wasn't up too early, so I had a long breakfast, filled a thermos with coffee, and timed my arrival to be around 8:30 and 9 a.m., around the time when I walked Trixie along the train tracks when the morning had warmed and the birds were feeding actively. I was under dressed for a still, gray morning, but I had the basics: hiking boots, fleece leggings, and tough Cahartt' work pants courtesy of the Salvation Army, along with a thick-hooded sweatshirt, a windproof fleece, and a blaze orange vest and hat that I'd picked up from Walmart when I got my hunting license. There would be time for more appropriate gear later, a proper hunting coat, and a training collar for Trixie, but for now I had the basics to get out and hunt.

As I parked my truck, I saw what the carpenter from South Dakota meant when he said that the land bordering the game preserve wasn't working. Where the game preserve fields were a thoughtfully maintained mix of unharvested corn rows along the edges, and neatly tilled soil sowed with winter wheat towards the center, the land on my side of the hedgerow was overgrown and mostly wild. It looked like corn had been harvested the previous season, but most of the overgrown clumps of topped grass provided good food and cover. The field stretched on for acres, an overgrown mess of dry weeds, framed on two sides by tall hedgerows of old-growth trees.

Out in the middle of the field, a mild swale provided some geese with a seasonal pond backed with a few small bushes and cattails, and Trixie was working her way out that direction when I called her back. I loaded my gun, zipped up my coat, and we set off along the inside of the hedgerow, protected from the wind.

Before we got too far from the truck I aimed at a ball of mistletoe near the top of one of the oaks in the hedgerow and shot as Trixie nosed around in some large fallen branches. The sound didn't seem at all loud out in the open, but Trixie looked back at me with a curious look before moving off into an open spot in the hedgerow. So much for being gun shy. I walked over to where some of the small greens from the mistletoe had fallen to the ground and put a clump in my pocket for post-holiday luck.

The field and hedgerow stretched on for about 400 yards before it began angling downhill and to the right until it finally met an old wire fence that divided the field from the beginnings of a wetland depression. The cattails and reeds eventually gave way to a pond with a thin layer of ice that looked to have great prospects for a bass pond later in the summer if there was shore access on the side.

Trixie and I walked, and I breathed in the cold air of the field and savored the reality of our first hunt together: the powdery threat of snow, the geese honking in the distance, the crunch of frosted grass beneath my boots, the sight of Trixie working in front of me, and the balanced weight of an over and under shotgun in my hands. I wasn't cold yet, but knew that the best way to stay warm would be a steady pace. I could see my breath, but we were nicely sheltered from the wind from the tree cover.

Out in the field before me Trixie was running hard, energized by the newly discovered open space and whatever mysterious scents that only dogs can smell in wild places. She was running faster and with greater range than I had ever seen her run, openly overjoyed to be working the field edge. Sometimes she'd charge into the thick cover of the non-working field, boldly jumping through the high grass. Then she'd work her way back to the tree cover, and she'd slow down and nose around a clump of brush in the field, or a thick tangle of weeds within the hedgerow before moving off. Each time she slowed down I moved up behind her with my gun ready, but each time she moved off without a solid or meaningful point.

At one point, she flushed a bird out in front of me but she was running so fast that I don't think she noticed. It was the first quail that I had seen in over twenty years and it flew through the air with the weighty authority of a small game bird. Its speed was immediately noticeable and I suddenly wished that I had taken more practice shots with my shotgun. We were both here to learn, I told myself. And the birds were here. That's what was important. I was disappointed that she hadn't caught the scent of the bird, but I figured that she was entitled to some beginner's mistakes, and as a young dog probably needed to burn off a little steam before getting down to business.

As we walked on along the hedgerow, Trixie worked the edges and occasionally bounded into the thick cover. As we neared the corner of the field I saw the unmistakable body language of a pointer getting birdy. Her zigzagging pattern in the thick grass grew tighter, her look grew more intense, and her small tail began wagging faster. Finally, she stopped dead in her tracks, rock solid as I walked up behind her with my gun ready. It wasn't the picturesque, high head with one paw raised stance that you see in sporting paintings, but there was no denying that she was on point. Her head was low, all four legs were down, but she was intent on a small clump of grass just a bit to her right near the corner of the field.

My gun was loaded and cocked, the safety was off, and I approached from below and kicked the brush in front of her nose to no effect. As I worked my way forward, I stamped and tried to flush something and finally heard the sound of wings behind me as two quail took flight to my left and directly behind me. The birds were weaving into the trees and out of range before I even got the gun to my shoulder and Trixie was chasing after one. I called her back and she had a frenzied look when she came back to me.

I knelt down and gave her some calming pats down her sides. She was shaking with excitement and anxious to get back to work. I offered her some water but she wasn't at all interested, so we set off again. The morning was warming a bit and there was less of a frosty crunch under my boats as I walked and the sun was trying to burn off the low cloud cover.

Trixie was a bit more methodical as we worked down the next line of tree cover from the corner, and within a few minutes she was on point again, a sudden but solid point with her head high in the air and a bit less restrained. As I walked up behind her, the bird flushed before me without me having to kick any grass. This bird didn't head for the tree cover but luckily set off out into the open air over the field. Without much thought I brought the gun to my shoulder and fired. The bird fell from the air in a still tangle of lead and feathers.

I didn't have high expectations for Trixie to retrieve the bird, but I was hopeful that she could at the least help me find anything that I'd shot, so I started walking to the general area where I thought the bird might've fallen. She definitely had the scent of something and within a few moments of searching in the thick grass she was nosing the bird with a predatory curiosity. I knelt down to pick it up and the bird was warm in my hand but was surprisingly light. I realized then that I didn't have a game bag, so I put the small bird in my sweatshirt pocket.

After that, the task was clearer for both of us. Trixie had figured out the scenting game and was getting more confident with what we were doing in the field, and I was getting a better handle on the nuances of wing shooting and how to approach a point. Her drive to find birds was great and her steadiness on point was impressive, but I knew that there were other things that I'd like to work on with her. Retrieving birds and steadiness to the shot were good eventual goals, but for now I had a perfectly serviceable hunting dog and our first outing together was better than I had imagined.

We walked down the remainder of the old wire fence and found a few more birds that rose in singles. I missed the first one but brought the next one down, and after Trixie found it, I put it next to its colder covey mate. After we reached the end of the fence line, we turned into the field itself to see if there were any birds away from the edges and began the long hypotenuse course back to the truck.

The taller grass had been mostly beaten down by winter but still made for fairly unsteady footing until I found a minor deer trail that we could follow as Trixie worked the dense cover on either side. As we got deeper into the interior of the field the excitement of our first hunt began to simmer down and the beauty of the scene finally sank in. Off behind me there was the ambient honking of geese from the bass pond. I could see the overgrown expanse of the field spreading out in front of me, framed by a cornered hedgerow full of bare old-growth trees. Near the top of the hill off in the center of the field, an impossibly huge sycamore stood, with a thick and white mottled trunk, bare branches and a crown that filled the gray January sky. I hadn't noticed it when I parked, I was so intent on our first hunt.

I stopped walking and did my best to savor the moment. My pretty young dog was working back and forth in front of me and the shotgun in my hands was a finely crafted treasure. There wasn't a car or building for miles. We were a long way from a walking along the trash-littered, power line riddled Salisbury train tracks. I breathed the winter air and felt my cold toes in my boots, and tried not to think about my life back in town, of the stack of unopened bills on my counter, or my precarious finances, all the more delicate now after a few unplanned expenses.

Fifty yards ahead, Trixie had picked up a scent and started working back and forth to my left, and without any kind of warning, a trio of quail just a few paces ahead of her flushed into the air. They were out of range as soon as they flushed, and I watched them fly off without attempting a shot. Trixie looked back at me, not even attempting to chase them down this time.

The morning had been a great one, but it had ended for us after that last flush. The ending wasn't out of bitterness or missed opportunity, but of knowing that we had reached our saturation point of learning and experience for our first hunt together. We had experienced success and learned how to hunt together. At that point, it was enough, so I broke open the barrels of my 12 gauge, removed the shells, and set off to the end of the hedgerow where we parked.

The worn over and under that complimented my sporty young bird dog had the patina and romance of a bamboo fly rod, and it felt comfortably balanced in the crook of my elbow as we approached my truck. The warmth of the mild winter morning had chilled to a stark afternoon, and as I poured a cup of coffee from the thermos I'd left in the cab, I was grateful to see steam rising off the surface before I took a sip.

After we packed the truck and headed south back to Salisbury, Trixie was fast asleep on the front seat next to me before we'd driven a mile. I had toweled her off and wiped her paws down, but she was still a little damp from her time in the field and there were a few burrs on her chest and ears. The heat was on full blast and I had all of the vents pointed at her. She looked tired but pleased. I reached over and put my hand on her, trying to pass on the incredible feeling of pride and gratitude I had for the morning that we had shared together through just a touch. When I got home, I put the shotgun shell from the first bird I shot over Trixie up on the window sill next to the sprig of mistletoe. Trixie drank up most of her water, jumped up into her spot on the couch, and was back asleep within minutes.

Later that evening in Don's, I sipped bourbon in pensive celebration and each sip had the relaxing warmth of a wood stove. Within the space of a month I had adopted a dog, bought a shotgun from the pawn shop, and received an unexpected invitation to hunt quail in a farm outside town. My sporting identity had shifted from a fisherman, to a hopeful winter dog owner, to a bird hunter. It was strange to feel newness in the dead of winter, and perhaps it was the bourbon, but I felt a warm gratitude to be beginning something together with Trixie.

It occurred to me that although it would be worth a shot to keep checking the field near Seaford out over the next few weeks, the hunting would continue to decline until more birds were released and unharvested. It felt like the crappie in the small spillway stream all over again, another one-dimensional option near home, but one that I was fortunate to have in January when choices were limited.

Because of this, or in spite of this, I found myself thinking of our family farm up in western Maryland where I'd hunted with my father and cousins before my teenage years took me away from outdoor sport. I knew that by the end of January, Backbone Mountain was long covered with snow, but for the first time in decades, I found myself thinking back to an old trail that lead down through the deep woods to an older homestead where grouse sometimes flushed from the thick cover near an old collection of pear and apple trees.

On another part of the property, I remembered the thick brush and thickets from new growth after the Westvaco Paper Company had harvested acres of timber along one of the access roads and I imagined the rebounding cover twenty years later, mostly impassable, and ideal cover for grouse. I pictured the small stream where I'd found crayfish under rocks and caught brook trout from the deeper pools.

As I drank my bourbon, I pictured Trixie moving lightly and happily through the woods on Backbone Mountain as I walked behind her with my 12-gauge. I wondered if the old hickory tree at the bottom of the hill was still standing. The next winter would come as an opportunity, not a sentence. Other hunts were now possible, and lasting the winter was not a sentence to be served.

Grouse and Rabbit Brunswick Stew

Our modern palates are so used to chicken, beef, and pork that rabbit and grouse are a pleasant surprise each time I eat them. Aside from being mid-winter sport, the mild gamey flavors sets them aside from the banality of grocery store-bought chicken. I once brought home a rabbit and grouse from a late winter hunt and, after skinning and cleaning them, I saw that a good portion of the meat had been torn up by the shot. With dinner plans altered, I elected to use what I could with the game in a pot of Brunswick Stew, probably where the recipe came from in the first place: a frugal way to stretch a small amount of meat into a full meal.

Ingredients

- Grouse breast
- Saddle and leg of rabbit
- Olive oil
- Garlic salt
- Flour
- Pepper
- Celery, diced
- Onions, diced
- Carrot, diced
- Potatoes, peeled and diced
- Garlic, minced
- Chicken stock
- Frozen succotash
- Canned tomatoes
- Salt and pepper, to taste
- Crusty bread
- Butter

Directions:
Coat a thick-bottomed pot with olive oil and heat with medium heat.

Debone and dice grouse and rabbit into small pieces. Season with garlic salt and pepper and divide into two portions. Coat one portion with flour. Add floured meat to pot and brown until crispy; then set aside.

Deglaze the bottom of the pan with celery, onions, carrot, potatoes, garlic, and remainder of uncooked grouse and rabbit.

Cook on low heat until meat is cooked through and onions are translucent.

Add chicken stock, succotash, and canned tomatoes. Simmer on low heat, stirring occasionally until potatoes begin to break down and meat begins to string.

Add pan-fried rabbit and grouse to pot and simmer for another twenty minutes. Add salt and pepper to taste. Serve with crusty bread and butter.

FEBRUARY

TAPPING MAPLES

Although each day in February is five minutes longer than the next there is nothing quite so optimistic as the winter crocus, rising from snowy earth and loam, early and unexpected as noon guests for a one o'clock luncheon. Spring is just an arm's length away as Lepus scurries at Orion's feet and maples run their sweetest. Early in the month a groundhog tells our winter fortune and later Valentines warm cold winter feet.

It is bad luck to burn sassafras
or apple logs in a fireplace.

J ust outside my kitchen window there's a chickadee tucked under the snowy eaves of an overgrown juniper. It's been making hurried trips between the bird feeder and the safety of the bush, and in the dim 6 a.m. light, I can see the faint traces of bark and needles in the snow beneath the branch it favors, small signs of warm February life.

A winter storm began yesterday afternoon, closing schools and businesses early and charging the region with the folksy excitement that comes with a snow day. Every year, despite the fair warning and recent frequency, the snow comes as a surprise. We hear the news over the television and radio, and we heed it well enough, but the sight of fresh snow causes something to rise within us with each falling.

Snow reminds us that it's possible to go to sleep one night and wake up the next morning in a world that's completely different. People don't change overnight—that's too difficult: it's the world outside, the grays and browns of a winter landscape that change so suddenly and impossibly. If when we were younger it felt like a snow came as a miracle saving us from school, it's because it was a miracle by the plainest definition of the word: a day changed completely by something that's literally fallen softly from the sky. Snow pushes inward, inside our homes and the concept of home, insulating us in a domestic slowness where little can be rushed, so long as there's food in the fridge, a fire going, and something simmering on the stove.

Downstairs in my fireplace, the fire from last night still has a few coals glowing and it doesn't take much prodding to get it going again. There's a decent stack of kindling and dry firewood in the mudroom, and nearly a full cord out by the garage if we need more, but for right now, the morning's fire is covered and there's no immediate need to think about boots and trips out to the wood shed. After the fire sets, I grind coffee for the french press as water boils on the stove and bacon begins to sweat in a cast iron skillet.

The window by the kitchen sink looks out onto my back yard, a nicely planned mix of Japanese maples, paper birch, and old oaks anchored by mulch beds and flagstone paths. Rhododendron and shrubs curve around the yard in a thoughtful frame and, depending on the season, tulips, hostas, and monkey grass add texture and depth to the yard of our small house in Gaithersburg, Maryland.

A landscaper owned the house before my wife Hannah and I bought it, so any credit for the dense and diverse layout should go to him, but since it's ours, I can look upon it with the pride that comes with owning a small piece of property. I did build the fence that borders the property and I put in some raised garden beds a few springs ago for vegetables and herbs, so I can claim responsibility for at least some parts of it.

With mostly bare trees, snow still falling, and about a foot of snow on the ground, it's difficult to imagine the blooming life that seems to race about the perimeter of the yard as the seasons change; how crocus give way to daffodils and tulips, which then give way to dogwoods, daisies, and tiger lilies, and finally the yellow-orange blaze of fall foliage.

Beneath the snow there's no sign of the edged mulch beds or the flagstone paths, and the yard has the stillness that comes with snowfall. There's no sound of wind outside, no sound of traffic, except for the occasional thunder of snowplows, and even the house itself with its tapping radiators and creaking, wood floors feels unusually quiet. I reach to turn on the radio, but my hand stops halfway to the knob.

The bacon crisps just before burning, exactly how I like it and without a single trace of soft, fatty chewiness, and I set it out to dry on paper towels while I toast an English muffin for a second time and eggs begin to sputter in the bacon grease. The kitchen takes on a smell that reminds me of my great grandmother, a Virginia waterman's daughter who liked her coffee black, her bacon crisp, and her English muffins toasted to a crispy, golden brown.

I eat my breakfast in silence while my wife and dog sleep upstairs and, near the end of my second cup of coffee, the growing light has dispelled the first chickadee's early wariness and the bird feeder has busied to a happy chaos. House sparrows have joined the mix and starlings bully their way through the smaller birds as the flock feeds happily. Occasionally, a pair of cardinals fly down from a high spot in the paper birch to feed politely.

Beneath the feeder I can see fresh tracks in the snow and the traces of spilled birdseed and the feeder reminds me of the grocery store last night: it has the same crowded excitement brought about by snow and centered around food. The snow seems to finally be tapering, but still falling lightly as the morning grays begin to lighten.

I watch the happy chaos outside from the warmth of my house and a kitchen that smells like my great grandmother's. The birds will probably empty the feeder by 10 a.m., sooner if the squirrels came, and as my thoughts drift to squirrels and their greedy plunder of birdseed, I notice a robin at the feeder.

Against the fresh snow any color leaps with sincerity, but even compared to the cassock red of the cardinal or the screaming cobalt of the blue jay, the understated burnt orange of the robin breast is a startling, welcome surprise. Migrational patterns and biology aside, the old saying about robins and spring is welcome, and even though there's nothing new or special about the bird itself, the sight of it in February feels meaningful.

As the light of the morning strengthens, I catch a glimpse of my reflection in the window. I realize that the circular, pensive scrutiny of winter birds and snow is one of the final challenges of February. Lasting the winter means having to last a moment, and winter's slowness and introspection tend to draw out a moment: an early morning watching the birds in fresh snow, their colors and pale auspices of spring, their loud happy chaos in the bushes near our patio, and the light traces of tracks and scattered birdseed in the snow beneath the feeder.

It's at that moment that I feel in my body that the winter has been a long one, and that it's time to spend a fairly uncomfortable day outside on the water. Regardless of the outcome or the improbable reality of hooking a fish, it's time to take an actual trip, if anything, in order to break the hyper-conscious scrutiny with action.

* * * * *

About a week after the winter storm, what would be our last big dump of the year, the days warmed into the high forties and low fifties, and all but the biggest drifts along the road and in the parking lots melted. These warming trends in February are good for tapping maples since the sap runs better on the warm days and the freezing temperatures at night still keeps it sweet. But while the sugarbush production kicked into gear and the snow turned into a memory, I wondered about the runoff into the Potomac River where I planned on fishing.

Just northwest of Poolesville, the Dickerson Power Plant operates on the eastern bank of the Potomac River. It generates power for Montgomery County and Washington, DC, and draws water from the river to use to cool its generators. The heated water from the plant is discharged into a canal that leads back to the river. Where river temps above the plant average in the high thirties and mid-forties in mid-winter, below Dickerson along the Maryland bank, temperatures can average in the fifties and sixties.

The happy result for winter anglers is the Dickerson Warm Water Fishing Area, a public park where anglers and kayakers can take advantage of these warm waters. In winter this area can draw fish like flies to a picnic, and this fishery can be consistent when most other local waters are empty or covered with ice.

Dickerson isn't always a slam dunk, though, and low water levels can make the fish skittish and closed mouthed in the clear water. But it's a good spot to try for no other reason than it's a better bet than most anything else in late winter: the smallmouth fishing can be great, the bluegill and crappie fishing can be spectacular, and if you're adventurous enough to launch a small boat or canoe, you might see enormous schools of carp or catfish finning in the deeper pools.

As fishing spots go, it's not at all a secret. The power plant is often written about in winter publications and commonly mentioned in area fishing reports. Despite that, and even though it's just a stone's throw from Germantown and Washington, DC, I've only ever seen a handful of winter paddlers in the canal, and just a few other anglers along the banks most of the times when I've fished there.

On the drive out through rural Montgomery County, March felt less like a vague rumor and more like a promise. Old stone fences lined the fields of some of the properties and there were traces of snow in the shady edges of the forests and hedgerows. Most of the fields had a tilled and thawed look to them that hinted at spring and in a few spots I could see small flocks of robins working the soil for earthworms. There were traces of buds on some of the hardier trees.

At Dickerson, I parked in the lot and began walking down to the river and saw that the waters of the C&O canal were still frozen in the tree-lined shade, despite the warmth. The path down to the river was a slick mess of mud and thawing ice that my felt-bottomed waders didn't grip with confidence, so I walked in the leaf and loam forest floor beside the path until I reached the river.

There might have been a hint of spring to the day, but it was still decidedly winter in the low-shaded stretch by the river. The waters, thankfully, didn't have the muddy look of spring runoff that they'd probably have in a few weeks and at that moment they were fairly low and shockingly clear with an occasional chunk of bank ice drifting by in the current.

A pair of ducks hurtled by in their weighty, muscled flight and reedy whistles. I watched them fly upstream and followed them until I found an easy spot to enter the river beneath an eddy that formed behind the trunk of a tree that had fallen out into the current. It looked like the crown had snapped off, and out in the open river, about forty yards off the bank, there were the remnants of another tree. Only its trunk and a few larger branches were left and the tangled bulb of roots was caught in the river bottom. Even from shore, I could see that a significant eddy had formed behind the roots, and I imagined a deeper hole behind it, carved from the river bottom by the current and stacked with fish.

The day itself was a mild winter day with temps in the 40s and the lack of wind let the warmth stay close. Between a hat, scarf, fleece layers, pants, waders, and jacket, I was warm and being on the water wasn't at all a hardship. Once I'd waded into position in knee-deep water I started casting upstream into the seams where the current met the eddy behind a large log.

After my second cast I was connected with a pale bluegill that hit a small clouser with all of the confidence and aggression of a much larger bass. I let it go and pulled a few more fish from that seam, along with one nice smallmouth from just above a downstream riffle. I had just been holding my fly above where the current began to pick up when it came out and hit the fly with a jarring strike. It was a beautiful smallmouth with bright red eyes and the beginnings of the distinct vertical bars that mature fish get. It had fought like hell coming in, heading downstream and west to Virginia as soon as I hooked it, and I actually had to let it run with a little line before I put it on the reel to fight.

I go into most winter trips resigning myself to fishing in empty waters, with only an outside chance at hooking or seeing a fish. The waters can seem empty on those winter trips, and I tell myself that it's the ritual of heading out that's important and that any fish seen or caught is an added bonus. Consequently, the amount of life and activity on the Potomac that day was surprising—not just the amount of fish caught, but the signs of fish throughout the river. There were occasional splashes out in the open water of the river, not the muscular splashes of large bass, but something lighter, smaller panfish or trout perhaps, and I could see thick schools of minnows holding in the shallow water near shore, scattering and holding among the rocks, mud, and broken branches. The water was clear and I could see the baitfish perfectly, so well that I knew the exact colors to use if I wanted to copy them at the vise: a sparse olive over tan calf tail, with a dark peacock herl lateral line to separate them, and a pale white belly. There was clearly something to the warm-water discharge.

Above the western shore and the bluff that rose above it, the dull, lead gray of the low clouds stretched out above the river giving off the muted, dreary light that fishermen welcome. Below me, the Potomac poured on and on, a clear, gray current-seamed giant heading southeast to Great Falls and the Chesapeake Bay. Mid-river ledges and boulders boiled the deeper currents back up to the surface while a bluejay screamed from across the river. I'd become so used to the Chesapeake tributaries, with their changing tides and multi-directional rivers, that the permanence of the current pulling me downstream to Great Falls felt intimidating. So much of the fishing I do tends to be from a boat or kayak that wading felt new and exposing.

The tangle of uprooted trees along the shore confirmed the power of the river and its one-directional fate. There's a saying about never being able to step into the same river twice, and I see this at its most evident on the Potomac. Even though some of the large trunks looked to be fixed into the river with a weighty permanence, their massive trunks creating significant eddies for a season and their ages impossible to tell, this woody structure along the banks of the river is in constant flux. Waters rising with hard floods scour the river banks and sweep through the mid-river islands inexorably, cleaning out the old and pushing a new big tangle along shore each year.

I stayed close to the bank for most of the morning and in the shoreline tangle of branch and boulders I found a few good holes that held crappie and sunfish. All of these panfish had the same winter paleness to them, but this paleness didn't at all hint at weakness: if anything, there's a predatory ferocity in Potomac River panfish that makes them unique. Often they hit the same flies that I use for the river smallmouth and in winter fly fishing, changing flies with numbed fingers is a nice chore to avoid.

Out in the rocks and current seams where the river current ran stronger, I pulled the occasional smallmouth bass. Most were on the smallish side —one to one and one half pounds—but one seemed closer to two pounds. There were plenty of fishy spots to cast to and I was honestly surprised at how regularly I'd been hooking fish, certainly not every cast, but common enough for it to feel like fishing and not just winter casting practice. The action was good along the rock shelf near shore, but I found myself looking out at the lonely tree trunk out in the open water of the river, the most significant piece of structure within sight.

It's a common rule in fishing to never leave biting fish to find more fish. Perhaps this is the angling equivalent of a Rorschach test and gives good insight into a fisherman's ability to be satisfied with the things he has; but for me personally, I've never found this rule to be an easy one to follow. Maybe this behavior is more natural than I think, but I can honestly say that it's never been a question of satisfaction or a quixotic search for bigger fish driving me away from a perfectly good thing. Because in plain terms, my standards are fairly low: most days I'm happy with a few small fish and to not get blanked. If anything, leaving biting fish is something I do for curiosity's sake. Most times, I see a place and want to check it out so that I know firsthand if a fish is there. If I wasted time and got blanked, so be it. If I would've caught more fish staying put, what exactly would I have gained?

In that way, the lonely tree trunk stuck in the river called me from the bank, a mid-river itch just off to the west. As I considered making a few casts at it, I saw that the wade over didn't look too treacherous and, despite the thaws from earlier that week, the water was the midwinter low before the big thaws and spring rains. Out from shore, the mud gave way to a consistent gravelly flat that was about knee deep, and just below me, boulders and stoney, ridged shelves extended out from shore into the current. I could hop along these for much of the way, and I'd only have to wade the last thirty feet to get into casting distance.

I reeled up and started working my way across river on the rock shelf that spread like a spine toward Virginia. The wading between exposed rocks was tricky but possible. Ice had formed on a few of the edges and pocked holes. Every now and then large, rounded boulders poked from the water and offered good footing as I grew closer to the enticing tree trunk. After a bit of effort, I was well offshore and making good progress to it.

There was a hairy moment as I stepped down from a rock shelf and the loose gravel gave a bit beneath my feet and, for a second, I felt the inexorable pull of the current at my winter-numbed knees and I felt myself slipping. The risk of drowning in cold waters and the privileged idiocy of leaving biting fish for potential harm all mixed together into one convoluted ball of adolescent danger and adult wisdom. I was alone and off balance in the middle of the Potomac River in February, momentarily scared and sobered, but still drawn to the eddy of the mid-river tree.

This range of emotions swept through me within the two seconds it took to slip and catch my balance in the current, and after an easy wade from the last piece of the rock shelf I found myself within casting distance of the tree trunk. From mid-river, the bluff on the Virginia side of the river rose up against the gray sky, and behind me the Maryland shore was a stand of bare tree trunks tangled with logs and winter mud. The river poured on from my right to left.

The slip in the river had scared and sobered me, but after most of the distance had been covered, idiocy started might as well be idiocy completed. Selfishly I wanted the crossing of so much water to be worthwhile. I wanted the payoff to be proportional to the risk, and more than usual, I wanted a big damn fish.

This type of pressure isn't common in my fishing. If anything, there's usually a mindless surrender to action and motion more than any truly calculated approach to my fishing or expectation of any kind. But as I stood there in the middle of the Potomac River in February with the fishiest lie of the warm-water area an easy cast below me, and a slip in the river current heightening my purpose there, I knew that my first cast to it would be infused with importance.

Much how weeks earlier in my kitchen where I cooked a slow breakfast and watched the birds feeding in the snow, the same midwinter hyper-consciousness came back to me then. Each of the details of that moment on the river stood out in perfect clarity: the sound of my reel as I stripped line out, the pull of the current against my knees and slack line, the perfect profile of the damp clouser minnow in my hand, and the finely built tension of the moment before my first cast as crows cawed from the Virginia bank.

I was just above and across from the old tree, an easy cast into the current seam where the fast water rushing around the base met the slow water of the eddy behind it. I thought that with some creative casting and mending I might even work the deep water of the eddy before the current dragged the fly downstream.

My hands took over and I cast down into the spot in the river just above where the current began to rush against the base of the root bulb of the tree. The fly landed in the fast water, sank and drifted downstream, and before it washed past the current seam behind the root bulb, I felt the pull of the fly swinging through current and the sudden, jarring strike of a nice fish. Without even seeing it, I knew that it was a big smallmouth, deeply bending my 6 weight to the butt as it fought in the current and headed downstream. When I got the fish close enough to net I saw that it was one of the largest smallmouth that I'd ever caught: a beautiful three- to four-pound fish with deeply mottled ochre and olive sides and a mouth I could almost fit my fist into as I removed the fly.

Before I released the fish back into the current I considered the impossible balance of the moment, of how symmetry in life was preciously rare but common enough to merit hope, and that a fabled payoff in a fishing story—whether it's written, told, lived, or imagined—was just as possible in winter as it was in any other season.

As the afternoon grew later and the day grew colder, I fished the spot until my hands grew numb. I pulled a few more fish from the lonely tree in the river: a pair of nice smallmouth, but nothing as large as the first, and even a short walleye. Just before I left, the snow flurries began. Nothing too serious, sparse flakes with the floating gravity of May cottonwoods. They floated weightlessly and aimlessly in the air as I worked my way back across the river towards Maryland and the warmth of my truck.

* * * * *

About a week after that trip to Dickerson and just a few days before leap year, I was driving to another power plant to cast flies at another warm-water discharge. I was heading to The Rips at Calvert Cliffs on a scouting trip with Captain Pete Dahlberg because he was curious to see if the decent fishing that holds there through the lean part of winter had been bolstered by some early migrants.

Now, a scouting trip was different than a typical guided trip, and meant that Pete would take on a few anglers for a half-day trip where we'd all split the cost of gas, and Pete would spend a bit of time fishing as well. Not all captains do this, but every once in a while when patterns shift and Pete gets curious about certain areas, he'll put word out for a scouting trip, if only to scratch an itch and check out things before he brings paying clients along. Expectations are low, and aside from the fairly low costs, there was the added bonus of feeling "in" with the guide when he extends the invitation. So before I really felt like the year had kicked off, I was driving through southern Maryland on my way to Solomon's Island.

The Rips is a well-known mid-Bay spot just a few hundred yards offshore of the Calvert Cliffs Nuclear Power Plant, where water that cools the reactors is pumped back into the bay—nearly 2.4 million gallons per minute when the plant is running at full strength. Much like Dickerson, there's a significant temperature difference between the water of the bay and the warm water discharged from the plant. But unlike Dickerson, there's an incredible current rip that sets up from the pipe a few hundred yards offshore.

Between a strong running tide, the rate of the discharge, and the potential crosswinds, the conditions at The Rips can be tricky, and depending on the combination, things can range from an easy anchor within casting distance of the current line, to a bouncing, bracing, carnival ride drift through the best water. There are spots that hold fish throughout the area, but most, like the best saltwater fishing spots, are in the hairiest water. Fishing here, in winter or any season, requires prudence and a watchful eye on conditions.

Although the temperature just a week before had been fairly mild, just a few days before the trip February tightened its grip on us as a final reminder that the contract on spring hadn't been signed yet, and that we weren't quite done with winter. The warm days where sap ran freely from the maple taps were gone, and late February felt...well, like February: cold gray days that didn't hint at snow or rain, a biting wind, and afternoon light that didn't have much more strength than the gloomy light of morning and evening.

We met at the boat ramp, three men in hats, scarves, and the thickest coats that we owned, waiting for the fourth of our group. The parking lot was cold and breezy and Pete was done up in a matching waterproof coveralls and jacket, typical guide-wear for someone who's on the water twelve months a year. The other guy was in jeans and a camouflage parka, the thick kind for duck and goose hunting. I was wearing a Filson˚ tin cloth jacket with a flannel shirt and wool sweater beneath it. I knew that it might not be the easiest jacket to cast in, but I was willing to sacrifice a little mobility for warmth.

The fourth guy ended up sleeping in and staying home, a standard winter casualty according to Pete. This firmed our resolve before heading out, proving that the three of us were serious fishermen and that most of the world was staying indoors still dreaming of spring. In short order, coffee was drained and cigarettes were finished and crushed under boots into the gravel parking lot, our rods were loaded up, and we were headed out of Solomon's Island and blasting north to Calvert Cliffs and The Rips.

Although Pete's cabin blocked the wind fairly well, the chill in a moving boat on open water was felt immediately. I found myself wishing for the thermos of hot coffee that I'd left in my truck and an extra layer of clothing. Luckily, the winds were light and from the southeast so the ride up was smooth.

Before long, the Calvert Cliffs rose above the water to our left. The park beneath the cliffs provide popular spots for winter beach combers, bird watchers, and fossil hunters and, despite the cold, we could see a few people already walking along the beach.

After we arrived we idled off The Rips for a bit and finished rigging up. There were two other boats fishing the area and we watched them hooking schoolie stripers with fair regularity. The boats would drift through The Rips, working the area above and below the warm-water discharge, and then they'd motor back up for another drift. We worked our way into the rotation, and things stayed nice and orderly for the entire afternoon: three boats drifting through the fishy water quietly, regularly hooking fish, and keeping an eye out for each other. It doesn't always work like this in spots like this, but's it's nice when it does.

The fish finder in Pete's cabin suddenly had the magnetic draw of a television during Super Bowl Sunday. We watched it intently as we motored up, noting the depth and temperature and the silent emptiness of fishless water. Once we were above the current rip the screen came alive with fish marks. Stripers were tightly packed within a small space, stacked as neat as winter firewood, and I imagined the fish holding in the warmer current like campers around a campfire. Nobody on the boat felt a single winter chill at that moment.

For the most part, I stayed on the port side of the boat while the guy in camouflage worked the starboard. Once the drift through was set up and we were through the hairy water, Pete would sneak back to make a few casts, but after a few bouncy drifts I think his instincts took over and he stayed at the wheel. Pete and the guy in camouflage were both fishing light tackle with half-ounce jig heads rigged with plastics. They were both into fish on our first drift.

Pete had advised us to fish the heaviest sinkers we had so I had my 9 weight strung up with a Teeny 450. I had to cast upstream to allow time for the line to sink, and after a long count into the drift, the line would belly out below me and I'd begin stripping the fly back to me in erratic, jerky strips.

My first fish finally came after I got the hang of the drift and how quickly we were moving through the water. Instead of rushing my retrieve and trying to get two casts in for each drift I slowed down so that the fly would be good and deep by the time we got closer to the discharge. My first striper of the year was a nice omen, a thick twenty-three-inch fish that fought like hell until Pete netted it neatly.

That was the drill for the next hour: cast, hook, and fight fish, then motor back up current for another drift. The steadiness of the fishing lulled us into a mindless rhythm, but at one point I looked up and noticed that the tide had picked up and that standing waves had formed. By mid-morning, the relative calm we'd experienced earlier had evolved into a fairly jostling drift where I had my knees braced against the transom as we rode through the fishy water of The Rips.

Although the plan was for Pete to get some fishing in, I think that the conditions were iffy enough for him to want to stay at the wheel, and he was polite enough to let us to handle the bulk of the actual scouting. I offered to take a turn at the wheel a few times, but Pete politely declined and worked us through each drift in his Judge 27 Chesapeake.

There was a point in the morning when Pete pulled some life vests out of storage and asked us to wear them for the rest of the day. It took a little getting used to, but there was unexpected warmth to them with the additional layer and insulation. As the tide increased and the warm water continued to flow from the discharge pipe, the fishing got better and better while the water got meaner and uglier. By then the wind had picked up a little and our drift had been abbreviated into a quick outside drift along the edges and I had put up my fly rod for a spinning rod.

It was around this point that the older man in the camouflage parka hooked into a serious fish and Pete let us drift through the tail of The Rips as he fought it. When Pete netted it, we saw that it was a beautiful fish, winter bright, perfectly lined, and measuring around thirty inches.

The three of us took a break then with a snack and drink, and although the bite still seemed to be on, we decided that this was a good enough time to call the day.

I don't know if it was Pete's seriousness when he asked us all to put on life vests, or if the slip in the river a week before was still with me, but the possibility of drowning felt very real to me on our way back and I found myself attempting to calculate my odds of dying like this. I considered how often I fished alone in winter and knew that there would be a point soon where my legs would weaken, my reflexes would dull, and my body wouldn't be able to unconsciously get me out of trouble so easily. I thought of the places where I fished and the people I fished with. With no actual math to base this on, I decided that I had a one-in-four chance of death by water during a winter trip. It seemed like a fair number.

This, I hoped, would be my last bout with winter hyper-consciousness, the last spiraling introspection where observance lead to thought, which lead to memory, and finally creative hypothesis.

"I've seen it worse," Pete said on our way back to the boat ramp. "But I've also seen it flat calm, so nice that we anchored just off the pipe and fished poppers in the easy water. I think we might've caught fish on every cast that day."

He shook his head at the memory.

Although I felt that winter had been shaken off over the past few weeks and that spring and the spawning runs were nearing, at that moment in the gray choppy stillness of the Middle Bay the thought of topwater action like that sounded like an impossible luxury, something as far-off unimaginable as summer.

* * * * *

ON BURNING SPOTS

Fishermen can be protective of their fishing spots. I think it's a natural thing to guard the places you love, but as a fishing writer there's an impossible balance to this. There's a piece of water that you like and you want to celebrate it, so the urge to write about it comes. There might even be a story to it. But the reality is that most Chesapeake Bay anglers recognize that the best seasonal spots aren't at all secrets. So it's not exactly locations that they (we) guard, as it is the times when the fishing is on, or when big fish are being caught in the area.

Winter complicates things further because fishing spots on the Bay are so limited. With just a few realistic areas that hold fish, competition increases. And when the word gets out that the fishing is good at one of these spots, these spots that typically hold around three or four boats comfortably, suddenly see more pressure than the area can handle. Consequently, the fishing suffers. Spots get crowded and the fish get closemouthed.

I've heard a lot of rationalization on why these spots shouldn't be promoted: they're small and can't support too much pressure, it's hard on the fish, and it's a cultural breach of etiquette to speak so publicly about a small fishing spot. I understand that and respect it, but if I felt for a second that this sentiment was truly based on a concern for the fishery, and not a sportsman's fundamental desire to keep other anglers off the water, I would have avoided writing about these spots completely.

In the end, how I rationalized the decision to write about warm-water discharges was that, despite the fragility of these spots, winter remains the most effective deterrent to keep crowds off the water, despite the good fishing at these spots at a time when good fishing is scarce. Try fishing either of these spots on a Wednesday in February and I'd honestly be surprised if you saw a mob scene. My guess is that most people are staying home where it's safe and warm, and you'd be part of the happy minority.

Maryland Crab Soup

There are times when recipes can be updated or re-imagined, but some are simply fine as they are, if only to bring you back in time. At an early age, and partly because of this soup, I was under the impression that Maryland crabs were special and somehow better than other crabs. The name of the soup wasn't just crab soup, but Maryland Crab Soup. Every time I eat it, I think of Holly's Restaurant in Grasonville, Maryland, where my family would stop on our way to Ocean City. This recipe isn't a new take on a classic: it's consistent and evocative and tastes exactly as expected.

Ingredients
- Seafood stock
- Canned tomatoes
- Frozen mixed veggies
  (corn, green beans, lima beans, carrots)
- Cabbage, cut into spoon-sized pieces
- Bay leaf
- Crabmeat, equal parts claws and backfin
- Old Bay Seasoning

Directions:

In a thick-bottomed soup pot, bring seafood stock, canned tomatoes, mixed vegetables, cabbage, bay leaf, and Old Bay Seasoning to a boil. Simmer on low heat until lima beans are tender.

Hold off on adding crabmeat too early. There should be plenty of flavor from the seafood stock, and the crabmeat is cooked already. Add crabmeat during the last five to seven minutes before serving so the meat stays together and doesn't string.

A Note About Stock: The key to any soup is a homemade stock. It's easy enough to keep a large Ziplock® bag of clam, crab, and shrimp shells in the freezer. Chicken bones and odds and ends of vegetables can help round out the flavor. Once I'm ready to cook a soup, I'll simmer all this with lemon, onion, celery, and carrots. The flavor that comes with homemade stocks simply cannot be replicated and the process is a slow and warm one that helps dispel a cold winter day. Once I'm ready to cook a soup, I'll simmer all this with lemon, onion, celery, and carrots for at least an hour. Then I'll strain the shells and leftover, and then set the stock aside.

My mind was a dogsled to the arctic,
my wrists had salmon leaping for spring in them.

—Diane Wakowski
Waiting for the King of Spain

SPRING

MARCH

SHORE LUNCH

Daylight savings at the beginning of the month gives us the gift of time. A growing wind blows across thawing fields, while forsythia brightens yards with the sunny yellow of crayons. Garden tilling and plantings begin, the spawn starts, and Saturn shines behind clouds in the night sky. Cancer can be seen in the Northern Hemisphere, a celestial reminder to Maryland that the blue crabs will soon be swimming beautifully in our tidewaters.

A watched pot never boils.

Wye Oak in Bloom, c. 1955. The Wye Oak in Talbot County was ninety-five feet tall, had a spread of over 165 feet and measured fifty-seven feet and seven inches around its trunk, one foot from the ground. The state bought the tree and a small plot of ground around it in 1939 for $6,150 and constituted it a one-tree state forest, the only one in the nation. It fell in 2002 during a summer thunderstorm.

There's a lie that's born each winter: the falsehood of March sounding off like a 12 gauge and spring starting with a bang. With fresh snow on the ground and weeks of winter still ahead of me I'll picture mild spring weather and a mad dash through warming water, willing fish, and sunsets well after dinnertime. Hope emerges like a crocus: spring will come, March will come, and the perch will charge upstream in hordes.

I tell myself this lie every winter and I believe it each time. Our first instinct after all is to pray for deliverance, not the strength to endure, so as February trails away and daylight savings gives us later sunsets, there's a plea inside me for spring to come suddenly, but I know with a cold certainty that relief won't be given right away.

Some years winter does shift quickly into spring, but most years I've found that the actual arrival of spring is a far more gradual process, and that it's rarely like a bang at all. February snow gives way to barren fields, stark trees begin to hint of buds, and ice begins to slowly thaw away from shore. This is a process that takes weeks, and because I watch so intently, the pot never comes to a boil, and winter ends with aching slowness.

If you go by the calendar, the first day of spring is marked by the vernal equinox near the end of March, but I've never viewed this event as a very accurate starting point to spring and my fishing season. For one thing, the vernal equinox never really seems to fall on a day that truly feels like the official beginning that it designates. Astrologically, I appreciate the symmetry of day and nighttime hours, and some farmers might argue that there's biological, if not cultural significance to the date, but as a fisherman, I've never found much use for it. Most years, the vernal equinox seems to come and go as an afterthought— sometimes early or sometimes late, but rarely feeling right on time.

My personal definition of the beginning of spring is based more on when the perch start running. This is usually sometime in March, after the last of the snows have melted off, and when the first daffodils have started to poke through the soil that's been faded by three months of winter. The spawn can shift from year to year, but broadly speaking, March is as good a time to look for it as any other, so I use the month itself as a target.

I've seen mild Februaries when the yellow perch ran early and we fished in light jackets, and I've seen hard Marches when late blizzards and cold fronts had the rivers frozen over and, while we waited for the thaw, the white perch must've snuck by under the ice. After the rivers thawed, the party was over, and it felt like summer was starting before we'd even gotten a taste of spring.

So the spring perch runs on the Chesapeake Bay are a timing game where the fish hold all the cards and the seasons make up the rules as they go along. We wait for the warming days, for rumors to start spreading at the bait and tackle shops, until finally there's the welcome sight of four or five trucks pulled over beside a bridge or turnoff beside a small stream that leads to a larger tidal river.

February may be the shortest month, but it can last the longest, so by early March, I'm desperate to grasp for any sign of seasonal progress. And after a winter of empty water and cold days, what could be more seductive than the mindless, lusty arrival of hordes of spawning panfish? We've dedicated three months to slow, pensive fishing and thoughtful preparations: the idea of a river full of small, aggressive fish can have the romance of a tropical beach scene, and the simple fishing and ample catching of perch helps to dispel winter and put it behind us.

So, by early March, the nearness of the perch spawn is as tangible as being able to smell snow coming in December, and the preparations for a year of fishing come sharply into focus. Fishing licenses are bought, if they haven't been bought already. Leaders are retied and fly lines are stretched out and cleaned, tackle gets cleaned off and organized. My 5 weight leans against the wall by the garage door expectantly, strung up with a clean line, fresh leader, and favorite fly just steps away from my truck and a trip to spring waters, expectant as a dog waiting for a walk.

In these last weeks before the spawn begins, flies are tied with a professional focus on output. This isn't a creative journey through ideation and materials on hand; this is serious production where known fly patterns and color schemes are listed, prioritized, and tied by the dozen. Producing flies in bulk might not happen every winter, but it's happened enough over the years that this has evolved from an accidental event to a fairly attainable goal. By March, I'll aim to have tied three full fly boxes of flies for the upcoming season: one large box of clousers and huge streamers for stripers on the Susquehanna Flats; one medium box full of buggers and poppers for largemouth bass and bluegill; and one small box full of small clousers, grass shrimp, and crazy charlies for perch and croaker. If I'm especially productive, I'll have a box of flies for redfish and seatrout, smaller clousers and mushmouths that lack the bushy corpulence of my striper flies.

Depending on a number of things like snow or overall focus at the vise, I might get all three boxes done, but the biggest factor rests with which winter fantasy is resonating within me: is it the thought of bluegill hitting poppers from the surface of a millpond, or the idea of trophy stripers hitting huge flies in shallow water that I'm fixated on? With March and the perch runs so close, the fantasy of fishing for spawning perch in our small tidal creeks is typically what takes hold, and most years I can count on these flies getting tied and this box getting filled while the others may have to wait, hastily tied the week before a trip.

Tying flies in winter is equal parts creativity and frugality. The desire to prepare comes from cabin fever, a necessary separation from the water, and the knowledge from a past year's worth of fishing. But winter also brings out the miser in me and drives me to prepare for spring, since I can do little else. At my desk I open last year's perch box: a messy, disorganized collection of last year's flies and hasty discards. I remove everything for examination and to let the foam heal for a few days. Anything rusted is thrown away, anything too mangled is set aside to be striped down, and anything that can be reused is set aside into piles of bead heads, cone heads, usable hooks, and dumbbell eyes.

If I can maintain the fantasy of perch and avoid the easy distraction of late spring stripers or summer bluegill and the flies that accompany them, within a few sessions at the vise I'll have a box full of small calf tail closers in chartreuse and pink, tan, and olive crazy charlies, short cone-head crystal buggers, and translucent pearl grass shrimp sparkling happily from their neat rows.

After the flies are tied and my tackle is ready for a day on the water, final spring preparations bring me outside. One year in particular, when the fantasy of perch had been especially strong, I was living in a small farmhouse on Kennersley Farm, an old horse farm just outside Church Hill, Maryland. On a gravel and dirt lane, and separated tastefully from the big estate house by a line of poplar trees, there was a line of small caretaker's houses. I lived in one, a retired couple lived in another, and the farm caretaker lived in the third.

The property owner had let me store my boat in one of the barns over the winter and early the following March I headed out to begin the seasonal preparations that boat owners begin every spring with crossed fingers and mild dread. Back then I owned a sixteen-foot aluminum johnboat with a 40hp Yamaha outboard, a humble fishing boat that served me well until it was stolen about five years later. This boat was a Polarkraft johnboat, with a modified V hull that handled the standard chop of the bay a little better than the average flat-bottom johnboat. On first glance, it was the kind of boat you'd see ten times a day on the Eastern Shore: a working-class, dark-green, aluminum boat with white registration numbers on the sides and a Minn Kota¨ trolling motor mounted on the bow. The main thing that set it apart from other boats like it was the center console that elevated just a step above any other johnboat on the water. Most johnboats were of the open, utilitarian variety, but the addition of the center console gave mine a lot of spirit.

The console itself took up a good bit of space on the deck of the small boat, but it offered up nice storage for all the things that would otherwise clutter the deck of an open hull with bench seats. It was well suited for the creeks and rivers, small for the open water of the bay, but also at home on freshwater lakes. It wasn't exactly perfect for anything, but it had the everyday versatility of a Swiss army knife, so I fished it just about everywhere.

Inside the barn I saw that the tarp covering the boat had a decent coat of pigeon and barn swallow shit from its three months in storage. Underneath it, some dry leaves had managed to find their way to the deck and a squirrel had hidden a decent store of acorns in the transom near my gas tank and battery. A shop-vac made neat work of the leaves and squirrel's winter savings and soon the deck of the boat was clean.

I hooked the hose and clamps up to the outboard and, after a few turns, the engine caught and began to idle while spraying water in a tight stream down to the cold ground. There was a mild sputtering from the old gas and fuel stabilizer burning off, but for the most part, the engine sounded strong. I let it idle as I examined the rest of the boat, checking fuses and switches and wondering what winter casualties would emerge from months of storage and disuse.

Miraculously the bow and stern lights came on when switched, and my fish finder powered on and seemed to be reading fine. Even the lights on my trailer were functioning—brakes, blinkers, the whole package. For a boat owner, these were auspicious signs of spring and a new fishing season. To own a boat on the Chesapeake Bay is to live a life of happiness tendered by fear. While the days on the water are gifts, the time between trips is spent with renewing registrations, rewiring spent connections, flushing and fogging carbs, and fighting the constant losing battle between saltwater, electronics, and internal combustion engines. No boat is ever 100 percent functional: anyone who says otherwise is either a liar or doesn't take care of it himself.

While the trailer was hooked up to my truck, I towed the boat down the dirt and gravel lane and onto the main road that led into Church Hill. Despite the cold it felt good to be towing a boat behind my truck again.

I bought a cup of awful coffee at the gas station, filled the spare tank with fresh fuel and oil, and put air in the tires of the trailer. The boat ramp to Southeast Creek, a small tributary of the Chester River, was just a short distance from the gas station and a stone's throw from Kennersley Farm, so with hours of daylight left I decided to take a quick scouting trip to run the boat and stretch its legs, burn of the old gas, and check if there were any early signs of perch in the creek.

The winter had been hard and drawn out, and the temperatures over the past couple weeks had been in the low forties with rare moments of afternoon warmth. I wasn't too optimistic on any strong signs of perch—although you never knew just how things would shake out until you got out—but heading out seemed like a worthwhile thing to do, if only to run the boat and see what the river looked like.

So with the boat hooked up, and not even fishing rod with me, I headed to the boat ramp at Southeast Creek. The parking lot was empty when I pulled in and, even on the border of late winter and early spring, the empty boat ramp was a welcome sight. There were no lines, no sign of other boats on the water, and no other fishermen to contend with despite the earliness of the trip—only a cold line of geese out in the water watching warily as I slid the boat off the trailer and headed out to the mouth of the creek, and into the flat, empty water of the Chester.

* * * * *

With yellow perch, the comparison to the white perch run is natural and difficult to avoid. Where white perch tend to be monochromatic, stout bodied and aggressive to a fault, yellows are brightly colored, longer bodied and a bit more reserved in how they hit a fly. Where white perch strike a fly with the aggression of a bass, a yellow perch will follow and then finally decide to inhale the fly: one second you're retrieving the fly slowly, the next you're connected to a wiggling fish.

Yellow perch usually spawn earlier than whites, and their run tends to be quieter than what comes later in the month. With the white perch run, there are just more fish in the waters, and on their runs there's often a splashy ruckus close to shore and in stream riffles, and a fish-on-every-cast action. Yellows fill the early spring waters, but their signs are not as obvious. You have to look for them, search the streams for where they're holding, and not every river is home to a spawning run.

So, the runs of yellow perch are smaller in scale and more subdued when compared to the whites, but because they come earlier each spring, there's an excitement around them.

The fish themselves are brightly colored panfish with golden yellow bodies and dark vertical stripes. They're also fine table fare and when taken from these cold tidal waters provide a firm, sweet meat.

Yellow perch run can sneak by each spring if you're not watching and there's a thin line between getting out early and missing it altogether. The fishing can be hit or miss, and sometimes you end up standing beside cold water with a few other anglers and an outside chance at the fish themselves—whether they're caught or not—seems to be a good enough reason to get out of the house.

About a week after my scouting trip on Southeast Creek it seemed like the wait for spring was over and I was driving east from Church Hill through Caroline County towards Greensboro. I had a 5 weight, a pair of waders, and a freshly tied box of small flies with me, but I had left my packed lunch at home on the counter. The sky was a mottled gray and everything about the day was inconsistent: the wind would pick up and then stop, the clouds would move gloomily overhead and then break with a high sun, and every once in a while a rain shower would start before fitfully trailing off. Consequently, it was impossible to dress for the conditions without either being clammy in a raincoat, wet in a fleece, or too hot in both.

The rumors of yellow perch had finally begun to circulate and a friend had told me that he'd seen trucks pulled over at Red Bridges, a well-known spot on the headwaters of the Choptank where perch were known to run. Whether there was any truth behind the rumors or not, I was ready to give it a try, and the emptiness of the previous week's scouting trip had been the cherry on top of a big helping of winter of silence. At that point, I think I would've fished happily elbow-to-elbow with a platoon of fishermen on the banks of a small stream if it meant that there would be fish in the water.

When I parked at Red Bridges, I saw that there were only a handful of other anglers along the banks—a solemn looking group of old men and miserable-looking young kids watching the water dejectedly.

It was around eight o'clock when I got there, a few hours after high tide, and the tide was beginning to fall and pick up pace as the water headed down river to Cambridge and Tilghman Island. On the trash-lined bank of a county park, that looked to be equal parts parking lot and riverfront, I found a spot where I could cast just downstream from the other anglers and started peeling line of my reel as I stepped into the water.

Some of the fishermen there were throwing jig heads tipped with minnows, others were throwing small beetle spins, and a few were tossing weighted bobbers and rigs baited with grass shrimp. The morning started pretty quiet, but as the day wore on and the tide picked up, I saw that fish were being hooked with a slow, begrudging regularity. Every once in a while someone would say, "Fish on," quietly with their breath steaming in the cold, morning air. Even the kids were fairly subdued in their announcements although they seemed to feel the perch with a bit more enthusiasm.

My first casts were ignored, but after I added a five-inch sink tip, I eventually got a half-hearted bump in the deeper water, and then on the following cast hooked my first perch of the day, a bright eight-inch yellow perch that reluctantly hit a mylar grass shrimp pattern.

The steady bite lasted for just over an hour, with most of my bites coming from a cast directly out into the deeper channel of the river where the current would catch the line as it sank and drifted downstream. By the time the line had reached the two o'clock angle of the drift, I'd begin retrieving the fly back in slow, jerky strips, and every once in a while a perch would commit. As the tide picked up, the bites increased and a few times I could see perch following my fly at the end of my retrieve.

Although the morning was quiet and there wasn't yet the carnival atmosphere that emerges later in the spring perch runs, the other anglers and I were talking openly, and there was a clear appreciation for other people's success. I guess that's one thing that winter and the perch runs bring out of us: after months off the water, sometimes it's enough to be fishing and see that fish are being caught for the day to feel like success; if we can catch a few ourselves, so much the better, but even if we don't, at least we've made it outside to where a few fish were caught and seen.

One of the Red Bridges regulars said that this was probably the tail end of the yellow perch run here on the Choptank and that two weeks before, it had been fairly strong. Since then, some commercial fishermen had put in nets down river and whether it was the increased fishing pressure or just the run trailing off, the size of the fish had decreased significantly from the nicer twelve- to thirteen-inch roes to mainly eight- to nine-inch bucks. All of the fish I saw caught that day were carbon copies of each other without anything of notable size: bright eight- to nine-inch fish that put a decent bend in my 5 weight.

That was the scene at Red Bridges: a small group of quietly talking anglers fishing on an inconsistent spring morning with a brief but significant bite on a falling tide. Nobody had heard much about the white perch yet, but we all knew that it was just a matter of time before things really took off—here and at other spots like it around the Eastern Shore. Eventually, the tide finished falling, the bite died off, and the other anglers on shore with me started packing up to leave.

I might've caught five or six yellow perch that morning in a few hours of fishing—all on a small joe's grass shrimp pattern. The action was slow by perch standards, but considerably higher than what I'd seen over the past few months, so I was happy with the end result. It seemed like as good a time as any to call it quits there, so I decided to head home to Church Hill since lunch was ready and waiting on my kitchen counter.

The next day, with yellow perch still on my mind and all my gear still in the back of my truck, I drove to St. Paul's in Kent County. This spot was a small millpond beside the St. Paul's Church that had a spillway stream that led down to Langford Creek, a small tributary of the Chester River. This was another locally known yellow perch spot just outside Rock Hall, and though I hadn't heard much about it that year, I'd fished it before and knew that yellow perch historically ran in this small stream.

When I pulled up, there were two other cars parked alongside the road, fairly light pressure by perch-run standards, and as I rigged up and pulled my waders on (still cold and damp with water from the previous day's trip to the upper Choptank) I watched as the two other fishermen tossed weighted bobbers and bait rigs up against some lay downs beside the far bank of the stream. In the time it took me to string up my rod they each pulled a few fish from the edge of the main spillway pool. Even from the distance I could tell that they were a nicer quality than the bucks from Red Bridges.

Other than the fish I was targeting, the scene could've been easily mistaken for a January or February outing. It was cold and the cattails along the far bank were dry, frayed, and tallowed like melted candles. The sky was a raw gray, and although the wind had been fairly stiff at my house in Church Hill, it was fairly protected there in Kent County. It was one of those days when, although the temps were in the forties, it felt colder. It wasn't the wind that cut though me, but it felt as if the last bit of deep winter coldness in the ground was giving itself up and dissipating up through the surface. Where the previous day had been inconsistent and back and forth between warmth and cool conditions, along the headwaters of Langford Creek, the day was uniformly cold, and even beneath a hat, scarf, jacket, and my waders, I was having a hard time keeping warm.

Just past the ditch and dry weeds of the roadside there was a small, rough sand point that made up the inside bend of where the stream curved away from the spillway. There were tracks in the sand and a few buckets near the water; one, I assumed for bait, and a larger one for perch. On the other side of the stream, and an easy roll cast away, was what looked like the deep part of the stream where the fish were probably stacked. A tangle of brush and dead honeysuckle choked the far bank, along with bare trees and tall, dead grass backing it. A larger poplar tree from the woods behind the stream had fallen that winter and one of its larger branches rested in the stream on the outside of the bend where the mild current flowed and the deep water of the stream lay. This seemed to be the spot that held the best water and the bait fishermen lightly tossed their rigs up into the eddies of the branches.

The stream there at St. Paul's isn't a huge spot and the two guys fishing there offered a friendly greeting as I walked up. It's nice to share a small spot with friendly anglers when the fishing is in close quarters and you can't give people the space you'd normally give. Fly fishing is still a relatively new way to fish the waters of the Chesapeake Bay, so it always seems to draw a look or comment when I walk up to the water with an eight-and-a-half-foot fly rod. This is especially true during the perch runs, when people are more talkative than usual. Although most people were curious about flies and fly fishing, some could be idiotic; but on the whole, most people were never rude about it, and these guys at St. Paul's seemed more curious than anything. After happily sharing a look into the contents of the larger bucket, they said that the bite had been on since they got there forty-five minutes before.

The bait guys watched me cast for a bit, but eventually they shifted their focus back to their ultralights and bobbers. It took a while to get my bearings on the stream and figure out the cast and drift into the eddies of the poplar branch. It always seems like when I have an audience I spend more time losing flies to trees or snags in the water, or untying knot after knot in my leader and making a mess of my cast. It's easy to chalk days like this as kicking off the dust of winter, but I think they're most common when people are genuinely watching. But finally, I had the right combination of cast, drift, and fly weight and I was into my first yellow perch: a chunky ten-inch roe that tried to head straight into the tangle as soon as it was hooked.

Fly shops especially like to talk about hot flies and how minor variations in a pattern can account for boatloads of fish. There's a pattern for every season and every body of water—the Pax special and crab-colored closer come to mind here—and often they have a place of regional angling folklore. I'm the first to appreciate a new and innovative pattern, but for the most part, most of my flies tend to be pretty traditional. I usually fish the basics and do well with them. Most of the time, I've found that just getting a fly in the right place typically had more to do with success than the fly itself.

That morning, however, while fishing for subdued early-season yellow perch, I found that one pattern out-fished everything else, including the small minnows that the bait fishermen were using. I'd started with a short white crystal bugger with little interest, and then I'd switched to a chartreuse clouser with little effect. After losing them both in the submerged branches, I finally tied on a pink crazy charlie, and my first cast yielded a fish.

My next three casts led to three more fish, and for the rest of the morning, no matter where I cast it throughout the stream—in the far bank laydowns, up into the fast water where the spillway fell from the lake, or just out into the main channel of the stream—the yellow perch there could not stay away from it. The fly itself was a simple tie: a short size 8 saltwater hook with bead chain eyes, pink diamond braid round around the shank, a short pink calf tail wing, and finished with red crystal flash and red thread.

The bait fishermen were doing well with their minnows and the three of us were in good spirits as the morning wore on and we hooked yellow perch with a surprising regularity. Since they were keeping their fish, I said that they were welcome to mine if they were interested, but once I made this offer, the magic of my pink crazy charlie began to wear off. The action slowed and the bite on the stream eventually fizzled out. I managed to hook a few more fish before calling it quits and, as I walked over to where they were standing, I saw that after the morning of fishing there at St. Paul's they had what looked to be a good mess of fish, but still within the boundaries of the ten fish creel limit.

The bait guys said that they were planning on having a family fish fry later that evening, and that their secret to fried perch lay in seasoned flour and peanut oil. The thought of small perch fillets fried in peanut oil sounded fantastic and I told them I'd try it the next time I had a mess of perch to cook.

Back in my truck on the way home, with the windows up and the heater on, I looked out on the thawing farmland as it rolled past me. Along the roads it looked like winter, but the season had the edges of spring to it—in feeling if nothing else. Spawning fish had been caught in the tidewaters with fair regularity and although my hands had been cold, I hadn't had to bust ice out of my guides once.

* * * * *

A week later the yellow perch run quietly fizzled out, much how the run began just a short time before: quietly and without flourish. Although most of the yellows had exited the headwaters, word was spreading around the Eastern Shore that the whites were quickly beginning to fill the space that they'd left. To the south, the Wicomico and Nanticoke Rivers were already awash in spawning whites, so it wouldn't be much longer until the Chester and Choptank systems were full of their share of these tough, aggressive fish.

Unlike how the yellow perch trickle in, do their business briskly, and then head quietly back down river, the white perch run is a more boisterous, sustained run. White perch have greater numbers, and each spring they show up in waves, extending the run for weeks and providing a larger window of when we can fish. Consequently, the atmosphere of the white perch run is more like a county fair: as more fish are caught and the weather becomes milder, the fishermen themselves are more talkative, and the banks of the rivers are as much a fishing destination as a cultural event. All in all, the white perch run is more like a party than a quiet outdoor pastime. Along with the minor details of fish and fishing, there's a clear sense of community, and that when you're part of the perch run here, you're part of the Eastern Shore.

By then, it was getting towards the end of March and the daytime high had risen into the steady 50s. The forsythia had begun to brighten the landscape with its happy yellows, the daffodils were blooming, and the winter wheat along the roads was more than a hint of green. On my trip to St. Paul's, the world had looked and felt decidedly like winter with spring at the edges, but within the space of just a few weeks, the season had shifted to spring with some bits of winter leftover. The mornings were still cold enough for a real jacket when you walked out the door, but by eleven o'clock with a bright sun overhead, it was warm enough to take it off if the wind wasn't blowing.

With word of the perch running, my dad had come down from Cumberland to visit. We were headed to a spot on the upper Chester River near Millington where the Route 313 bridge crosses the Chester River, just south of town. This was a well-known white perch spot, and with easy fishing just steps from the parking lot to the river, it was a convenient spot for my dad.

I think he was in his late sixties at the time, not elderly quite yet, but there had been a string of health issues he had to contend with— heart, hand, and one mean winter cold that left him thin and weak— so our fishing trips had lost some of the expeditionary qualities that past trips had provided. Over the last two years, he had graduated to a kind of pedestrian fishing: piers, river access points close to parking lots, and the occasional dock on a lake or pond—all which as a dedicated bait fisherman, suited him just fine.

I sensed on the drive out that he'd reached the age where it's not the end result of fish caught that gives him the most pleasure now, but something broader: a break in the monotonous routine of retirement and the basic joy of being out fishing on a beautiful morning. He watched the awakening farmland roll by as we drove east in my truck, his hands in his lap holding a cup of coffee that he barely drank. And although he didn't say it, I knew that he was just content to be in a truck with me on our way to fish somewhere.

As expected, the white perch run on the upper Chester had the festive atmosphere of a county fair. Although it was a Tuesday in late March, there were already a handful of cars and trucks in the parking lot and the banks had good numbers of anglers casting and hooking fish with a noticeable regularity. People were talking back and forth, the river was low and clear, and the morning was warming up nicely.

I helped my dad get set up along the bulkhead, conveniently next to a few other old timers, before I headed downstream for a spot where I could at least cast into the river without snagging a branch or crossing someone's line in the water. I watched him between casts, smoking cigarettes and standing beside one of the pilings where his rod leaned.

Once I saw that he had finally hooked a fish I felt like I could stop watching him so closely. It wasn't that I thought he needed help or supervision; I think I just wanted to make sure he was having a good time and see that the fish were cooperating.

It's a strange contradiction of fishing and fly fishing that even when I fish with someone—and even when there's a significant crowd like here on the upper Chester—I do my actual fishing alone. I might meet a friend at the water or we might make the drive together, but as soon as we're rigged up and ready to fish, there's a quick and often mutual separation at the water. There might be an occasional check in, more typically words exchanged back at the truck at the end of the day, but for the most part, the fishing is a solitary experience. On one hand, I think the solitude on the water is a base element of fishing, but with fly fishing especially, and the need for a little room to cast, I think it's fairly natural to head in separate directions from a companion.

With my dad, this wasn't a change for us because we'd always gone in separate directions, even before I started fly fishing. Growing up, fishing was one of the things that he wanted to share with me and he would let me wander off to fish and fool around, catching crayfish and salamanders, and exploring the woods and streams nearby while he fished bait in some quiet corner of a pond or lake. Thirty years later, he was still fishing bait on an ultralight, and I was still fooling around next to shore.

The river there near Millington was simply loaded with white perch. There were splashes throughout the river and common hoots and cries of, "Fish on," from the anglers on shore. I still had my pink crazy charlie from my trip to St. Paul's and I could cast sidearm along the bank to work the murky water just off the shoreline. Within a few strips I was connected to my first fish, a short, bright perch with nickel sides and tarnished edges.

After that, I was conscious of the direct fulfillment of the winter perch fantasy: the constant bite, a river full of fish, and a warm day. This simple fishing during a special event was what I imagined during the last, cold, toothy phase of winter. There was an acceptable vulgarity to the mindless perch fishing, but one that I had wanted badly.

The bait and light tackle guys next to me seemed to begrudgingly admit that flies were especially effective in these conditions. The crazy charlie I was fishing was exactly what the perch seemed to want. It worked the shallow water well, there was no time lost with baiting and re-baiting, and the fish seemed to respond favorably to some actions that grubs and spinners simply couldn't replicate, the pulsing, jerking action of the fly followed by a pause that always seemed to trigger a response.

After the silence of winter and the subtlety of yellow perch, it was a shock each time to feel the strength of these fish and to see how small in size they were when they came to hand. Most of the fish landed were smallish bucks, although a few of the fish that my dad pulled in with his night crawlers looked to be some of the larger roes pushing eleven inches.

Some time before lunch, fully sated with perch and catching perch, I slowed down and started watching the other anglers around me. My dad was reeling in another stout perch and one of the old timers next to him said something that made him smile. Although it didn't seem like the numbers of people there had grown, it was clear that there had been a steady ebb and flow of fisherman, but that the total number had remained close to what it was when we'd arrived. The faces were different, the cars in the parking lot had changed, and the volume of conversations had lowered.

On the other side of the river there was a man in hip boots standing on a slim point that probably disappeared in a higher water. He was fishing an ultralight and casting a small jig head with a curly tailed grub downstream and he was hooking perch on nearly every cast. Although we were all hooking fish with regularity, it was clear that his was the best spot there in Millington: he could cast well into the river channel, and into the tail of a riffle that fed to the bridge pool that we couldn't reach from our side of the river.

The guy in hip boots knew he was putting on a show. He had the exaggerated actions of someone aware of an audience and the loud vocal excitement that's only really excused during the perch runs. At one point as he was reeling in a perch his rod jerked violently and bent for a few moments before his line broke. Nearly everyone on shore saw it happen, and nearly everyone had the same thought: striper.

Every piece of water has a spot like this: the one spot that everyone vies for and looks at longingly. The guy in hip boots was clearly a local and his had probably been the first truck in the parking lot that morning. I imagined the relief he must've felt when he saw that he was the first one there that morning, and I envied the first half hour or so that he had by himself, where by all rules of fishing and nature, his first few casts yielded good fish and the day had been his and his alone.

The bite that morning never really turned off, people came and went, fish were caught, but eventually we had gotten our fill of the blessedly mindless perch run so we decided to head home for lunch. On the ride home, my dad talked about the guy in hip boots and the luck he'd had. He wondered at the size of the fish that had hit the doomed perch the guy was reeling in. Two miles out of Millington it started raining and my dad was snoring in the seat beside me.

Back in Church Hill, my yard smelled like rain tilled earth, cut grass, and fresh mulch. The caretaker had been at work in the fields and grounds of the estate, and my neighbors had been gardening. My small yard looked a shade sloppier in comparison and I moved yard work up in my unwritten list of domestic priorities. I'll get to it after dad leaves, I thought. After dad leaves and when the perch stop running.

* * * * *

As fishermen on the Chesapeake Bay, boats are often a logical and necessary extension of the experience. And for as long as I can remember, my father has loved boats and being on boats, but he's always been intimidated by them. The maintenance, boater safety courses, trailering, and navigation were all things that he just wasn't comfortable doing, so he never bought one. But I know that he loved them.

Me owning a boat made much more sense. He could have the access and enjoyment without the realities of ownership. For a long time I judged him for this, for letting fear and discomfort stand in the way of a world of open water and good fishing. It took over twenty years for me to understand that it's completely normal to love something without ever being completely comfortable with it, and that a son with a boat was a beautiful thing to a father, perhaps in some ways, even more beautiful than a boat of his own.

The next morning, instead of rejoining the masses on the banks of the upper Chester, we launched my boat on Southeast Creek to see how the perch bite was close to home. I hadn't heard much about Southeast Creek, but then again, I never heard many rumors about Southeast Creek, and I liked it that way.

With high tide just after one o'clock, there was no serious rush to get out early, so we took our time around my house, had breakfast, and I went outside to pack the boat up while my dad did the dishes. Outside, the day didn't have the crisp spring blue freshness, but a low, gray stillness that feels more appropriate to fishing. When I came back inside, the kitchen was clean and the newspaper was spread on the kitchen table. My dad was standing at the kitchen sink looking outside.

"Ready?" I asked.

He nodded and put his coffee cup down on the table.

The trip to the boat ramp took all of five minutes after I hitched my boat up. Living within sight of the water I had come to know Southeast Creek fairly well over the past two years and knew that while there wasn't a perch run like in the headwaters of Millington, the waters in the rip that formed just off the north point of the creek mouth still held perch in good numbers once things got going.

There was a nice moment on the short drive to the boat ramp that emerged over the years I lived there at Kennersley. I would drive down the dirt and gravel lane, with the comforting ocean sound of the gravel beneath my truck tires and the metallic creak of the boat trailered behind me. At the end of the lane: if I turned left I would be fishing the home waters of Southeast Creek, and if I turned right towards Route 213, I could fish anywhere else: the Chester, the Choptank, the open water of the Chesapeake. It struck me then, and it still strikes me now, that both choices were fantastic. To have the intimacy of home waters or the adventure of unknown waters broken down into something as simple as a left or right-hand turn was something special; having it so close to home made it a blessing that I've never forgotten.

A short time after turning left at the end of the lane, I saw that the boat ramp was empty except for one truck that had already launched its boat. The launch must've been an early one because there was no telltale sign of wet tire tracks and a dripping trailer from the ramp to the parking area.

I made the familiar U turn, back-up, and launch, and within a few moments, I was parked beside the other truck. My father waited until after I launched before stepping down unsteadily into the boat from the bulkhead. He sat immediately on the console seat and leaned back contentedly.

I didn't blast off in a hurry to get the boat up on plane, but took my time and motored easily down to the mouth of the creek. I took a lap around the small island there to show him an abandoned cottage. From there we picked up a little more speed to get to the water off Deep Point, the northern point where the mouth of Southeast Creek met the Chester River. A sandy beach there dropped immediately off into a deep channel and a great rip formed here that held fish for most of the year.

Like the process of launching a boat on a familiar boat ramp, anchoring in this spot on a falling tide was something I could do with my eyes closed. I dropped anchor in the shallow water of the creek, well above where the rip formed and we drifted down with the falling current before the line grew taught and we were positioned just an easy cast above the rip.

From the stern of the boat my dad baited up and cast down into the current. Just a few seconds after he reeled in to tighten the line and set the rod in one of the rod holders, the rod was pulsing and he reeled in two perch hooked on the top and bottom hooks of the rig.

We'd planned to keep a few fish for lunch, so the larger of the two fish went into the bucket we'd brought with us. As the day wore on, we'd keep some of the larger perch, and when we were all said and done, I think we had around six good-sized perch in the bucket. We let a handful of the smaller ones go because we honestly just didn't need so many for lunch.

I was fishing an eight-foot 5 weight custom perch rod built by a rod-maker friend, Joe Cap. One winter he and I had talked at length on what the perfect perch rod would be: a 5 weight that could throw a light sinking line but still light enough to let panfish show off, the lower end built with stainless steel instead of the standard wood reel seat that saltwater would eventually corrode, and under nine feet long for fishing in tighter quarters when the perch were way up in the headwaters. Before spring arrived that year, Joe had built the rod that we'd talked about and I still have it. It's the one rod I will never sell.

With a stainless steel reel seat and fighting butt, it looked like a scaled-down saltwater 8 weight with a refreshingly progressive action that threw a 175-grain sinking line effortlessly. If you slowed down and cast the rod the way it wanted, it would throw a light sinking line a mile, and with a small grass shrimp at the short leader of mono, casting was a dream there in the windless morning. After a few weeks of fairly steady fishing and some practice casting out on my lawn, my form was coming back and I could make some of the longer casts that had challenged me earlier in the month.

A few fish came from the rip below us, but I found that if I cast to the shore, as my fly drifted down, it would work its way down the edge that dropped off quickly. Some good fish came that way: heftier, darker white perch that were a full step above the small bucks we'd caught at Millington the day before. I got snagged a few times fishing this drop-off and looking in my fly box that had been so well stocked at the beginning of the month, I thought that I might need to tie a few more flies. I still had a good amount of perch flies, but after having a full fly box for so long, the empty spaces called out to me.

The action there on Southeast Creek wasn't the every-cast nonstop action like it had been on the upper Chester, but it was just a beat slower, which can be better in some ways. You stay a little more aware of your retrieve, since not every cast yields a fish, and it's nice to have a pause in the action every now and then to talk and take a natural break. Dad would alternate between holding my spinning rod and setting it in the rod holder to sit and smoke. I'd make a few casts, catch a few fish, and sip from the thermos of coffee we'd packed.

At one point, a pair of deer stepped out of the woods and marsh grass and walked on the quiet beach there on the creek. A boat would motor by occasionally on the Chester, but the small waters of Southeast Creek stayed empty for the most part.

I caught fish on grass shrimp and small chartreuse clousers steadily that morning. Dad caught perch, singles and doubles on his bottom rig, with one early-season catfish and a lonely looking yellow perch thrown in for good measure. At one point in the morning when the tide was running the strongest, we caught a few baby stripers, all of which we released, although dad had gut-hooked one and felt sorry as hell about it.

With the fish still biting and the tide still running, we reeled up, pulled anchor, and motored the short distance to shore where we beached the boat on Deep Point. I jumped out of the boat and peed up against the reeds on shore. Dad was sitting on the padded console seat looking out over the water towards the small island and marina just beyond it.

"Let's cook lunch here. I brought everything."

He looked confused for a second, but then pleased and mildly amused.

In many ways, I keep clean and organized tackle and gear if only to show my father what a slob he is. Where his garage is full and cluttered, and his rods are tangled and strewn about, my garage is clear and organized, with most things in a proper place.

The stove and fuel, pots and pans, cutting board and utensils are the main pieces of hardware. After that, the pantry items just take a little creativity: frying oil in a small plastic bottle, a can of baked beans, and a few potatoes. Even a few salt and pepper packets left over from fast food restaurants help to add the finishing touches to a shore lunch. All of this can fit into a small backpack, and I had packed that into the boat without him noticing earlier that morning.

Standing on the beach, my Dad used the raised deck on the bow of the boat as a work station and started working on the perch we'd kept. He filleted them neatly on a cutting board with the educated precision of his surgeon's hands. Even with the nerves of one hand badly damaged, he still filleted a fish neater than I ever would with perfectly functioning hands, and within a few minutes there was a modest pile of fillets off to the side.

On the beach beside him I had a two burner Coleman camping stove set up in the sand beside an old stump. On one burner was a small pot of baked beans, and on the second was a small pan with peanut oil heating up. I cut two potatoes into rough french fries as the oil began to heat

Dad tossed what was left of the mess of fish that he'd just cleaned up beside the reeds for the muskrats and snapping turtles and took a few handfuls of river water to wash the fillets and cutting board. Squatting by shore he washed his hands in the creek and washed his face as well—a habit that I mirror almost perfectly.

From the backpack I handed him a large Ziplock® bag with flour and seasoned salt in it and he dropped the fillets in to coat them. The fries were almost done cooking through, and I set out two plates to divide them to dry. The beans were simmering by then and I took the pot off, covered it with the small lid, and set it in the sand.

"Do you want to do the fish?" I asked.

"Sure," he said smiling. After the surgeries and sicknesses it was good to see him in such good spirits.

Much how a sandwich made by your wife always tastes better than one you make yourself, fish cooked by my father always seems to taste better than any fish I ever cook or order in a restaurant. I don't know if it's psychology, how he cooks them, or the meat from the freshly caught fish themselves, but he can make a river perch or pond-caught bluegill taste like dover sole.

With the oil still hot from the french fries he set the fillets in the pan gently and let them fry and bubble steadily before flipping them neatly with a fork. After a few batches in the small pan we had a sizable pile of small fillets on each plate beside the fries. I spooned a few helpings of beans beside everything and finished them with some salt and pepper.

Before we ate, Dad dipped his hands in the water by shore as if to wash them and then set them over the two plates of food dripping a few drops of water onto them.

"Lord, bless this food to our use. Thank you for these fish and this day," he said unexpectedly.

"Amen," I said.

There wasn't a ton that we spoke about over lunch. I think we talked about the nicer size of perch there on Southeast Creek, and Dad mentioned the angler in hip boots there in Millington and the striper he had hooked into for a second.

We ate our lunch, which would've been nothing to write home at anywhere else, but on the beach looking out over Southeast Creek, picking the occasional fish bone from our mouth, it was sacramental. We'd fished and caught fish, and now we were eating a shore lunch in the sand. It would have been simple enough to just head home and cook the same lunch there in my kitchen, but cooking that simple meal there on shore infused the trip with significance and special meaning.

"It's good," he said.

We were running out of beach as the tide rose, and after finishing up our plates of food with a few fillets left over we rinsed the dishes and packed everything up in the boat.

It was just before noon by the time we pushed off the beach and headed home. The morning gray had burned off while we cooked lunch. The sun was high in the sky and the temperatures had risen to the low 60s. At some point in the morning I had taken off my jacket and rolled up my sleeves. The new feeling of warmth, the early start that morning, and a belly full of fried fish, potatoes, and baked beans all added up to a drowsiness that only comes after a morning of fishing. After we got to the boat ramp, Dad sat in the truck while I strapped the boat down and readied it for the short drive home.

We had barely gotten half a mile from the creek and turned onto Clabber Hill Road before I noticed that he had nodded off in the seat beside me. Once we pulled up to the house, he wandered into the house drowsily and fell asleep on the couch.

I put the leftover perch fillet into the fridge and looked at the newspaper on the kitchen table. The weather section was out and it looked like my dad had been reading over it before we left. It had the weather five days out—rain coming—along with the tide table that they posted every day. A brown ring from the coffee cup he'd set down circled an old-fashioned graphic of the sun with the words, "VERNAL EQUINOX" written beneath it.

The date on the newspaper said Wednesday March 20, 2002. Despite my doubt, spring had in fact come like sudden deliverance, dead center on when the stars and the calendar said it would. The weather had warmed, the farmland was a pulsing state of green and unexpected color, and the perch had filled our rivers from beginning to end. Although I had been right in the gradual stages leading up to this moment, I had been wrong about the tipping point: that a tangible, definable moment—small or otherwise—would come and it would clearly define the beginning of spring and put winter firmly behind us.

In the small farmhouse at Kennersley Farm my dad snored on the couch as a lawnmower ran outside. We had lasted the winter and it was undeniably spring.

White and Yellow Perch Scampi with Saltine Crackers

White and yellow perch fresh from the Chesapeake Bay and surging up tidal rivers to spawn have the clean, flaky meat that comes with anadromous fish and tends to taste more like stripers than freshwater panfish. Most of the time, it takes longer to fillet a mess of perch than it does to catch them. I typically try to keep a few decently sized bucks and let the fatter females go. Depending on the size of the fish, this recipe calls for between eight to ten perch, and the fillets from each side of the fish should cover the bottom of a casserole dish nicely.

Serves eight to ten

Ingredients
- · Mess of white or yellow perch fillets, enough to coat the bottom of a casserole
- · Salt and black pepper, for seasoning
- · Garlic cloves
- · 1 stick salted butter, room temperature
- · Butter or cooking spray (if desired)
- · White pepper, for seasoning
- · Parmesan cheese
- · Fresh basil
- · Flat leaf parsley
- · 1 sleeve Saltine crackers

Directions:
Heat oven to 450°.

Fillet perch and set aside in bowl. Hold each fillet under a running faucet to wash any excess scales and feel for any missed bones. Once rinsed and inspected, set on a cutting board and pat dry. Season with salt and pepper.

Using a garlic press, press four to five garlic cloves into a small bowl holding one stick of salted butter raised to room temperature. Blend and set aside.

Coat the bottom of a nine-inch casserole with butter or cooking spray. Lay one layer of fish down so that the bottom is completely covered. Lightly season with white pepper and spread pats of garlic butter on top. Repeat layer with the remaining fish and garlic butter. Coat liberally with Parmesan cheese.

Bake uncovered on the top rack for fifteen minutes or until fish is flaky and white, butter is bubbling, and Parmesan cheese has begun to turn golden brown.

Remove from oven and top with thin ribbons of fresh basil and flat leaf parsley.

Serving Suggestion
Fork small servings onto saltine crackers as an appetizer or as a main dish beside mac and cheese.

APRIL

HOPE AND RAIN ON THE SUSQUEHANNA FLATS

Rain falls a thousand miles to the north, finds its way to a Pennsylvania stream, and joins the muddy Susquehanna to head south to Maryland. Behind the clouded spring sky Mars slides behind the sun and out of view. Below, as the soil awakens after the last frost and warning rains, gardens take root, seeds poke meekly from the ground, and an early chorus of frogs sing long into the night.

If the cows in pastures are lying down,
it's a sign of rain.

Susquehanna Mist, c. 1950.

From the inside of a tent it was difficult to tell if the rainfall came from the clouds, leftover drops from the leaves above, or a little bit of both. I could hear a staticky drizzle on the nylon fly of my tent as I woke, along with an occasional heavy drop from the new oak and maple leaves from the trees above. The sound was compounded by the leaves rustling above, along with the drops hitting the thick leathery leaves of the mountain laurel around my campsite. It wasn't at all ominous and didn't hint at threatening weather to expect; it was just the random and ambient sound of a tapering rain with few bolder drops every now and then dripping from the leaves in the trees high above the campsite.

We had arrived at the campground late the night before, coming in hot from a highway sprint up Interstate 95 in an over-caffeinated buzz, and barely making the 10 p.m. cutoff point at the Elk Neck State Park ranger station. After we checked in, we set up our tents in the stark, overexposed beams of our truck headlights, lit the obligatory campfire, and roasted a few hotdogs for a late dinner. Shortly afterwards, David and I turned in, tired from a long week of work and a late drive, and anxious to get out on the water the next morning.

Our trip to the Susquehanna Flats that year had come together quickly. On Wednesday a work obligation of mine for the weekend dissolved, leaving me with some unexpected free time. I called David that night to see if he was interested in trying to get up to the flats with me, and after some back and forth, he committed enthusiastically to the trip. David might be the last guy in the world who would ever plan a fishing trip, but he's usually the first to jump at the chance to get out.

The weather and tides didn't look ideal, and there hadn't been enthusiastic reports of the flats fishing because of the rainy spring we'd had, but with our fairly complicated work schedules and ever-increasing home and family obligations, it was looking like this could be our last shot before the flats season ended, so we went.

* * * * *

The Susquehanna Flats are at the northern end of the Chesapeake Bay near Havre de Grace, Maryland—about 200 miles from the mouth of the bay near Cape Charles, Virginia. The waters of the Susquehanna River spill from the Conowingo Dam and flow into the flats from the north, while the North East River enters the shallow brackish estuary from the northeast. As its name implies, the area is mainly a shallow saltwater flat, roughly six miles by eight miles, with two main channels working up the eastern and western shores and a network of smaller guts woven throughout. Much of the water is less than ten feet, with many portions as shallow as three feet or less where the healthy weed beds can be seen reaching up towards the sun. In the summer, you can see the mats of the weed beds all the way from the US Route 95 bridge.

Our moody and unpredictable mid-Atlantic springs make the fishery somewhat touchy. Wind can churn the shallow waters quickly, temperature drops can push the fish into deeper waters, and runoff from the Susquehanna River can all put the fishing off for anglers fishing flies or light tackle. Along with local rain and runoff, there's the considerable drainage of the Susquehanna River to the north to consider. If eastern Pennsylvania, and even southern New York see their share of rain and flooding, all of that muddy water flows downstream to the main stem of the Susquehanna River until it spills over Conowingo Dam and into the Susquehanna Flats.

Beneath the threat and reality of spring rain there's the undercurrent of the spawn. By then we've been warmed up by perch and tempered with the arrival of stripers. There are also the side plots of shad on a few select rivers and on our lakes and ponds largemouth bass and bluegill start finning out nests. After the silence of winter, all of this effort to procreate in the face of high muddy water sounds especially unstoppable. It's a good feeling to know that the runoff might hinder the fishing, but it never really stops the spawn.

I don't consider the flats to be local water, and it's taken years for me to get even a minor understanding of the fishery. It can change drastically from year to year and from day to day. At this point, I have a basic understanding of the area and what the fish are doing there, but I'm far from an expert. Biology and sheer math are luckily the main contributors to most anglers' success up there.

The tidal creeks and rivers of the Chesapeake Bay are the principal spawning areas for striped bass along the mid-Atlantic coast. Each spring stripers return to the Chesapeake Bay after wintering off the coast of North Carolina. They work their way into its tributaries to spawn where some stay for the summer and fall, but others return to the ocean. Some of the fish veer off to spawn in main tributaries like the Potomac, the Chester, and the Choptank, but others keep working north until they hit the flats.

For fly fisherman, the black and white math of the fishery simply can't be ignored. Each April during trophy season, a huge number of fish enter the relatively small and shallow body of water of the Susquehanna Flats. Some of these fish can be in the thirty- to forty-pound class with others comparatively smaller, but regardless of their range in size, they're all stripers, and after long winter, they're ready to gorge on the ample supply of herring on the flats.

For many anglers, this is an incredible opportunity to catch trophy stripers in easy-to-access shallow water. Rich and poor, young and old, when the bite is on, the flats can fill up quickly. On nice days, I've seen everything from cabin cruisers and pleasure boats, to center consoles and small aluminum boats powered by 10hp outboards out fishing. The regatta can be jovial when the days are mild and the fishing is good and it's similar in feeling to the perch runs. Other times when April feels more like a closer relative to March than June, the waters are cold and stained, and the anglers are scattered.

Even with the outside chance at a trophy striper, it felt good to be fishing the bay again. The perch and largemouth trips I'd taken had been good ones, but it didn't really feel like I had started the year until I woke up at Elk Neck.

* * * * *

So often there's an excitement before a fishing trip that can keep me up at night. And on a domestic level, there's the strangeness and moderate discomfort of sleeping away from my bed and wife that can make for a strange night's sleep. But I woke up incredibly comfortable the next morning. I wasn't cold, I wasn't at all damp. I was perfectly warm and dry inside my tent and sleeping bag, and glad for the extra padding of the sleeping pad that I had purchased that winter.

I'm not entirely sure why, but I always sleep incredibly well at Elk Neck. Maybe it's the time of year, late spring when it's usually pretty temperate, not the harsh winter cold or summer heat that can make some camping trips test a man's constitution. But each time I camp at Elk Neck, when I sleep in its mountain laurel enclosed campsites on bluffs that overlook the Chesapeake Bay, I wake incredibly rested after a deep, uninterrupted sleep. Much how some wild places can feel innately haunted or sinister, Elk Neck has the opposite effect, as if the forests and waters there have a healing and rejuvenating power born into the area.

The sound of rain and my overall comfort made rousing myself a little harder than usual, but within a few minutes I heard David fart loudly from within his tent and soon I heard the sound of his tent zipper as he started waking up and digging through our lukewarm cooler.

Our trip that year had a haste and overall lack of preparation to it that left us mildly embarrassed. Along with this were unspoken and moderately low expectations for the fishing itself. We had remembered to bring the basics—rods and tackle, kayaks and paddles—but we had each forgotten a few key items. David had left his sleeping pad, so he slept on the ground in his sleeping bag, and I had forgotten tippet material and my headlamp. We had a cooler with us, but it wasn't packed well or incredibly tempting: inside were some bottles of water, the remainder of our hot dogs and soggy buns, some bruised bananas, and the remnants of some barbecue chips. Clearly, we hadn't thought this through, not all of the details, and the seriousness of spring trophy season made us feel even more unprepared. Despite all that, the basics were there for a fishing trip and we were there to give it a shot.

Breakfast was a necessity, but it wouldn't be pretty given our available options. The campground store wouldn't open for another couple hours and probably didn't have much for breakfast anyway. There was a McDonalds about ten miles up Turkey Point Road in the town of North East, but driving there and back seemed like a waste of time, so we cooked up some hot dogs, forced down some mushy bananas and finished what was left of the chips before heading out on the water, agreeing to eat a warm meal once we got off the water around lunchtime.

We launched our kayaks at the state park beach and paddled out into a still gray spring morning. There was a low fog and the water of the flats was calm. Our initial plan was to work the relative shallow water of the middle portion of the flats, targeting a few of the minor channels that acted as back roads to the two major highway channels that lead up the eastern and western shores.

The surface on the open water was mildly choppy from a stiff breeze and the temperatures felt noticeably cooler down on the water than from the protected forest of the campsite. At least we'd both remembered our waders.

The water clarity near the beach wasn't great. It was stained that muddy and turbid brown from the runoff of four mid-Atlantic states, but it improved a bit once we got out into the main channel. Behind us, the bluffs of Turkey Point rose into the fog and light rain. Although I couldn't see it, I knew the light house was there, but its light no longer warned ships of land.

Our paddle out wasn't too bad. The wind was with us, and the tide was beginning to rise. After more than a few perch trips that year, along with a handful of early bass trips on some local lakes, my paddling stroke felt strong and consistent again and winter's dust and cobwebs had been knocked off. David was ahead of me in his kayak, a light poking from his milk crate shining in the early morning gloom, and two nine-foot fly rods rising into the air from their rod holders. After we crossed the channel and ventured into the flats we began casting.

David was about thirty yards away in his kayak when I heard something between a laugh and a gasp. I looked over to him and he had a scared look on his face.

"I was just about done my retrieve and was about to make another cast when I saw a fish was following my fly. It was huge. I could see its eyes and...and it saw me."

The morning was so still that his voice carried over the water without much effort. I nodded and smiled, paddling west, deeper into the weedy, shallow flats, glad to hear that the morning looked promising. Finding fish was a great start, because even though the body itself wasn't expansive, the flats can feel like a big, empty place sometimes.

We fished hard in the gray morning in the dirty water. I was fishing a big chartreuse cactus striper fly and David was fishing a chartreuse over orange clouser tied with yak hair. We stuck to the lower half of the flats that morning, drifting north with the rising tide, watching our depth finders, and paddling back into position to fish the minor channels that we were targeting.

David got two stout fish that morning, in the higher twenties, he guessed. I landed one and lost two before we decided to head in for lunch. By then most of the fog had lifted and we could see the western shore and the houses of Aberdeen in the distance.

By the time we had paddled back, dragged our kayaks up the steep hill from the beach, and loaded up David's truck we were absolutely starving. We found a diner in North East, ordered breakfast, relaxed with a cup of coffee, and followed up by ordering burgers.

* * * * *

More than any time of year, hope swims in the water of the Susquehanna Flats. Because of the sheer number of fish that have entered the area, every cast has a real potential to end with a trophy fish. The fishing is more like entering a raffle than buying a lottery ticket and it's impossible not to be conscious of this. Faith moves to the front of the fishing and it's common to see an ebb and flow of that faith out on the water.

Fishing earlier in the season is just honestly easier in a boat. When water temperatures are still in the low forties, it's a common tactic to look for pockets of warming water where fish might be holding, and on tougher days when the runoff from the Susquehanna River is a factor, it's necessary to move from place to place in search of improved water clarity. It's touchy fishing early, but the fishing can be fantastic when it's on, and I've had some incredible days. It's not unheard of to see pictures of guys holding forty-pound fish that they caught in early April on a popper.

Other times when the weather's mild and the fishing's been fairly stable, the fishery is no secret. On these days there's a carnival atmosphere, along with a relative armada on the small body of water. People are talking back and forth between boats and everyone can have a good time.

One spring I was fishing with Brandon White, a highly connected angler and entrepreneur on the Chesapeake Bay. Brandon was a leader in the *dotcom* explosion back in the late '90s, and I was fortunate to be one of his partners along for the exciting ride. We were one of the largest and best fishing sites on the Internet at one point, with an incredible collection of content, an active online community, and we were fishing from his twenty-one-foot Parker, a simple and stable center console popular with local anglers.

It was still early in the season, and winter hadn't given up its hold on the area quite yet, so water temps were still fairly low and the fishing hadn't really broken loose. We had spent most of the morning on the eastern side of the flats, fishing hard and barely talking as we cast and worked the water from spot to spot. I had hooked and lost one decent fish early and there had been little action since. After eating a quick lunch, we had moved over to the western side of the flats just a bit north of Turkey Point.

I was still going through the motions of casting and retrieving when I felt the dull, indescribable connection to a huge fish. I set the hook, leaned into it, and felt the loose line on the deck of the boat disappear through the guides. The fish had barely even woken up and already it was on the reel and sloshing at the surface with its head out of the water like a tarpon. The fish ran, turned, and then decided to stay put for a second, letting me feel its considerable weight.

I can remember everything about that morning: the rod I was fishing, the fly I was using, even the jacket I was wearing. And I can still distinctly feel that moment when that impossible fish spit the hook and left me and Brandon looking at each other in shock and disappointment.

I remember Brandon saying, "That fish was every bit of forty pounds."

The stillness at the end of the line was shattering. I remember having to sit down afterward. I've caught and lost a ton of decent fish over the years, but that fish was the fish of a lifetime. Brandon excitedly told me to keep working the water since more fish might still be in the area, and when I stripped in the line to make another cast, I saw that the hook point was still sharp, and that it hadn't been bent straight.

We fished through the rest of the day, and didn't have much luck. That had been our shot and it hadn't panned out. There can be quiet days on the flats as well as incredible ones. Losing that fish stayed with me for a long time, but it also gave me an early glimpse of what's possible up there, and fuels me to come back each spring.

* * * * *

A few years after that April with Brandon when I lost the big fish, and before my hasty camping trip with David, there was one April when I camped for three days up on the Flats by myself. The winter before had been hard with a number of blizzards and ice storms, and it was common for the region to be out of power for a few days as utility companies worked to repair the power lines that were knocked down from falling trees.

Elk Neck State Park had seen a fair share of tree casualties and the cleanup there had been significant. That year as I drove to my campsite, I could see where a number of trees and limbs had fallen, along with bare areas with muddy sawdust and overturned stumps waiting to be removed. Rather than trucking out a winter's worth of firewood, the park workers had left huge stacks of firewood at each site.

The wood wasn't seasoned or split, but it was thoughtfully cut into logs that burned well enough once the fire was going. After I lit my first campfire I don't think it ever fully went out for the three days I was there with all that wood available. I'd keep it going during the day, and each afternoon and evening when I got back from fishing, the coals and half-burned logs would just need a little prodding to get going again. It might have been overkill for one guy, but part of me wished that I had brought a dutch oven and a cheap roast so I could've let that cook over a smoldering campfire all day while I fished.

This trip was in the middle of April, after the heavy rains had pushed through, but there was still a trace of that raw March breeziness and the weather hadn't begun to warm significantly. The mornings would be cold and still as the last of coals from the night's fire smoldered in the fire ring. The mountain laurel surrounding the campsite was a deep green and a few were tipped with white blooms. Above the small green buds of the maples and oaks began to unfold into the stillness. As the mornings progressed, the wind would pick up, steadily churning up the water of the flats, but dying down around dusk. All this made for tough conditions on the water, but fairly comfortable time in camp.

Before that trip the impeller to my outboard had some issues, so I dropped my boat off at my marine mechanic's and brought my kayak with me to the flats instead. I was a little disappointed in not being able to execute the plan I'd been working out in my head over the last few weeks, but it felt mildly liberating to have everything I'd need loaded into one truck in less than fifteen minutes before the trip. Although towing a boat lends a trip an expeditionary quality, having everything self-contained and self-propelled added a sense of old-school minimalism that, as a fly fisherman, I could appreciate.

I launched from the beach there in the state park, and aside from the intimidating hill down from the parking lot, there wasn't anything else to contend with, and I was a short distance to some prime water on the lower part of the flats. This part of the state park was mostly empty at this time of year. At its busiest, on a Saturday afternoon, there might be a few families letting their kids run off some steam, or a bird watcher looking for the pair of nesting bald eagles that made their home on a bluff overlooking the water. This was a significant change from the area boat ramps during the trophy season, which could be as crowded as mall parking lots during the holidays, and tended to bring the worst out of people rather than the best.

Just a short paddle from the beach I was crossing the deep water of the channel and marking a few fish on my fish finder along the western edge. Soon the water began to shallow from twelve feet to six feet, eventually evening out to a four-foot flat. The water clarity out in the weeds was noticeably improved, and in a few spots I could see the tops of the weed beds poking up from the muddy depths.

There wasn't much surface activity, but I began casting into a hole there in the shallows, a small depression that dipped into eleven feet in a flat that was mostly five feet deep. A fish on the first cast of the day is one of fishing's finest moments, but a moment like that on the flats after a long winter is an incredible gift. My first striper of the season was an even thirty inches, stretched across my outstretched legs in the kayak, and measured against the ruler marks on my paddle. Three more fish came from this spot before I paddled deeper into the shallowing water, searching for significant channel depressions. Before the morning was complete, I had a handful more fish in the mid twenties, and I lost a nice fish at the boat as I was trying to land it.

The morning was finally beginning to warm and the early, cloudy skies were giving way to a clear, sunny blue. To the north across the flats, I could see Havre de Grace in the distance waking for a day's work and the shine from the small cars on the Hatem Bridge catching the sun. To the south, I could see the armada setting up, a group of boats anchored in the tide and acting as a blockade to fish entering the flats from the bay.

I headed back in, paddling with the falling tide and a decent breeze at my back as I worked my way southeast. After I dragged my kayak up the hill from the beach, at least 200 yards up a steep incline after a morning of paddling close to six miles, I relaxed in camp for a few hours.

This was the first time that the light bulb went off in my head on what the fish were doing there and how I could target them better. Up until that spring I had been focussed on the spawn, assuming that the fish were there, but moving through in pulses, either heading north into the river or south back to the main stem of the Bay. I'm sure that might be the case in some instances, but lately I've come to think that the Flats are more of a staging ground, and that once there, the stripers simply act like stripers—they want deeper water to hide in, they'll move into shallow water to feed, and because they're gluttons, they feed quite often and will hit a fly if you can get it in front of them.

So now I work the water away from the crowds, deeper into the weedy, shallow waters of the central flats, and silent as a heron in my kayak. Silence in that shallow water has paid big dividends for me over the past few years, with an overall increase in quality and quantity of fish caught.

* * * * *

The late winter fishery of the Bay Bridge Tunnel and the spring trophy season on the Susquehanna Flats make for nice bookends: fly fishers begin and end the Chesapeake Bay striper season casting big flies to trophy fish, while the rest of the year has more moderate expectations and surprises.

December and January can end the season on a good note with a final shot at big fish. Some years I'll head south in December to the Chesapeake Bay Bridge Tunnels around Cape Charles, Virginia, to fish for large ocean-bound stripers heading south to winter off the Outer Banks. Often down there, and much how we will four months later be in shallow waters to the north, we'll fish large eight- to nine-inch mullet patterns tied with yak hair on huge 1/0 hooks.

The class of fish is incredible, with fish in the high twenties average, fish in the thirties common, and fish in the forties completely possible. It's an amazing time of year to fish and an exciting way to end it. And it always ends abruptly. There's this crescendo of big fish possibility and then silence. Within a short amount of time, anglers on the Chesapeake go from headhunting to being snowed in.

Very often as I settle into the inevitable late winter fly tying routine with temperatures in the twenties and a foot of snow on the ground, I'll open up my large fly box with its big trophy streamers, culling out the ones that are too rusted or mangled for future use. I'll tie up a few in anticipation of the spring Susquehanna Flats season, thinking back to fishing my 9 and 10 weight rods and the incomparable thrill of hooking these large wild fish. As I fill my large fly box with huge flies, I'll think forward to spring and the Susquehanna Flats.

The flies I tie for the flats can vary. I've always enjoyed fishing Joe Bruce's cactus striper fly because I've had good success with it and because it's a relatively easy fly to tie, but lately I've been more and more into larger profile flies like high tie bunker flies and large buck tail deceivers. These flies aren't the production ties where I aim to tie at least a dozen in one sitting. They're each custom jobs, and I'll restart my tie if I make a mistake or don't like the way it's turning out. This approach is fine, because I can't keep more than the usual amount of these flies in my fly box reserved for trophy flies, and don't really need that much variety anyway. It's not a game of subtlety and detail, it's about grabbing attention, and letting a hungry predatory fish do what comes naturally.

* * * * *

After David and I ate our lunch in North East, we stopped at a convenience store and got a decent cache of food, and then we headed back to the campsite. I put some coffee on and checked the tide table at the picnic table. The tide would be rising late in the afternoon, and we agreed to try to be in position by the time the current was moving.

By three o'clock that afternoon we headed back out. We landed a few small fish off the main channel edge and then paddled deeper, looking for the secondary channels braiding throughout the flats. We could hear splashes as we got deeper into the weedy shallow water. As the sun began to set, fish began rolling in the surface, enormous twenty-inch and thirty-inch fish that were splashing and jumping in the shallow water of the weed beds. It was one of the most memorable sights I've ever seen on the Chesapeake Bay.

As beautiful and intimidating as the scene was, the fish weren't hitting anything we threw at them. I tried the cactus striper fly I'd been fishing, switched to a yak hair herring pattern, and ended with an unweighted buck tail deceiver that pulsed seductively in the water and proved to be the most weedless of the three. David fished a big half and half and switched to a popper at one point. Nothing tempted any of these active fish. Between the vegetation fowling the hooks and the fish clowning around in the shallows, the fishing was an odd mix of frustrating, amusing, and breathtaking.

After the sun went down, we paddled back to the beach in the growing dark; we both couldn't believe what we'd seen even if we hadn't caught anything.

Once we loaded our trucks, I headed home, but David had decided to stay on for one more night. He had gotten the striper bug pretty bad after that last outing on the flats and the next morning he landed a good fish from his kayak. He didn't measure it, and he didn't have any way to weigh it, but he guesses that it was just under twenty pounds.

"It was heavier than a full gallon of milk, but lighter than a stocked cooler," he said over the phone the next day, as if either of those comparisons gave me any kind of clear reference.

Family Chicken

Along with being known for its fresh produce and Chesapeake Bay seafood, the Eastern Shore of Maryland is also known for its ample chicken production. Barbecuing chicken is one of the first things in spring or early summer that mark the beginning of warming weather. As the evenings lengthen, I like having my grill going while I begin the new year of yard work. There are few things that feel quite so satisfying as the smell of cut grass, a charcoal grill going, and overturned soil.

My nephew, Isaiah, named this recipe because he felt that every family should have its own barbecue chicken recipe to share and pass down.

Ingredients

- **Chicken:** mess of chicken thighs, one-half boneless and skinless or mess of chicken wings broken down into wingettes and drumettes

Marinade
- Olive oil
- Brown sugar
- Garlic, minced
- Liquid smoke, dash

Spice rub
- Salt
- Onion powder
- Garlic powder
- Paprika
- White pepper
- Black pepper

Directions:
Marinate chicken overnight in olive oil, brown sugar, minced garlic, and a dash of liquid smoke.

Combine spices for spice rub into bowl, mix thoroughly, and add spice mixture to a spare shaker.

Prepare grill. Light charcoal in charcoal chimney. Once coals are lit and glowing, spread on one side of the grill and cover.

On hot side of the grill, sear and brown chicken, turning as needed. Once the chicken has been seared thoroughly and the skins have been crisped, move chicken back over to the cool side of the grill and cover, flipping the chicken every five minutes and applying more spice rub with each turning. The overall goal is to get a good sear on the chicken and grill on indirect heat until the skin is thick and crispy and the tendons of the chicken have broken down. Chicken thighs will stay moist through the process.

I like to eat the thighs with skin and bones first, leaving the skinless and boneless ones for leftovers or cold sandwiches.

MAY

TRUCKS AND A SLOWNESS AGREED UPON

Memorial day brings Virgo high in the night sky, and picnic tables so laden with food that only the red gingham borders of a tablecloth can be seen at the edges. Plates of fried and barbecue chicken, bowls of potato salad and coleslaw, and hard rolls stuffed with ham begin the season of eating and cooking outdoors. The spawn has reached inland, orioles begin to mate, and spring courses, like fish upstream in our veins.

"Sloth, like rust, consumes faster than labour wears, while the used key is always bright."
—Benjamin Franklin

I n between spring and summer there's a moment that comes each year when I notice for the first time that it's warm enough to drive with the windows down. This is my internal sign that spring is nearly over and summer is about to begin and, when I notice, it's invariably evening and there's the smell of cut grass in the air and the sunset is noticeably later. I might be coming home from work, or back from the post office, or the grocery store, and if I'm coming back from a fishing trip, there might even be the beginnings of the season's first sunburn on the back of my neck and arms, and a few foam poppers stuck in the brim of my hat.

It was early May one year when this moment came to me. I was driving through Montgomery County, in the well-to-do Potomac farmland along River Road. It was an early Sunday afternoon and I was coming back from a slow but satisfying trip to the Potomac River. I had started the day late, driving out to Pennyfield Lock where I parked and headed upstream in my kayak in the slow water of the C&O Canal for a few miles until I reached a small landing where I portaged down to the Potomac and began the float back.

From there I could work my way back with the river current, down to Pennyfield, fishing the mid-river structure until I reached the small creek that led up to the lock. Although the fishing was better upstream near Harpers Ferry and Brunswick, this stretch was nice for a quick half-day trip, and didn't require the standard two-truck coordination between anglers that most Potomac trips needed.

I had hoped to take some smallmouth bass on poppers, but the fishing was slow, although the conditions were perfect. The river was clear, the vegetation was waving lazily in the current, and early blue damselflies skimmed over the river waters. The water still had the coolness of spring, but the warm temperatures made it feel more like summer.

I started with a popper, but nothing much was happening in any of the current eddies or ledges that I cast to, and all of my offerings had been ignored. I switched to a clouser, and when that didn't work,

I tied on root beer crystal bugger. But it didn't make much difference. I worked the river eddies, ledges, mid-river boulders and shorelines with nothing to show for my efforts. Quite simply, the fish weren't biting, and for whatever reason, that seemed okay. I had all summer to get the timing right, and this seemed to be a fair price to pay for a mildly impulsive trip.

It turned out to be just a nice, comfortable day to float the river and near the end of the float, I took a pair of small smallmouth from a shoreline stump eddy on a black hellgrammite pattern, so the day wasn't a total loss.

Back at Pennyfield Lock I loaded my rods and kayak into my truck and began the drive home, consciously enjoying the season's first truly warm day as I drove with my windows down. The rich farmland passed by in an allegro of green and late spring blooms. Lilacs bloomed near new mansions, forsythias faded from yellow to green beside the impeccably fenced horse farms of southern Montgomery County, and all about, small plots of farmland were making the adolescent shift from spring to summer.

I was about halfway to Gaithersburg when I felt the engine of my truck lose power in a steamy, labored gasp, shattering the windows-down reverie that I'd been enjoying. The inevitable breakdown was a risk that came with owning an old truck, and at the time I was driving a 1987 Toyota 4Runner with just over 200,000 miles on it.

There had been a few mishaps here and there, nothing too serious, but enough for me to have a cheap mechanic that I knew by name and his business card in my wallet. In the four years since I'd bought it, I'd only had a new clutch put in, replaced the shocks, and gotten a tune-up. For the most part, it had been a solid truck and had served me well, considering its age, mileage, and the small amount of money I had invested in it.

I pulled over and called for a tow truck to come pick me up at the next gas station and while I waited inside, it seemed like every other person who came into the small store there was damp with river water. The bright, warm Sunday had brought out the swimmers, tubers, and canoeists to enjoy the day on the Potomac, and each time the door opened, there was a burst of laughter and the squeak from wet flip-flops as kids came in and bought beer or suntan lotion. Girls came in with bikini tops and wet cutoff jean shorts and baseball hats, and most of the guys weren't wearing shirts.

Inside, everyone was young, fit, and incredibly happy, while outside my ugly, old truck sat wounded in the parking lot and I sulked in a corner booth watching Keno numbers change on the television screen.

The windows-down optimism of my trip had vanished completely by the time the tow truck got there to pick me up, and the ride home went by quickly, since the driver wasn't much of a conversationalist.

As the tow truck idled in front of my house, I unloaded my kayak and fishing gear before it headed south to Silver Spring and my mechanic's garage. I looked at my old 4Runner hooked up to the tow truck in the late afternoon sun. The valence below the front bumper was fairly mangled, but bent back into shape by hand, the hood had a few dents, and the antenna was bent from a close call with a wild turkey in flight. On the driver's side, the bracket for the side-view mirror had weakened to the point that the wind bent it back in the summer months when the heat caused the joint to loosen.

Inside, the dust from only one state road coated the cracked dashboard because I rarely drove it very far from home. The air-conditioning didn't work, the radio didn't have knobs, and most of the carpet in the back had been torn out leaving the truck bed bare. Outside, the gray paint was rough and mismatching in some areas where some rust had been treated and painted over. The removable top was leaky in hard rains, but still serviceable with some rusty edges at the sliding windows.

It was a "beater truck" in the truest sense of the term; a purely utilitarian vehicle with little-to-no cosmetic value, but a ton of history and personality. Anything new or squarely mounted on it, like the front bumper or the back turn signals, were only in good condition because they'd replaced old parts that had failed completely.

Most people thought the 4Runner wasn't much to look at, some people thought it was a poorer investment than the brand new Jeep that it had replaced, but a few people appreciated the decision as well as the aesthetic. Even in moderately decent shape, the design of those first generation 4Runners was still eyebrow-raising for the right kind of people (read old Toyota enthusiasts) and buying it had been a conscious decision from the beginning.

The next day I spoke to my mechanic and at first it looked like it might just be the radiator, but then he delved into things a bit deeper as mechanics do, and later that week the bottom line was that a full engine replacement was necessary. The rest of the truck was fine, omitting all the cosmetic stuff I mentioned before, and he could find a refurbished engine fairly cheaply if I wanted him to go that route. I told him I wanted to think about it.

Four years before, through a trifecta of bad credit, frugal logic, and deeply ingrained juvenile aesthetics, my decision to buy a beat-up old truck became one of the best decisions I'd made in early adulthood.

(There had been a few false starts into adulthood, but this last one was the one that took.) I didn't want a car payment, I didn't want a significant portion of my income tied up in a car, and since I was living and working in Washington, DC, I really only needed a vehicle for fishing trips since I rode the bus and metro to work.

I was on the market for the cheapest truck possible, and a coworker said he had an old 4Runner that was in pretty rough shape but tagged and drivable, and just sitting in his garage. It wasn't exactly love at first sight when I took a look at it, but it was a serviceable truck, and at the price he was asking, beggars couldn't be choosers. So I bought it. A few weeks later as I was driving to fish north of Frederick, I realized that the combined worth of my tackle was worth more than the truck I was driving.

Sure, there was always a little trepidation about driving too far from home, or getting nervous about every little sound I heard from the engine, but as I look back on those years with the 4Runner, I remember fishing with healthy regularity. The rare occasions when I had a breakdown or had to change an old tire certainly came up, but I can honestly say that there was never a point when it really let me down or when I was embarrassed to drive such a beat -up truck.

But what made the 4Runner an especially good fishing truck was that along with the overall rough four-wheel-drive exterior and spirit, it enabled me to actually get out and fish. I wasn't scraping by with gas money and struggling to make car payments. Largely in part because of that first decision to live cheaply and reasonably, I had made some headway since buying it. I'd established my career, I'd gotten married, and we'd even bought a house.

And there in the May evening outside my house, I looked at it hooked up to the tow truck in the slanting light, and I didn't think for a second that this would be our last trip together.

* * * * *

Before the beat-up old 4Runner, there was a Jeep Wrangler Unlimited that had great potential as a fishing car, but didn't quite match up with my lifestyle—which is a polite way of saying I couldn't afford it. This brand new Jeep was an impulsive purchase that lead to unlucky times and I struggled each month to make the payments.

Throughout our time together, we suffered through two repossessions, a mysteriously cracked window that happened days after the warranty expired, and a faulty starter. On the outskirts of vehicular concerns, there might've been a layoff and a breakup in there as well, along with a friend's suicide, a stolen boat, and having to put an old dog down.

For three unlucky years there was never a moment when I felt like I was getting out from beneath the calamity of the Jeep. Each month I walked the tight line between chaos and the beginnings of order: I slipped behind on my payments, did what I could to catch up, and all the while the bank called and late payment letters came in the mail while my stomach filled with acid and the ulcer in my stomach burned nervously.

As bad as things were with the Jeep, things were never so terrible that I couldn't fish, although the frequency I was used to was certainly decreased. If I learned anything during this time, aside from the hard lessons of financial management, it was how to sniff out a public spot close to home that didn't require too much gas.

Back then I was living in Ellicott City and for much of that time, I remember fishing the upper Patapsco quite a bit since the nice stretch at Daniels was just a few miles from home. This part of the river was a nice combination of smallmouth bass and trout water, and a welcome change of pace after living on the Eastern Shore for ten years. I could cast poppers and hoppers in the slow water of the shorelines for smallmouth, and in a few of the riffled sections I could drift nymphs for stocked rainbows. In one of the deeper pools one morning, I remember catching five species of fish from the same spot: a smallmouth bass, a brown trout, a rainbow trout, a rock bass, and a pumpkinseed.

To the south, there were Rocky Gorge and Triadelphia reservoirs on the upper reaches of the Patuxent River. They were both deep, cool freshwater lakes with undeveloped shorelines that had good populations of largemouth and smallmouth bass. After ten years on the Eastern Shore and focussing mainly on striped and largemouth bass, I remember this time as being a smallmouth bass period for me, where I'd jump at any chance to fish for a species of fish that was suddenly readily available.

Occasionally, there were times that driving the Jeep was honestly a joy, and taking the top down and removing the doors in the spring and summer always softened the sting of the payments, and made the difficulty of owning it seem somewhat bearable. And sometimes if I looked at it at the right angle, quartered from the front, the Jeep looked beautiful, not like a curse, and not like a factory stock vehicle begging for a two-inch lift or bigger tires.

As I look back on those years with the Jeep, it sounds like the difficulty that comes with a beautiful but expensive girlfriend. It's probably unfair to blame the overall tone of those years on the Jeep, but I can trace back the beginnings of a difficult time to that initial bad decision to buy a car I couldn't afford, and that subsequent bad decisions stemmed from this first one.

Conversely, good things seemed to happen as soon as I sold the Jeep and bought the 4Runner. Along with being a cheap and humble vehicle, the 4Runner had been lucky at a time when luck was scarce. And more than that, it was a symbol of getting my act together. I knew that getting something more dependable made sense for me now, but I was worried that the good fortune I'd gained over the past four years might have stolen off into the night, hooked to the back of a tow truck headed to my mechanic's garage in Silver Spring.

* * * * *

Before the Jeep, there was a 1979 Ford F-150 Lariat that I bought with my summer savings after working in a restaurant in Ocean City. As the tourist season was winding down and my friends and I were planning on heading back to college, there was a rumor that a number of the rental places in Ocean City unloaded their beaten and abused wares before closing things down for the season. One of the waiters I worked with found a flyer, and underneath the heading, "DELMARVA END OF SUMMER COMMERCIAL AUCTION!" it said they'd be auctioning summer rental items like bicycles, surfboards, hot tubs, mopeds, and jet-skis.

Among the Ocean City locals, the goods were rumored to sell pretty cheaply and that it was worth going if you were open to the risks and charms of other people's junk. The following weekend I drove out with my friend Mike. He and I were roommates at Washington College and he'd worked with me at the seafood restaurant that summer and had made good money waiting tables.

Out in the chalky white glare of the crushed oyster shell lot, there were rows and rows of the sad detritus of hourly beach rentals baking in the August sun. There were pop-up campers with torn mesh screens and signs that listed known problems. There were jet skis and mopeds that the tourists had ridden hard all summer, packing about five years of casual use into one summer's worth of hourly use entertainment.

Mike went off to look for scooters and mopeds, and I walked down among the beaten and abandoned trucks and campers. At the end of the row beside a string of white trucks from a plumbing company that had gone belly-up, there was an old brown farm truck with the telltale wooden stake sides along the side of the bed. It had the bold and corpulent lines of a late '70s model Ford pickup, and compared to the group of newer, rounder white Chevys with commercial caps over their beds, it looked either dull or dignified—I couldn't decide which.

I had an image in my head of a Delaware farmer who had used the truck for years in the flat coastal farm country north of here until finally retiring it to the occasional Sunday drive to church or the drugstore. I saw it parked underneath a shade awning out of the sun beside a simple rancher. How the truck had ended up at the auction was tough to say. Maybe the farmer had died, maybe he'd had enough of his wife complaining about it sitting out in the driveway, maybe his farm was about to be taken by the bank and unloading it had been a necessity born of circumstance.

Although the plan when we drove out was simply to see if we could buy cheap mopeds for easy college transportation, I had decided that if I was going to bid on anything, it was going to be the old brown farm truck.

Mike came down to look at the truck with me and called it a grandpa truck since it didn't have the big tires and aggressive 4-wheel-drive look that most trucks on the market had back then. Compared to the Chevys, it had a low and lean look to it with a fading brown and beige paint job and a dull, pitted chrome strip running down the middle. A pair of large sideview mirrors poked out from its sides like a set of embarrassing ears and the wood slats along the bed made it look as country as a gingham table cloth. It wasn't a truck for off-roading or traditional male vanity, but it gave off the impression of honest work and reliable service. It was certainly old—close to 20 years old—but it was actually in pretty good shape considering its age.

I opened the door and there was a dry, dusty, sweet -smelling saddle blanket cover thrown over the bench seat. The keys weren't in the ignition, but taped to the window was an auction slip that said, "ALL VEHICLES SOLD AS-IS. 1979 Ford F-150 Lariat. 147,000 Miles. Strong runner. Starts, runs, and drives. Passed Delaware State Vehicle Inspection." Looking closer, there were two cassettes in the glove compartment: *CCR Chronicle* and a *Greatest Hits* by Blondie, nice bonuses, but my image of the old Delaware farmer shimmered like a mirage.

Off in another row Mike poked around a few of the mopeds lined up beside some lawn mowers and bicycles. The vinyl seating to most were cracked with the weathered yellow of cushion foam showing through. Some were missing headlights and rearview mirrors, and a few of the seats were patched with duct tape. Sun-faded surfing stickers decorated any flat area that could be covered.

"These things are pretty mangled," I said.

"So we buy two cheap and between them we'll have enough parts to get one running," Mike said. "I just want to be able to get from the dorm to the gas station downtown to buy beer and I heard that you can't get a DUI on one of these."

Mike was a musician philosopher with an eccentric streak. His American-Italian good looks and charm had kept him busy that summer and had made him a small fortune in tips at the restaurant. I liked his creative approach to student transportation, although I felt that his logic here might be flawed.

"I wish there were one with a sidecar," he said with a far off look. "Think of the possibilities."

The moped plan that had seemed so rational on the drive out of town, suddenly felt shaky as we stood there in the auction lot. The sun was high in the sky by then and there wasn't an inch of shade anywhere on the oyster shell lot. Both of us were sweating through our T-shirts.

"I think I'm going to bid on that old truck. If I can get it for under $1,500, I'm going for it."

I had saved around $3000 that summer and was willing to spend half of it on a twenty-year old truck that looked as honest as a handshake, but had the words, "AS IS," clearly posted on the window.

Once the auction began, we joined a group of people following the auctioneer around. An old speaker was mounted to the roof of a golf cart as a fat man in a baseball hat drove down the rows and spoke in his rushed auctioneer's cadence that's exciting at first, but looses its charm after a few minutes.

The auction crowd followed along as the golf cart droned on into the August heat. Our group looked pretty down on their luck, but occasionally I'd see a roll of cash come out of someone's pocket that looked like something out of a drug movie. I felt pretty suburban with my checkbook.

Mike ended up getting two mopeds for less than $100 (both ran just fine and I think that he still has one of them in his garage) and I walked away with the farm truck after spending nearly all of my summer savings on it.

I drove that old F-150 for six years, through my college years and the early professional years of my late twenties. And although I was hard on it, with long drives on nearly empty tanks and longer periods between oil changes, the truck, as advertised, was a strong runner. I think the only serious alteration I made to it was removing the wooden stake sides, and in the six years I drove it, only a handful of minor issues arose outside of standard maintenance.

* * * * *

On the Eastern Shore of Maryland, a Ford pickup truck is as synonymous with a working man's identity as a docked workboat, a wet Labrador retriever, and a broken-in pair of Carhartt coveralls. Extending that aesthetic into the history that comes with older trucks, my old F-150 had the rare combination of blending in perfectly and tastefully standing out. Over the years, I got a lot of waves on the back roads and appraising comments in gas stations and parking lots, and the conversation it stirred seemed as natural as commenting on the Orioles, or how high the corn was. Fairly often, when someone complimented the truck, they seemed to always mention the color first, the two-tone brown and beige paint job that unknowingly complimented the faded yellow-orange of the blinkers perfectly.

I met a girl at a breakfast diner one summer in Chestertown, and I remember that one of the first things she ever said to me had to do with the color of my truck. It was a Sunday before Memorial Day, and I was sitting at the breakfast counter in Sharon's Diner, incredibly hung over after a lively session at the Bluebird Tavern the night before. I was trying to undo the previous night's drinking with a heavy breakfast and I sat there unshowered with my hair in my eyes and my beard a thick mess, wearing the same clothes from the night before that smelled of sweat and cigarettes. In between sips of coffee and staring blankly at the newspaper, I noticed a pretty girl come in and sit at the breakfast counter. She looked like the polar opposite of how I felt: freshly showered, neatly dressed, and probably on her way to church.

"Well, look who's here," the waitress behind the counter said as she sat down.

"Hello, Sarah," the pretty girl said.

"Sit down, let me get you something to eat. Look at you, Ellen, a young lady now! What can I get you?"

"I think I've been a young lady for around ten years now," she said with a little embarrassment, "but I'd love some orange juice."

Sarah moved efficiently behind the counter and had her drink in front of her quickly, while still seeing to the other guests.

"How are things in Wisconsin? I thought you graduated."

"Minnesota. I'm still in Duluth. I graduated a year ago, but I finish my master's next year."

"Oh, that's wonderful. How long are you home for, Ellen?" the waitress asked.

"I'll be here for the summer. I'm closing up things at my Aunt Ruby's house."

The waitress stopped and put her hand on her chest.

"I'm so sorry, sweetie. I wasn't even thinking. I knew she passed this spring and I just saw you walk in and I was so glad to see you that…" Sarah walked from behind the bar up to where Ellen sat and touched her hand.

"It's okay," Ellen said. "My dad said that we're going to sell the house on Queen Street so I'm here to help clean things up and get it ready. Mom's been so busy with my sister and Dad just can't take any time off work, so I figured I'd come home since I had the summer free. A lot of her stuff I think we can give away or sell, but some of it I think we should keep in the family," she said from the stool. Her shoulders shrugged, "So, I'm here."

"Well, I'm glad that you're home. Even if it's just for a little bit, and even if it's to say goodbye."

The waitress moved off to table some food and my plate was among a few that she brought out. If Sarah and Ellen kept talking I didn't hear it, because all of my attention was on the heavy plate of food in front of me: white toast smothered in cream chipped beef, and hash browns piled to the side.

I took my time with breakfast and glanced through the rest of the paper. After a bit I swallowed what was left of my coffee, left some cash on top of my check, and headed for the door looking forward to a shower, my couch, and the dim, shady coolness of my living room with the blinds drawn and the curtains closed. Ellen-from-Duluth was leaving behind me, so I held the door for her as we walked out of the diner and into the parking lot.

"Thank you," she said.

"You're welcome."

I started walking over to my truck and she followed in my direction. It looked like she had parked near me and we were walking together, so I felt like I should say something else.

"I heard you talking to the waitress. Sorry to hear you're in town for hard reasons."

"It's okay. It's a little strange to be back, especially like this—staying in my aunt's house without her—but it's not all bad. It's good to be home."

"There's worse places to spend a summer, and I imagine there's not a ton of crab joints out there in Minnesota."

"No crabs and no sweet corn. But there's plenty of snow and even moose up north, I hear. It's really not all that different. There's lots of water and boats, lots of rednecks and trucks."

"Rednecks do love their trucks," I said.

"And that's a very nice brown one right there," she said referring to the truck I was standing next to, placing mocking emphasis on the color brown.

I looked at it with a little pride and embarrassment, the desert tan and chocolate brown bisected by a pitted chrome strip.

"Brown color palettes were big in the 70s. Not real common these days. Most everything on the road now is either black or white or red."

She seemed to consider that. "Some of the advice I got from my aunt had to do with color. The stuff I remember, at least. She said, 'Always wear white to a picnic so you think about what you eat' and 'Never trust a man who drives a red truck.'"

"So, I guess that means you can trust me, since I drive a humble, brown truck," I said.

That got a good laugh out of her, a genuine sound of surprise and amusement that, coming from a pretty girl, might be one of the best sounds in nature.

"Not likely. You have a wayward look about you, but I do like your truck. Enjoy your Sunday," she said with finality.

And then we were both inside our respective vehicles and heading off into very different Sundays; me to sleep off a hangover on my couch, her heading, I assumed, to church to sing hymns and take communion with the rest of the community, clean and fresh as a prayer.

* * * * *

I went to Sharon's Diner for breakfast with more regularity after that, hoping to see her again. Some morning's I'd just get a quick cup of coffee to see if she was in, on others I'd sit down at the counter to get a full breakfast, stretching out my time there with hope and a second cup of coffee.

Through my years in Chestertown I had frequented Sharon's for breakfast, but I was never what you'd call a regular. I got to know the waitresses over the next few weeks, and I think they could tell immediately why I was suddenly underfoot in their restaurant.

Sarah was the younger of the two waitresses at the diner. She was divorced and lived outside Chestertown with her daughter. She was a flirty, wry, walking encyclopedia of town history and family doings and knew all the dirt and all the gossip, past and present, of nearly everyone who came in to eat.

One morning as we were talking, she told me that she only slept around four to five hours per night since helping with her daughter's homework could last until nine, any housework that needed to get done crept until eleven, and she needed to get up around 4 a.m. to start the breakfast shift at Sharon's around 5 a.m. She did this six days a week and had the endearing and deserved bitterness that came with single mothers who worked long hours for little pay or recognition.

Jessica was older and more pragmatic, and tended to sit on a stool behind the counter moving only when necessary. Somehow things got done and the guests were never really wanting for anything, and she ruled from behind the breakfast counter with a heavy-set authority. Early on, it was obvious that she didn't approve of me and she seemed to guard Ellen with a nun-like silence.

Each time I tried to raise the subject of Ellen they evaded it: Sarah with more tact, and Jessica with a scowling reluctance. After a few weeks I was getting desperate to see her again and I knew my budget couldn't support this much restaurant food indefinitely. A chance meeting with Ellen was certainly possible in our small town, but I was getting impatient. Finally, one morning over coffee, it occurred to me that while gates are meant to keep people out, they can also let people in. I decided to use the waitress gatekeepers to my advantage and with no better plan to meet her, I wrote a note on a torn corner from a paper placemat.

Ellen,

We met here at Sharon's Diner a few Sundays ago. I was the trustworthy man with the brown pickup truck; you were lovely, and in from Duluth.
   Have dinner with me sometime. Or breakfast here. Anything.
   Tell Sarah what you're open to and I'll check back later this week.

No hard feelings either way,

Brett

I handed the note to Sarah and asked if she could give it to Ellen the next time she saw her. She looked amused, but didn't object. It was another approach, I thought.

I waited a few days before heading back to Ellen's Diner and I knew right away that my note had hit home when I saw Sarah's face as I walked through the door. She had the restrained, but gleeful look of a shared secret and I saw that there was a folded piece of paper underneath my coffee saucer when I sat down at the counter.

Mr. Brown Truck,

If you can answer this, I'll have dinner with you. No cheating. I'll know.
   "I run and run but never flee.

I'm often watched, yet never see.
Long, I bring boredom.
Short, I bring fear."
What am I?

I had to read it a few times to realize that it was a riddle. I hadn't even thought about riddles since grade school, and I remembered our teacher's drawn-out delight in having us puzzle over these brain games and my contempt for one of the smarter kids in the class who always seemed to figure them out before anyone else.

Over the next few days the riddle repeated in my head like a song,

"I run and run but never flee.
I'm often watched, yet never see.
Long, I bring boredom.
Short, I bring fear."

It even felt like there was a line missing at the end to complete the rhythm and rhyme with see, and I found this distracting. I considered things that ran and could be watched and measured. I felt that the answer was water-based at first, so I fixated on that for a while—rivers, oceans, rain—but deep down I knew I was off. It didn't fit perfectly, but I was almost there. I grew closer to the answer, circled away from it, and then backtracked. It was maddening.

I began to see that Ellen had me cornered. I could forget the whole thing and hope chance would bring me before her. It wasn't a big town after all, and there was bound to be a time when we'd eventually meet. But she'd know that I chose not to play the game with her, and that would be a mark against me.

And it would have been easy enough to find the answer online or maybe from a book in the library. I wanted badly to see her again, but something in me believed her note: I knew that she would know if I cheated, that after I gave her the answer and she agreed to meet me, all she'd have to do was ask, and without even listening to my response she'd look at me and know that I'd lied to her before our first date even began.

The only meaningful option was to answer her riddle honestly and go from there. It wasn't going to be easy, but I had to admit that it was a fair and clever way to screen a candidate.

I knew that the best way to approach a riddle was in knowing that some words drove to the heart of the answer, other words were there be cute, and some words were only there for misdirection. The trick was in knowing which was which.

I drew circle diagrams trying to find commonalities. I tried imagining subjects that she might like to use. Like my initial idea of water, nothing fit perfectly, and it was a maddening few days between work and driving and sleep and time on the water. My mind was completely consumed with this girl and this riddle.

Eventually, the answer came to me after I finally stopped thinking about it. I was in the grocery store buying chicken and frozen peas and, suddenly, the answer was alive and pulsing excitedly like a fish on the end of the line.

Time.

The next morning I drove to Sharon's Diner for breakfast and my truck rumbled happily over the antique bricks in downtown Chestertown as I parked on a side street. After I sat down at the counter I tore a corner off of one of the paper placemats and wrote a note to Ellen with my phone number on the opposite side.

I slid the note across the counter to Sarah.

Ellen,

The answer is "time." I thought it might be "tide" at first, but it didn't quite fit.

That's a shame. It would've been nice for time and tide to be married here:

Neither waits for any man, but I'll wait for you to call.

Looking forward to dinner,

Brett

"Did you figure it out?" Sarah asked when she took the folded paper.
"Yes, ma'am."
"Did you cheat?" she asked.
"No," I said, with a straight face and an honest heart.
She unfolded the paper and read it. After half a beat she snorted.
"You knew the answer?" I asked.
"Where do you think she got the riddle from?"
This surprised me, but I should have know. When I invited Sarah into the game, I should have known she'd happily conspire with Ellen to make the sport more challenging. She looked pleased with herself and I honestly liked her for it: she could've thrown the note away or cautioned Ellen to stay away from me, but she chose to make a fair game of it.

"And what if I hadn't gotten the answer?" I asked.

"Well, I guess it would've been a win-win proposition for all of us: She'd know you for an idiot or a quitter, you'd be steered clear of her, and I'd get a good laugh either way."

When Sarah brought me my check that morning there was a note attached with a paper clip.

Brett,

My aunt's house is on 238 South Queen Street.
    Her number there is 301-778-1900.
    Call me and let's work out when you can take me out to dinner.
    I'll eat anywhere with you, but I'd love to get out of town if we can.

Ellen Barroll

* * * * *

On Friday evening I could hear the creak of old wood flooring as Ellen came to the door, and when it opened she was wearing a collared summer dress with a belt around her waist. She hadn't put on shoes yet, so she seemed smaller than I remembered.

"Brett," she said, and it sounded like she was saying my name out loud for the first time, testing it.

"Ellen," I said, and it sounded more like relief.

"Come on in. I'm just going to get my shoes on and we can go. Give me a second?"

And then there was the sound of her footsteps on the stairs and more of the creaking hardwood floors above as she moved about upstairs doing the things that girls do before dates. Her aunt's house had a faint smell of sugar cookies, lemony wood polish and fabric softener. It was a womanly smell, but not motherly, without the chaotic potpourri of men, pets, and children that a family's house can absorb into its walls.

Aunt Ruby's living room was an odd mix of lived-in clutter and bare spaces. I could see a few cardboard boxes where Ellen had begun packing things: books and framed pictures mostly. All of the furniture was gigantic and wooden: a piano was up against a wall, a walnut and velvet-looking couch dominated the floor, and a roll-top desk anchored a corner near a window that faced the street. I didn't envy the movers who would eventually need to move these items out. Part of me doubted they'd even fit through the front door.

I could see dark rectangles in the wallpaper where large frames had been taken down. Some leaned against a wall by the stairs. One was a still life of fruit, another looked like a colonial painting of a family member, and one was of a sporting dog on point with what looked like pheasant in flight.

Ellen was back downstairs fairly quickly. After the riddles and note-passing, there was an element of polite scrutiny between us: We were each looking at each other with new eyes and trying not to be obvious about it.

She stood in front of me, only slightly taller than she'd been in bare feet, a small, athletic-looking girl with the muscled definition of a swimmer and the distracting curvature of a healthy woman. Her brown hair was back in a neat ponytail and her eyes were a surprising amber color, not quite brown, and not hazel, but something like a deep caramel that grew rusty at the edges.

"So, where are we going? I'm starving."

"How's Waterman's sound?"

"That sounds great," she said and I could tell she was happy with the choice.

As we got into my truck to head out to Rock Hall for dinner she slid across the bench seat of my truck with a natural ease and sat directly next to me, leaving the space immediately next to the passenger-side door empty.

There are unspoken gestures and cultural holdovers from youth and within our memories; they lie dormant and forgotten in a back corner of our minds. Once unearthed into the light of adulthood, the impact of their foundational echoes can ring true as Sunday church bells.

Ellen sliding across the bench seat of my truck to sit next to me was one of those gestures, because I had grown up in the country, too, and I held this image of a man and a woman in a truck with unexpected regard. On one hand there was the flirtatious closeness and the subtle hint of physicality, and on the other there was almost a pageant quality to it—that this was how grown-up girls rode in trucks with boys, and that the image of a girl with a ponytail riding directly beside a bearded man in a truck was as much for our intimacy as it was a public declaration.

On the easy twenty-minute drive to Rock Hall, we talked in my truck as the sun slanted in a yellow-orange light over the maritime corn fields and the cracked windows of my truck gave space for the wind to come in lightly and move her hair in loose bits about her face. The smell of her, clean and freshly showered, mixed with the sweet smell of the saddle blanket seat cover, and she sat close to me the entire time, her leg almost touching mine and a small yellow purse in her lap.

We sat on the crab deck at Waterman's Crab House and a summertime reggae band played off to the side. The sun had nearly set by then and the sky was a red-orange riot over Rock Hall's small harbor, and out in the open water of the bay I could see the lights from the green and red channel markers blinking in the distance. We each ordered a bottle of beer and looked at our menus.

"Let's split some clams. They sound so good. And I love the hush puppies here. Can we get a basket of those?"

Any nervousness I had about the formality of our date had been disarmed by the ride out and her excitement over eating there.

"That sounds great," I said.

I forget what I ordered for dinner, but I remember specifically that she ordered a soft-shell crab sandwich and requested it on white bread, not a roll. After her first bite, she looked out towards the water and said, "My aunt took me here on my eighteenth birthday and we sat over there," she said, pointing with her chin to a table along the edge of the deck with a good view of the small harbor.

"I ordered a soft-shell crab sandwich because she ordered one, and back then I assumed that this was what grown-up women ordered in restaurants. I thought it was a mature thing to order like a martini or raw oysters." She took another bite of her sandwich and washed it down with another sip of beer.

"When our food came out to the table I saw these little legs poking out from under the bread and it looked like my sandwich was about to scurry off the plate."

Her fingers fluttered over the table to prove her point.

"I didn't want to look scared, and I told myself, 'It's just a crab. You've eaten hundreds of them.' So I took a bite and it was just a blue crab, the same that I'd eaten all my life, but there was a new and unfamiliar texture to it that I didn't know how to react to, a new reality to it that made it taste and feel different."

Ellen picked up a few Old Bay fries and dipped them into some ketchup, but before she took a bite, she looked at me and said, "I had just turned eighteen and I was sitting there with my aunt eating a sandwich that I wanted to like, but didn't like quite yet, and I remember thinking about the first time I kissed a boy. There was the exact same newly discovered reality as the soft shell.

"When you're young, you see people kissing on TV all the time, but until you do it, you don't really know that it's a mouth and a tongue, and that there are these logistics like breathing and saliva. And I thought about that first time with Tommy Miller when he kissed me outside of Downey's after we got milkshakes, and I remembered that

I didn't really like it at first, there was that same new reality to it, and it was just too strange to be immediately enjoyed."

Our waitress came to check on us and drop off another round of beers. Ellen was nearly finished her sandwich.

"Well, it looks like you got over your discomfort with soft shells," I said after a while.

"Yes," she said smiling, "And kissing, too."

"That's good," I said, and her comfort with kissing floated around the table for a bit.

Ellen leaned back into her seat and sipped a fresh beer.

"Why are the best things so strange at first?"

"I don't know. Another one of your riddles?" I said.

"Not a riddle exactly, just wondering why things work that way."

We both looked out into the lights on water and watched a few boats come back to port.

She took another sip of beer and smiled. "Besides, they were Sarah's riddles, not mine. She had more, too. Way harder ones. You're lucky I didn't pick some of the others."

"I wouldn't describe myself as lucky exactly," I said and scratched my beard.

"You're here, aren't you?" she said, looking at me and around the restaurant playfully, and driving the point home with her interesting amber eyes.

And sitting with Ellen Barroll at Waterman's Crab House, with a second bottle of cold beer in my hand on a deck overlooking the sun setting over the middle Chesapeake Bay, I realized that I was, in fact, very, very lucky.

We talked through dark and shared some ice cream, then we walked down the pier and along the bulkhead along the harbor. There were big pleasure boats docked and the sound of happy voices from the cabins came up from them every now and then.

After a while we turned back towards the restaurant and walked until we found ourselves back at my truck. And again, she slid across the seat next to sit next to me on the dark ride back to Chestertown like it was the most normal way in the world to ride in a truck with a boy.

There wasn't an awkward pause when I parked in front of her house. Without the smallest hesitation or worry she said, "Thank you for a lovely dinner," and she kissed me before getting out of the truck. And for the first time in a long time, kissing a woman felt new and disturbingly real. I was fairly sober, her hand was on my chest, and the kiss was slow and brief. But as she broke away, she turned her head quickly to leave and her ponytail swung behind her, slapping my face as she got out of my truck. Whether it was an accident or a planned affectation, the ponytail slap got me good, and I thought about it, along with the kiss, for the next few days. But unlike the riddle, there was no answer to work out.

* * * * *

For the rest of the summer, when I drove to her Aunt Ruby's house and knocked on her door, it felt like courting. I didn't have a working definition of what courting was, but it certainly wasn't dating as I knew it, or the casual way that I'd gotten together with women in college. And it wasn't just friendship because there was a formality to it, along with restraint.

Slowness was the term she used for our agreement, and she said it first in my truck. I had taken her to a truck stop outside of town near the Delaware state line for pie and ice-cream, mostly as an excuse to take another long drive with her sitting beside me, and she was kissing me good night outside of her aunt's house when she put a cool hand on my chest and pushed away from me.

"I want us to move with a slowness this summer. Let's agree to that now. Can you do that?"

Asking Ellen why we should move slowly seemed beside the point. We'd known each other for just a few weeks and moving slowly seemed like a fair thing to ask, except that it wasn't a very common thing for a woman to directly ask at the time. And much how I was clear from the beginning in wanting to date her, she was clear in her willingness and the pace of that willingness.

So I agreed to the slowness. I probably would've agreed to anything that summer, but that was the one thing she asked.

Slowness had nothing at all to do with any sexual hangups that either of us had. Ellen was a young, healthy, intelligent woman. After a few weeks of long drives through the country and lengthening goodbyes in my truck, it was painfully clear that she was comfortable with her body, and liked what it did for me, as much as what it did for her. But she was clear headed in how she wanted us to conduct ourselves. We were moving slowly, and one night on my way home I realized that our slowness was as anachronistic in the late '90s as the old truck I drove, and I liked it.

The majority of our time together that summer was spent during daylight hours, and this helped to curb most of the wickedness I felt like exploring with her. At the time, I was working at a daily newspaper about thirty miles away in Easton, and my shift was from four-to-twelve. So much of my morning and early afternoon was wide open, while my evenings were spent in the office until I got home around one or two in the morning.

Sometimes I'd visit her briefly in the mornings with coffee, and on other days I'd help with sifting through her aunt's accumulated wealth and garbage: bagging things, boxing things, and driving to the dump and Goodwill. One day as we were heading back from a landfill outside town, I joked that the only reason she was keeping me around was because she just needed a man with a truck.

"That actually might be more accurate than either one of us knows," she said.

We were driving with the windows down through the cornfields outside Chestertown and an irrigation system was spraying water in arcing pulses like a giant sprinkler. It was a hot day and we each had our windows down, and as I watched the water spray from the large irrigator I saw that part of the arc of water reached the road. I slowed down so that I timed our drive through the spray of water and Ellen saw what I was doing and laughed and rushed to roll her window up. She was too late to stop the full splash of water through the window and we were both fairly drenched. She slid across the bench and sat next to me, damp with water and sweat.

* * * * *

On Friday mornings we made a ritual of eating breakfast at Sharon's diner where we talked with Sarah and let her see what she'd had a hand in creating. We were both adults and each lived alone, but there was something we enjoyed about having an older person keep tabs on us. I guess it wasn't really a courtship unless an older person was there to supervise and neither one of us had family in the immediate area, so Sarah filled that role perfectly with her smiling attention, wry admonishments, and motherly pleasure at having the two of us come to her place to eat.

So vetted by riddles, and chaperoned by daylight and waitresses, I got to know Ellen Barroll as I'd never gotten to know a woman before. She set the pace and I respected it, and often in the truck we'd kiss and our young summer bodies would begin to voice their objections to the slowness agreed upon. One of us would break away, and we'd sit there on the bench seat of my truck with our foreheads touching, struggling and questioning, taking calming breaths, until we'd start up again.

If I had been younger I would never have been able to handle the arrangement. I would have stormed off in frustration and hurt, maddened by the closeness of her and the boundaries we'd defined. And there were times when I did, especially near the end of the summer. But with Ellen, at that time, the slowness was bearable and I enjoyed being able to match her self control and frustration step for step, and not breaking under my body's need for her. And likewise seeing her so frustrated was a satisfaction all its own: Ellen in the cab of my truck, pulling back from me as we kissed, biting her lip, sighing, struggling within the fences of her creation.

* * * * *

One morning in July, Ellen came out on my boat with me on the Chester River. We had trailered it to the boat ramp in Cliff City and on the drive out she didn't slide over to sit next to me, but stayed on her side of the truck with a smooth brown arm hanging out the window. I wondered if this meant she was displeased with me.

When we got to the landing she surprised me by being perfectly familiar with the process of launching a boat. She got out of the truck with me and knew exactly what to do with the bowline and walked down the pier as I backed down the boat ramp and slid my boat off the bunks and into the water. By the time I pulled up into the nearly empty parking lot and walked back down to the bulkhead, Ellen had the boat tied neatly against the pier with the engine trimmed down and idling quietly.

It was late in the morning and the tide was high and slack, so I wasn't too optimistic about our fishing prospects out on the water. Despite that, it was a good day for boating and by 9 a.m., the sun was nearing a comfortable high point in the sky but hadn't yet begun to put off the midday heat that would drive us into the shade later in the afternoon.

"I love that smell, that marsh and river smell with tide and tar and a little bit of outboard exhaust," she said and breathed deeply beside me as we began to motor slowly southward, away from the launch and towards the mouth of the Chester. That was the morning when I really understood that she was from Kent County, and that this was home for her. As much as I'd found and built a home there on the Eastern Shore, I would always be an outsider from the mountains of western Maryland.

Running a boat on flat morning waters is a joy that has never faded for me, but sharing that joy with Ellen that morning was something new and intoxicating.

We raced south with the wind in our hair and the flat expanse of the lower Chester spreading out before us. She had one hand bracing herself on the console, and another around my waist. Channel markers and crab pots rushed past us and the healthy roar of my outboard filled our ears until after we turned north around the southern tip of Eastern Neck Island, and I pulled back a bit on the throttle and began looking for a protected cove where we could get away from the boat traffic.

Like launching a boat, once we anchored I didn't need to explain anything about fishing to her. She took one of my spinning rods out of a rod holder, cast the soft plastic and jig head out and let it sink until it hit bottom. She began jigging, snapping the rod tip back smartly as she reeled the line back in, and impossibly she hooked a small striper after just a few casts. I knew she was from Kent County and that she'd spent time on the water, but we hadn't talked much about how much fishing she'd done as a girl. Without a word, she lipped the fish and released it back into the water.

I was fairly surprised that she'd hooked a small striper there. I had honestly picked the spot more for privacy than the fishing. I had just wanted a piece of open water where we could drift or anchor without being close to a lot of boat traffic. We were on the southwest side of Eastern Neck island, well off the shoreline, but inside the green can marking the channel. It was a Tuesday in July, and there weren't a lot of boats on the water, but those we saw were well off into the channel.

I picked up my 7 weight to see if I'd have any luck and wondered if there was something to this approach; that by picking the last place I thought a fish would ever be, during the worst possible time and tide, perhaps there was some kind of backwards logic to it.

After I stripped out some line I began casting and she watched with curiosity.

"What's wrong with fishing bait or lures?"

I was standing back behind the center console of my boat on the raised bench, casting in towards the shore and the beginning of the drop towards the channel. I counted the fly down and began working it back to me.

"Nothing's wrong with bait or lures. I use them sometimes, I just prefer fishing this way," I said, "I think a woman like you can understand that, doing something a specific way."

"Sort of. But you can catch more fish like this, though. Right?" She held the spinning rod out as she asked.

"It's not about catching as many fish as possible. Some days, at least. Catching one fish, or twenty fish, or no fish, with a fly rod, is just how I prefer doing it."

I made another cast, stripped the fly back to me, still not hooking anything. I had hoped to hook a nice big striper to prove something and impress her, but the time and tide were all wrong.

"And plus when you do finally hook a fish like this, with the line held in your hand, there's no comparison to other rods and other kinds of fishing. You're connected to the fish for that instant. You can feel all its wildness, all its strength, and it fights that connection as much as it can and you can feel every pull and pulse. And then you let it go."

That seemed to answer her question and, after fishing for a bit, she brought a beach towel out from a tote bag and spread it across the raised bow and laid back to read. She'd taken her shorts and T-shirt off to get some sun, and although I was very familiar with her body and the shape of her figure by then, I was shocked to see it in its entirety: the lines, the fullness, the perfect skin, and the surprising look of strength to her. After a while she put her book down. Her eyes were hidden beneath the baseball cap that she'd lain across her eyes to block the sun.

"Brett?" she asked.

"Yeah?"

"What's whole, but when you remove the whole there's still some left," she riddled sleepily.

I had stopped casting by then. I was behind the center console of my boat just taking in the sight of her. Semantic deconstruction and word play were impossible then. As I looked at her laid out on the bow of my boat, I couldn't help but think that at that moment the only things keeping that bikini on her body were a few loosely tied knots and my decision to let them stay intact. I'd seen Ellen breathless and frustrated in my truck, I'd seen her Sunday proper and laughing over breakfast, but this was the first time I'd seen so much of her, and with the top of her face covered by my hat, my eyes enjoyed their freedom.

"A donut? A wheel? Something along those lines?" I asked.

"Not… even… close…," she said stretching, putting both hands behind her head, bold as the devil on a Saturday night. Her legs pointed out over the water and her stomach stretched tightly with the motion as she took in the July sun on her skin. A few larger boats passed by us in the channel and soon the sound of the water lapping at the aluminum hull of boat increased as the waves rolled against us.

I opened the cooler and took out a small bottle of water. The small sip made me realize how thirsty I'd become in the sun and growing heat.

"I don't know. What?" I asked.

"Wholesome," she said, and she peeked at me from under my hat, turning on her side a little to face me, exaggerating every curve she had. My fly rod felt strange and heavy in my hand. And then she laid back and was quiet for a while as I cast out into the water again, counting my fly down into the deep water, like a fevered man counting slowly for patience or regaining self-control.

After a while Ellen got up and dove off of the bow of the boat into the mouth of the lower Chester where it met the main stem of the Chesapeake Bay. I watched her swim for a bit, effortlessly treading water with the natural technique of a swimmer. I dove in after her, but she headed out farther.

I didn't follow her and I swam back to the boat.

Ellen swam for a bit and I watched her from the boat, her arms raising out of the water with a practiced regularity, her distance from the boat a function of confidence and comfort. After some time she came back to the boat, her hair dark and slick against her head, and her rusty, amber eyes looking up at me with a native brightness from the waters of the Middle Chesapeake.

"Help me up," she said treading water beneath me, she was a little breathless from the swim.

I reached down into the water off the stern and pulled her up into the boat. She stood there dripping. I had kept my shirt off to get some sun and could feel the beginnings of a sunburn on my chest and shoulders after just an hour of being on the water. I was mostly dry by then but she was happily cooled down and dripping with bay water as she put her arms around my neck and kissed me beneath the strengthening July sun. My arms circled around her and I could taste the saltwater on her lips.

"Your lips are cold," I said.

She murmured agreement into my mouth.

Behind her, my fingers found the string hanging at her back and started pulling.

"Don't you dare," she whispered, eyes closed, still kissing me.

"Okay," I said, still pulling slowly, and then the knot gave and the only thing covering the skin on her back was the paint brush tip of her wet ponytail and my hands moving slowly forward to her sides.

* * * * *

We did our best to maintain the slowness, but August loomed before us with a certainty that became harder to ignore. Soon after our morning near Eastern Neck Island there was an especially trying night when I came over to her aunt's house late after work. Night visits had been a rarity, but as our courtship continued and summer moved closer to fall, the agreed-upon slowness began to hasten.

It was before midnight on a Thursday and because I didn't work on Fridays or Saturdays, my Thursday nights had the liberating feeling that came with the end of a work week. I'd finished work early, but before I left the office I called Ellen to see if she was still up.

"Yeah, I'm still awake," she said. "Come over. I'm done dealing with boxes. Done. I boxed up what had to be twenty years worth of *National Geographic* magazines today. I called all around and nobody wanted them. Not the library or the Goodwill or even the jail. I called the freaking Kent County Detention Center to see if they could use them and even they turned them down. I made two trips out to the recycling center so the basement's almost done now."

"Are you hungry, do you want me to bring you something?"

"I could really go for a beer."

"I'll pick something up," I said, and moments later I was on the road with my truck rumbling in its loud steady breath up Route 50 towards Chestertown, and half an hour later, as I crossed the Chester River Bridge, the tires of my truck sang the familiar three note tune passing over the open metal grates of the drawbridge. I parked on Queen Street and as I walked from my truck to her aunt's house I noticed how still and quiet Chestertown was. The sound of my car door closing, my feet on the old steps to her porch, and even my knock on her door felt especially loud in the stillness downtown.

By then it was mid July and the late summer thunderstorms had begun to threaten the evenings with increased regularity. The silence in town felt like it was about to break as the heat lightning flashed with pouty infrequence in the sky above, and the thunder complained about the still heat under its breath.

In the grass between the road and the sidewalk in front of her aunt's house I noticed a "For Sale" sign for the first time.

When Ellen opened the door she was in her pajamas—an old pair of Kent County Field Hockey athletic shorts and a tank top—and it looked like she'd just taken a shower; her hair was still wet, and in the summer humidity, I knew it would still be damp come morning.

Inside the living room, much of the clutter from earlier that summer had been reduced to just a few pieces of furniture. The piano, couch, and dining room set had been sold, and only the roll top desk remained off in the corner near the window. The emptiness made the house seem bigger and the smell of sugar cookies and lemony wood polish had faded. Although I had never met her, earlier that summer I could still smell traces of Aunt Ruby inside the house, but in the emptiness of the living room that night it was hard to imagine her in these rooms. It just felt like an empty house now and our voices inside echoed a little.

"Let's sit outside," she said after she took the six pack from me and put it in the refrigerator.

We sat on the swing underneath her aunt's front porch and within moments a downpour started, a hard, vertical drenching rain that blotted out the rest of the town. The deep porch roof and a big magnolia tree just beside the house sheltered us from most of the rain, but ahead of us in the street we could see it coming down in weighty drops. It had been a few weeks since a good rain and I imagined the corn and soy in the fields sighing with relief.

The porch swing was just in front of a big bay window, well away from the railings, so we stayed dry and comfortable. Across Queen Street the street lights and window lamps were obscured in the pouring rain and, although the July night seemed refreshed by the rain, it was still unmistakably hot and our clothes seemed to stick to us as weighty reminders.

"My aunt used to have hanging baskets on this porch every summer. She'd have ferns and fuchsia and by July they were so full, the tips nearly reached the bannister. Every one of those hooks would hold something."

"Let's get a few tomorrow. You're still living here, might as well dress it up a little for some curb appeal."

"Maybe," she said. "But I'd want to fill it up with plants like she did and…I can't think about adding anything else to this place right now. I'm supposed to be packing it up."

She sat sideways in the swing with her legs on me. There was a slow creak to the chain and beam as the swing moved that back and forth had the suggestive squeak of a rocking bed frame.

The beer bottles were cool in our hands, nicely satisfying after a day of work, and it struck me at how pleasant ending the day with Ellen felt. Between the heat, the rock of the wicker swing, the sound of the rain, and the cold beer in my hand, a calm relaxation settled into me. Ellen looked comfortable too, leaning back into the curve of the swing with her legs stretched out. Her toes were painted, although I couldn't quite tell what color in the dark. I thought of the smudge of toe prints on the dashboard and windshield of my truck where she'd stretched her legs out in the same fashion as we drove back from Cliff City.

"How was work tonight?" she asked.

"Fine. Crazy. Stupid. But I got out early and nothing went wrong, so that was good."

"Do you like working there?" she asked.

This type of domestic reality was new to both of us. Usually there was just a flirty tension and friendliness to our days with coffee or work or food to fill the space between us and then slow goodbyes in my truck. The rain and the dark had made us brave and intimate.

Like fly fishing, she had been curious about the newspaper where I worked because she knew that writing was important to me, but I had shrugged most of her questions off that summer without giving her many good answers.

"I think that I like saying that I work there more than I actually like working there, if that makes any sense," I offered.

"That makes perfect sense. It's pretty much how I feel about school now. I like saying that I'm in graduate school to people who don't know anything about engineering, but I think I stopped really liking it last year. Now I just want to finish."

Every once in a while the trace of a southern drawl emerged in her voice, usually after a few beers or when she spoke with certain people in town. It was never contrived and seemed more unconscious than anything else, and the reminder of her Kent County roots was emerging as she relaxed, smooth and twangy as a slide guitar.

As we talked in the porch swing we were both touching something lightly. For the most part, we'd successfully avoided the vague realities of our lives outside the context of Chestertown and our summer together. Like the riddle that she and Sarah had chosen (purposefully, serendipitously?) we were both watching time from the corner of our eyes and knew that it was running short. As if by instinct we both wanted to retreat from the domestic direction our talk was heading and reset to something less threatening, something that didn't have the uncomfortable reality of a soft-shell crab.

We finished our beers and she went inside to get two fresh ones from the refrigerator. When she came back, she sat next to me and the mood lightened for some reason. We talked a little more about her day clearing out the basement and my evening at the paper, but soon we were kissing in the porch swing.

The rain beat down off the thick, papery magnolia leaves and the roof, and soon her hands began pulling at my shirt as the rain fell and the aluminum gutters drummed. The rides in my truck, the sight of her on my boat, all the restrictions and polite abeyance of the summer were cast aside.

Ellen shifted beside me in the swing and slid her leg over me so that she straddled my hips. She had both hands on my face as she kept kissing me, fevered now, frantic. After a few moments she leaned back and pulled her tank top over her head and just after I leaned forward to kiss her, a gust of wind and rain came in from the side of the porch soaking us both with a July rain that was both warm and sobering.

We laughed and our damp foreheads touched as we smiled and kissed. It had only been a brief gust of rain, but we were both fairly drenched. My hands felt the rainwater on her back and legs and we enjoyed the feeling of so much bare skin touching.

Headlights appeared out of the rain and darkness on Queen Street, the beams flashing down the siding of the house as Ellen laughed with surprise. She jumped from the swing, grabbing her shirt from the floor of the porch as she headed for the door. I followed her inside and saw her standing by the stairs. She hadn't put her shirt back on and the sight of her standing there glazed with rain water moved me closer to her. We started to kiss again but the slowness had worked itself back between us. The moment on the porch swing had passed and inside the living room, there was a cool hand on my chest lightly pushing me back.

"Let's go upstairs," I said, hopeful, desperate, pleading.

"No. Just a bit longer." She shook her head and pulled her shirt back over her head. "You should go."

I was beside myself with frustration and surprise.

"This is insane. We want each other."

"I know. I'm sorry. I didn't mean to let things get like that. I'm sorry. Just, please go. Let's talk tomorrow."

So I drove back home to my sweltering apartment and I thought ten different things about Ellen Barroll before I finally fell asleep that night. Our slowness was no longer charming or playful; it was starting to feel baseless, and like waste.

* * * * *

I met Ellen for breakfast the next morning. Even before nine o'clock the day had a humid exhaustion to it, but inside Sharon's Diner the air conditioning chilled the air so that hot coffee felt possible.

My anger and frustration had subsided, and sitting across from me in a booth in the diner Ellen looked fresh and beautiful. She was wearing another one of her belted dresses and in the familiar daylight I was happy to be with her.

"Why are we doing this?" I asked after Sarah had brought us our coffees and moved off behind the counter.

"We're just…Taking. Our. Time." She spaced each of those words as if she were figuring out the answer as she said it.

"Until?"

"Until we absolutely have to have each other," she said, but this answer was rushed.

"Well, I absolutely had to have you last night."

Ellen seemed to consider this.

"I know. I know." She looked away from me. "I wanted you. I still do. That wasn't easy for me, either," she said.

We sat in silence for a few moments and then Sarah took our order. I thought she sensed that we were having a talk and didn't linger.

"That's my point. I just want to know why we're doing this now. I know why we started with the slowness. I've never had an issue with that. I just want to talk about why…now?"

There had never been a moment where it seemed like she didn't know how to articulate herself. Ellen was well-spoken and sharp as a tack, but in this, she struggled. She started to talk a few times but stopped, like an engine turning over trying to start, as if her mind needed priming before her reasoning could ignite. Finally something caught.

"I want to say something and I hope you understand it because I don't know how else to say it. It's weird, but it's the only way I know to put it: To see how the butterfly works inside, you have to kill it first."

She let that sit for a while and I thought about it, but I didn't see what it had to do with sex.

"We're here together. It's wonderful. We're taking our time. I don't want to scrutinize every why and what between us because once we start, things will be different. We'll start asking about what we are, if there's anyone else, how much time we have left, and what we're going to do come fall. This will turn into that. All that—everything that comes with looking inside a butterfly. I just want this summer with you to be one good thing that's separate from all of that for as long as possible. Because once we start asking those questions, we'll get the answers we want, but we'll kill the butterfly."

She sipped her coffee and I looked at her, not quite making the connection.

"Sleeping together is part of all that. More closeness, more questions, but soon we'll kill the butterfly."

It seemed to make sense vaguely, in a circular, withholding, in-the-present kind of way. By not addressing the immediate future and stringing out our courtship for as long as possible, we kept the threat of fall and domestic realities at bay, and sustained the moments of our attraction.

But I wanted her, and I knew she wanted me. That part of the question still sat between us, like a riddle unanswered.

"So we're taking our time until we absolutely have to have each other. And I know that you don't need a promise or anything, and that all of this has been, well, different. It's been different for me, too."

She reached across the table and held my hand for a moment and looked directly at me with her unsettling amber eyes that I'd never quite gotten used to.

"I know the summer is almost over, but trust me when I say that I want you and that we will have each other," she said, and there was a finality to her last statement that I found a little intimidating.

Breakfast came to the table just as she finished. Pancakes for Ellen. Eggs, bacon, and wheat toast for me.

* * * * *

On one of our last nights together that summer, on our way to get pie and ice-cream, we drove out towards Broad Neck landing to sit outside in the dark, starry, ripening country to look at the stars since it was clear. We took a straight road through Kent County farmland that dead-ended into the open water of Langford Creek, and once we got there, I backed into the rough gravel landing so the bed of my truck faced the darkness over the water. I lowered my tailgate and we sat looking out over the water and dark expanse of sky with our feet dangling.

It was a clear night, and far away from the lights in town the stars spread out in fine detail above us. Even some of the smaller, fainter constellations were visible and it was possible to pick some of the planets out from the stars. The moon above us, a full August moon, was also called the Moon When All Things Ripen in the farmer's almanac I'd purchased at the beginning of the year. I could see its muddled reflection in Langford Creek along with a few of the brighter stars, and what I thought might be Saturn low and bright on the horizon.

I thought about pointing out Virgo and Capricorn to see if she knew them, but after two months of courtship something had tempered between us and by August our words became more measured and less rushed. We sat in silence for a while before either one of us said anything.

"If it were hot, we could swim, but tonight's actually kind of cool. Fall might come early this year," I said.

"Too early," she said, squeezing my hand a little. "We can swim if you want to, though."

"No, your hair will smell like river water for the rest of the night," I said. "I didn't bring any towels, anyway."

"Poor planning, Mr. Brown Truck. Looks like you missed your chance to go skinny dipping with me."

"The summer's not quite over, and the night's still young."

"Ever the optimist," she said.

"I doubt that's how you'd typically describe me."

She seemed to think about that.

"Maybe you're a pessimist that's trying to be an optimist. Or an optimist disguised as an pessimist."

"The former, if I had to pick."

"But maybe the latter. I remember you hunched over your breakfast the morning we met at Sharon's. I thought about you later: a brooding man with an honest brown truck, who looked drunken and wayward, but capable of good behavior."

"I think I've been exceedingly well behaved these last few weeks."

She nodded. "I think we both have," she said.

She yawned and stretched before jumping off the tailgate, the gravel crunching beneath her shoes.

"Come on. If you're not going to swim with me, you can at least buy me some ice cream," she said, grabbing my hands and pulling me down from the tailgate.

Inside the cab of my truck there was a buzzing and brightness in the overhead lamp as we opened our doors. I waited a moment before I turned the ignition and pulled a note out of my shirt pocket and gave it to her. We had begun with a note and I felt that ending with one held a symmetry that she'd appreciate. And there were things I wanted to say, things better written than spoken.

Ellen,

It's August and near time for you to head back to Minnesota, west and away from the fields of Kent County and the slow-spun torture of my hands.

   Between us there have been far more questions than answers but I wanted to revisit the first, Sarah's riddle about time:

Tabled and drawn we never wait,
Pulled by the moon but not by fate
Slack we dampen
High we hasten
We're watched and worked but never late.

Time and tide brought us together.
Perhaps they'll do so again.

Brett

She kissed me quickly and then just held onto me before I started my truck. We finished our drive out to the truck stop, and she sat directly next to me in my truck as she had on our first date, but by early August, my hand rested on her knee with familiarity.

Hours later, in a nearly empty house on Queen Street, Ellen stood in the doorway to her Aunt Ruby's bedroom mostly undressed, half a dare and half a present. One arm was against the doorjamb as she leaned forward, the other was against her side and the curvy exaggeration of waist and hip.

Her legs were crossed in front of her, her long hair was down against her shoulders, and there wasn't an ounce of insecurity or shyness about her as she looked at me from the doorway.

This wasn't a girl playing at womanhood, dressing up in her mother's high heels and borrowing her big sister's makeup. And this wasn't a woman numbed and emboldened by drink, brusquely throwing herself into a man, hoping to be caught in the current of mannish lust. Ellen knew exactly what she was doing and I remembered the confidence of her arms rising above the water of the lower Chester as she swam in the open water of the Chesapeake Bay, far away from my anchored boat.

We had walked up the creaking stairs in her aunt's house together and I finally understood the slowness agreed upon as each noisy step brought us closer to the finality of the bedroom. Amidst the lust of trucks, boats, and porch swings there was suddenly a sadness that made me want to pull her closer to me in a new and different way. Our slowness that summer hadn't been decided out of propriety, but from the desperation that comes with holding on to someone briefly before having to let them go.

As she stood in the doorway, Ellen looked at me with the certainty of time and tide in her amber eyes. Her hand moved behind her back, unfastened her bra, and she stepped toward me.

* * * * *

Anywhere there are cornfields and small towns there are men who choose to drive old pickup trucks, and there are women who love these kind of men. Forget the anthropology of American ranchers and the working-class archetypes of traditional husbands and wives.

Forget the daily application of filling the open bed of a truck with hay bales or lumber, and the implied nobility of dirty hands and weather-worn clothes. Driving a truck like my old F-150 said as much about my values and my perception of myself as a man as a three-piece suit and a Rolex watch would for another man.

Those few slow summer months with Ellen are important because my old F-150 played such a role in them, and to tell the story of that truck is to tell that story, too. If I had been driving a different car Ellen might not have remembered me after we spoke outside of Sharon's Diner, or slid so perfectly across the bench seat to sit next to me as we drove to Rock Hall on our first date. Later, I might not have endeared myself to her by helping her with trips to the dump and Goodwill, and by taking her out to the truck stop for pie and ice-cream, and into the ripening farmland at night to see the summer constellations from my lowered tailgate.

And perhaps at the most basic of levels, the Kent County girl inside of Ellen might not have responded to me if I had driven something other than an honest truck with a fading brown paint job bisected by a dull, pitted chrome strip, and a set of big side-view mirrors that stuck out from the body like an oversized pair of ears.

Of course, that old truck was much more than one summer in Kent County, and if I had to quantify all of my trucks over the years with trips made and fish caught, the F-150 would be the clear leader. I was fishing the tidewaters of the middle Chesapeake Bay a lot back then, and gauging my quality of life on how much I fished each week, not in trips each month or each year.

During the time that I drove it I had the good fortune to live in beautiful country, near waters that I grew to know intimately. Along with the tidal bays and rivers of the middle Chesapeake, I loved fishing the farm ponds of the Eastern Shore, and I developed a nice little network of ponds where I had gotten permission to fish from friends and strangers alike. And I'm fairly sure that in a few cases, it was the truck itself that eventually wrangled permission to fish a few of these ponds.

One time specifically, I remember the farmer looking out to his driveway from the front porch where we stood, and after I asked him for permission to fish his pond, I could see him almost look through me to appraise the old truck in his driveway. I couldn't read his mind, but I imagined something like, "Shit, he can't be half bad if he drives a truck like that."

During the term of that truck, the truck of my early to late twenties, I began writing, I began fly fishing, and I laid the important foundation of how I saw myself as a man. In that time I also learned the important skill of trailering a boat, a skill like working a clutch or building a fence.

Two weeks before I left the Eastern Shore for a new job in Washington, DC, I got into an accident on Nanticoke Road just outside Salisbury. I was coming back from the Hebron Fireman's Carnival, where some friends and I had met up to play bingo and eat the oyster fritter sandwiches that the carnival was known for.

As I was coming back into town I started to pass a slowly moving flatbed truck when it began to turn left onto a small side road. I couldn't slow down, and I couldn't do much else than turn off the road into one of the fields to avoid colliding with the truck. The ditch I hit slowed me down some before launching me into the freshly tilled field. I landed fairly square, but when I got out I saw that steam was rising from the engine, the front end was askew from the impact of the ditch, and the bed of the truck just looked off.

I was glad that I was sober and unhurt, but fairly sure that the truck was finished and, about a week later, when all was said and done with the insurance company, my truck was considered "totaled" because the cost of the repairs outweighed the overall worth of the vehicle.

The thought of that truck rusting slowly away in some Eastern Shore junk yard fills me with shame and sadness now. By all rights, if not fully restored, at the very least, it should be in a barn somewhere beneath a tarp, awaiting someone with the vision and budget to bring it back to its original dignity.

At the time, I remember feeling a bit of relief; that with the death of the F-150 the Eastern Shore part of my life was officially over, and that I was moving on to a brighter future in greener, urban pastures. So when I moved out of my house in Salisbury, after ten years of living on the Eastern Shore, I left town driving the U-Haul' I'd rented without a car to my name.

A week later, I bought the unlucky Jeep using the minor payout from the insurance company as a down payment. Within the space of a few days of buying it, a good friend committed suicide, and shortly after that my boat was stolen from behind my house and the company I had just started working for had to let half of its staff go.

It was the beginning of unlucky times, but I was in a new part of Maryland with new waters to fish.

* * * * *

After my truck broke down and I was firm in my decision to buy something else, I donated the broken-down 4Runner to a Vietnam Veterans group. I had tried to sell it as a fixer upper, but nobody seemed to be interested. I considered holding on to it and eventually restoring it, but I knew that once I moved on, I'd never really come back to it. Before the tow truck came to pick it up, I went out to make sure I had everything out of it that I might need: some jumper cables, a first-aid kit, and a few other things from the glovebox.

As soon as I opened the door there was the familiar smell of an old truck, impossible to describe, but as personal and comforting as the smell of a familiar bakery, an elementary school cafeteria, or an old dog's collar. I knew that a tow truck was coming for it, but there was something in me that was grateful for the opportunity to formally say goodbye.

Giving the 4Runner up felt like a necessary betrayal, and I sat inside for a second, my hands on the steering wheel and the familiar knob of the gear shift, torn with doubt. I considered calling the donation off, and just sinking half of the money I was planning on investing in a new car on a new engine and some body work.

But deep down, I knew that the decision had been made, and soon I was outside with the tinny sound of its door closing, and I took one last look at some of its strange features from another time: the triangular wing vents at the window corners and the faded red manually locking hubs in the wheels. With my hand on the hood, I wished it well, I thanked it for good fortune, and I prayed that its next owner would fix it up and drive slowly on flat country roads, in fourth gear, where it was happiest.

* * * * *

Between the old F-150, the new Jeep, and the beat up 4Runner, I had experienced a few different extremes of car ownership: a classic American pickup, a brand new vehicle fresh from a dealership, and an efficient Japanese beater truck. All three had their pros and cons, and each had a meaningful history associated with it: one beautiful, one tragic, and one, thankfully, about redemption.

As I considered my next vehicle, with no clear allegiance to brand or make, I vacillated between a late '80s F-250 and a mid-to-late '90s Toyota Land Cruiser. Both were appealing for different reasons. I liked the solid strength and power of the older F-250s, and how iconic they were of trucks in general. And with the Land Cruisers, I liked their no-nonsense heritage of capable off-roading and weighty quality.

I found myself leaning towards the F-250, possibly even something as old as a 1965 model. Even though there were clear elements about driving a truck that weren't easy—simple things like being able to leave my strung up rods in the back without having to worry about them being stolen, or not having a ton of room in the cab for dogs, kids, and groceries—a pickup truck was still an icon of individuality and masculinity that I couldn't quit.

There were compelling, logical arguments for a man, whether he's a fisherman or not, to own anything but a truck, but they carried little weight with me. I heard them, understood them, but steadfastly refused them. Hell or high water, I wanted to drive a truck and like that summer with Ellen Barroll, there was no reason to kill the butterfly to understand the reasons why a pickup truck was the answer for me.

But, in the end, I decided to go with a late '90s Toyota Land Cruiser. Even though I was forever in love with the rugged individuality of a pickup truck, I knew that the day-to-day sacrifice would be too much of an issue and that four doors and a place for a car seat made more sense than the honest, straightforward romance of an old truck with an open bed.

The Land Cruiser I found was being sold by a man in northern Virginia. It had nearly 200,000 miles on it, but the engine had been replaced around 185,000. The owner had taken decent care of it, and had modified it significantly over the years in the hopes of eventually taking it for extended trips into the Appalachians and out west. He told me that he had taken it on a few weekend trips, but he had never really gotten around to taking that big extended trip he'd always wanted. I said I knew what he meant.

The owner realized that he liked working on the projects with his son far more than actually taking the trips themselves, so he was unloading the '97 Land Cruiser I was looking at to make room in his garage and free up some money for their next project, a white mid-'80s FJ60 that was sitting outside.

Out in the driveway, the Land Cruiser still had beaded water on its gray paint from a thoughtful washing before I stopped by. It had a conservative but noticeable two-inch lift, upgraded shocks, and tastefully oversized tires. There was a solid-looking ARB bull bar bumper replacement up front along with a safari roof rack on top. The running boards had been removed and a matching spare tire had been mounted to a swing-out rack on the rear of the truck.

All in all, the proportions of the car had been just slightly filled out and extended to exaggerate the form into something that looked more complete, and looking at the finished product, I couldn't help but think, "Why didn't Toyota just make them like this to begin with?"

Inside, the gray leather seats were fairly worn and scratched, but not torn or sagging. The third row of seats had been removed, but he had them if I wanted them. I wouldn't have known what to look at when he lifted the hood, but he did because that's what you do when you look at a car, and once the hood was up, there was the cleanest engine I'd ever seen. I knew enough to see pride and maintenance.

Like most Land Cruiser nuts, he mistook my appreciation for fellowship and assumed I knew what he was talking about when he launched into the mechanic's language of locking differentials, winches, and expeditionary overlanding.

The gas mileage for these trucks wasn't great, but it was beautifully set up and felt very strong when I drove it, nothing at all like the light four-cylinder efficiency of my old 4Runner. With four doors it was fairly practical, in fishing terms it was versatile, and in domestic terms it was approved because it had air conditioning, a professional paint job, and room for a baby seat.

I had done enough research to know that this was what I wanted and after a few weeks of being without a car I was ready to make a decision. I wrote him a check that day and drove it home without any haggling. It was a fair price and I liked the guy, even though I barely knew him.

So three weeks after my 4Runner broke down in a steamy, labored gasp just a few miles from the Potomac River, I was whole again. By then I was anxious to get out of the house, and looking forward to taking my first trip with the new truck. I'd driven it around town for a few days and it was starting to feel like mine, but I hadn't loaded it up with rods and tackle and set off on our first trip yet, an important milestone in the life of a fishing truck.

By then we were nearing Memorial Day, the blue crabs were long finished with their spring molt, and I knew that with the upcoming full moon, the May worms would be swarming near the surface of mud and oyster shell flats. About a two-hour drive from home, there were a few spots in some of the tributaries that were open to catch and release fishing where these worms were known to swarm in good numbers and the fishing, could be on or off, with little range in between.

In waters where the worms were swarming, there was so much forage in the water that the fish were simply gorging themselves and you were either there when they were feeding, or you were there after they'd eaten. I'd seen fish slashing through the surface in a mindless orgy of food, and I'd seen some large fish finning slowly through the leftovers with all of the energy of a post-Thanksgiving living room.

Fishing during the May worms swarm could be a tough time of year to fish, because, let's face it: it's tough to compete with that much bait. But I had experienced enough good times when the fishing was extraordinary to keep heading back for the May worm hatch. Even if the fishing was off, the May worms on the Little Choptank gave me a target, and after three weeks of being laid up at home, a target was really all I needed. It would be an interesting natural event to witness, even if the fishing was off.

So on the last Saturday in May, I set off early for the Little Choptank, a small underrated river just west of Cambridge that's a little hard to get to and not really known for a ton of great fishing. I had been anxious to get out for weeks, but once I got on the road, I found myself slowing down, very conscious of my drive and the journey between home and the Little Choptank. I stopped for gas and coffee before the Bay Bridge, and soon I was crossing over the Chesapeake.

Towing my boat, with a lunch in the cooler and a few of my favorite rods packed in the back made the new truck feel more like mine, and the drive on Route 50 towards Cambridge made the trip feel perfectly familiar. I thought about my previous trucks and the stories that defined them and I wondered what was in store for me and this Land Cruiser, and how I'd eventually describe it once it was time for a new truck.

I hoped that this one might be the truck that would take me on one of the big trips I've always imagined, an extended summer road trip to the Boundary Waters Canoe Area or a fall trip through the Adirondacks as frost began to touch the northern woods. I pictured taking my son fishing once he was old enough to hold a rod, driving up to a pond in Allegany County where my father had taken me in a pale-blue Jeep Wagoneer. And I thought about all the simple trips that really define a life of fishing; the trips to waters known and unknown, all within the scope of a well-marked local map.

At a stoplight in Easton I looked around the inside of the new truck and I wondered if I'd ever be in a spot in life where I could return to a time when an old pickup truck somehow made sense. My hands were on the steering wheel, but I found myself still reaching into empty space for the gear shift of my 4Runner.

One day you're twenty-something with a pretty girl sitting next to you on the bench seat of an old truck. The summer is long, the windows are down, and there's nothing but fish and fields ahead of you. The next moment, you're waist deep into your forties, driving a newer truck, and towing a different boat. There's gray in your beard and a graveyard of Cheerios˙ and toys on the floor of the back seat. Part of your heart reaches for the days of a weathered pickup truck and the simplicity of a one-bedroom apartment, but then you realize, you're still on your way to fish somewhere on the Eastern Shore, in a truck that still has a good story inside it to tell, and other than some gray at the edges, not much else has changed.

Soft-shell Crab Sandwich

There are things that as children you can't appreciate: brussels sprout, stillness and quiet, and soft-shell crabs. I think that the best soft-shell crab sandwich focuses on crab itself, a crispy, fried delicacy with just a few toppings to freshen it and soft thin bread to hold it together.

Ingredients
- Soft shell crabs
- Milk
- Eggs
- 1 stick butter
- Vegetable oil
- Flour
- Old Bay Seasoning
- Lemon
- White bread
- Mayonnaise, spread as desired
- Tomatoes, thinly sliced
- Cucumbers, peeled, deseeded, and thinly sliced
- Butter lettuce

Directions:
Depending on how you get your soft shell crabs, it's possible that you may have to clean them. This basically means lifting the top shell to remove the gills, removing the apron from the bottom, and snipping out the eyes and mouth from the front. The devil is in the details, and whether it's you or your local seafood merchant who takes care of these minor steps, it can make an important difference in a sandwich meant to highlight the sweetness of blue crab.

Whisk milk and eggs together in shallow bowl. Place soft shells into mixture and let marinate for one hour, turning over once.

Coat the bottom of a cast-iron skillet with vegetable oil and add one stick of butter. Heat to medium high heat.

Mix flour, Old Bay Seasoning and dredge crabs until coated evenly,

Add crabs to hot skillet. Fry two to three minutes per side or until golden brown and crispy. Remove from heat once cooked through and set aside to dry. Squeeze lemons over fried crabs and dust liberally with Old Bay.

To assemble sandwiches, spread mayonnaise on two slices of white bread. Depending on the size of the soft shells, place one to two on bottom slice of bread. Top with thinly sliced tomatoes, cucumbers, butter lettuce, and second piece of bread.

…I fell back into the full flood of summer, into the full tide of feeling in which we drifted in a kind of breathless ease, like a strong, massive, deep current which didn't hurry but which had an irresistible weight of water behind it, and over which the days and nights passed like flickers of light and shade.

—Robert Penn Warren
All the King's Men

SUMMER

JUNE
SMALL WATER

Ursa minor and Polaris circle each other in the night sky, their histories and feuds forgotten with a rising strawberry moon. The summer solstice near the end of the month reminds us that with ripening comes reaping, that even the fleshy permanence of June gives way to the harvest. For now it is a time for corn to grow, for tomatoes to ripen on their tangled vines, and tiger lilies to reach for the sun from shady hedgerows.

Always keep a horseshoe above the front door for good luck to all who live there

Tomatoes, c. 1935. Tomatoes ready for canning in Cambridge, Dorchester County.

J ust southeast of Kent Island, there's a crooked island tucked away from the big water of Eastern Bay, and a small tidal river with three names flows around it. Each arm of this river is some variation of the Wye and early in each summer these waters are a nice spot for stripers during that delicate in-between pattern of late spring and midsummer—that period right after the fish have invaded the rivers and finished spawning, but before summer strangles the region with its ninety-degree heat and muggy persistence and pushes the fish to deeper, cooler waters.

Unlike most Chesapeake Bay tributaries that begin upstream in small headwaters and trumpet their way down to the bay in curvy, ever-widening carriages, the Wye River stretches into Queen Annes and Talbot Counties with a logic that's hard to follow. The mouth of the Wye joins the mouth of the Miles River—although in this case, it's fairly difficult to tell where the mouth of the Miles River starts and Eastern Bay begins—and from there, it quickly branches into the Wye River and the Wye East River, not the East Wye River.

To the north and the east, the rivers flow around Wye Island, impulsively spreading into coves, pouring around points, and tapering off into smaller secondary creeks in a series of moves that are hard to predict. To add to the confusion, the Wye branches off again above the northern edge of Wye Island into a piece of water called the Wye Narrows, which eventually meets back with the Wye East River at the eastern tip of Wye Island.

Taking all of this into account, most anglers just call the whole thing the Wye, and amidst all of this repetitive and ambiguous cartography, it's nearly impossible to tell exactly where anyone is fishing at a conversational level. Whether this is a contrived stance for secrecy or an honest accident of confused geography, it's impossible to tell.

Wye Island itself is a Natural Resources Management Area and much of its shorelines remain undeveloped. Although the city of Annapolis is just thirty miles away and the dock bar oasis of Kent Narrows is a mere fifteen miles distant, any time spent on the Wye River gives the impression of being much farther away from civilization. Along each side of the river there are the occasional dock and bulkhead poking out into the water, with miles of undeveloped shore and marshland, and the occasional houses that you see from the water have the understated affluence to them that Talbot County is known for.

The shores are lined with marsh grass and forests. Points and coves provide character to the water itself, and the river is surprisingly deep for such a narrow tributary—with a channel averaging nearly twenty feet deep in the lower sections. Although the depth of river makes it stand out somewhat, the Wye is typical of what I call small water: a secondary tributary of the Chesapeake Bay where the fish tend to be small, the waters are mostly ignored, and most days the only other boats you see on the water are pleasure boaters heading quickly past, or crabbers finishing a day that started with a 4 a.m. launch.

* * * * *

It seemed like for the past few years at least, spring had made an abrupt leap from the wind and rain of March and April straight into the muggy heat of midsummer. This quick transition had magnified the feeling that the early summer fishery on our tidal rivers was balanced on a knife's edge: the warmth and sunlight that we wanted so badly in February suddenly becomes too much of a good thing, driving the fish from the shallows into the deeper, cooler water before we've even had a chance to legally fish for them. So with the rivers not officially opening until June 1st, and a natural affection for fishing the rivers themselves, there's a rush to get out on the water before the pattern slips past us.

But this year, June took its time. In between dawn and dusk the corn stretched eagerly for the sun, the winter wheat washed the fields in a deepening green, and the tomatoes ripened on their tangled vines. This mild entrance into summer removed the typical panic to get out on the rivers. So there was a conscious luxury to the mild weather, and for the first time in recent memory, there was hope that the shallow water river fishing might last into July.

Mild weather aside, it had been a good and steady spring. The spring perch run had started things off nicely in March with a good push of yellows up into the headwaters of Langford Creek, and in

Southeast Creek the whites had shown up with a thick ferocity. We messed around with these fish on 5 weights and small flies as soon as the word got out that they were there, and before we knew it, winter was behind us and the waters were filling with fish.

A few weeks later in April, we were driving up to Havre de Grace to fish the Susquehanna Flats for trophy stripers with substantially heavier tackle and flies bigger than most of the perch we'd been catching. Later in May, and much closer to home, we'd even managed to squeeze in good trips to some local farm and mill ponds for largemouth bass as the waters warmed and the fish moved into the shallows.

So before I knew it, it was already June, and the seeds from a productive spring had been sown. And although the itch to get out on a local tidal creek for stripers had been there since the dead of winter, it wasn't until the middle of the month—a few weeks after Memorial Day—that I finally got out on the Wye River.

* * * * *

I launched early one Wednesday from Kent Narrows and made the short run south to the mouth of the Wye. Bennet Point reaches down like a finger and separates the Wye River from the southeast portion of Eastern Bay and the Miles River, and just off its tip there's a bar that's marked by three cans. This bar holds baitfish, and stripers will hold along the edges during moving tides. As I motored up I saw that there was another boat there with a few light tackle anglers and I could see them hooked up occasionally—a good sign.

My first drift there went unnoticed, but on my second, I felt my fly hitting the bottom as I drifted over the bar; I stripped it aggressively back to the boat and, suddenly, I was connected to a strong fish. After the initial run I hand-lined it in to the boat and lipped it, and admired my first locally caught striper of the year, a thick fifteen-inch fish that came off a tan and white clouser.

I worked that bar for another thirty minutes until another boat showed up with a few more fish coming to hand. Most were on the smallish side, but one was a keeper just a hair over eighteen inches. I thought about keeping this fish, but ended up releasing it. I watched the other fishermen for a few moments before casting again. Three boats certainly isn't a crowd in June, especially on the accessible water of Eastern Bay, but after a few drifts and only one short strike, I decided to head into the Wye to see how the lower river bars were fishing.

Over the years I've found that the lower portions of the rivers fish best in June where submerged points extend out and drop off into deep water; so much of my fishing at this time of year is with my 8 weights and fast sinking lines—a Teeny 350 at a minimum. I don't fish an 8 weight because of the size of the fish I'm catching, but mostly because of the kind of water that I'm fishing. A 6 or 7 weight rod would have handled most of the fish just fine, but because the stripers were typically holding in deeper ledges where the current moves fairly quickly, I like to use fast sinking lines to get the fly down into the strike zone as fast as possible. An 8 weight just casts and handles these sinking lines better, but later in the fall when the fish are along shoreline drops and dock lights, I'll fish a lighter 6 or 7 weight with an intermediate line as the fish are rarely over twenty inches and mostly in the teens.

Drift is everything when fishing over bars and more than any other types of fishing on the bay, working these lower river points is equal parts drift, depth awareness, and boating. Wind and current can quickly cancel out an effective cast, so there are two kinds of awareness necessary: being conscious of what your boat is doing in the current and being aware of your line in the current. There are times when a natural drift can illicit a strike, but I've found that an aggressively retrieved fly yields the best results.

It occurs to me now that this is probably why most people ignore the lower portions of the Wye and tidal rivers in general. It's a fair bit of work for what anyone in the area would call average fish. Sometimes it's just easier to head out into open water, anchor up with a chum bag over the stern, and wait for the fish to come to you.

There are times on these river bars when it's possible to set up and anchor on the up-current side of the bar for an easier presentation, but this isn't always the best tactic. These spots aren't really big, the fish can move or hold in different spots along the bar, so I usually just resign myself to having to reposition after a few casts.

I also think that that the noise of anchoring can spook a school of fish more than a few drifts of a boat twelve feet above. So most of the time, I choose to drift over anchoring. It's quieter that way and it keeps more options open. These bars are often thin points that reach into deeper water. The end point is often the best spot, but the ledge that leads up to the point can often hold fish, too. Often, I'll start drifting at the submerged point, and I'll work my way inland to see if any fish are holding along the edge.

Once inside the mouth of the Wye, I motored above the first bar inside the river and put the outboard in neutral. It idled quietly as I cast up current and began counting down as my fly sank, and soon the current caught the boat and began pulling it back downriver towards the mouth of the Miles. By the time I was drifting over the bar, my fly was at least ten feet deep and I was stripping it in short, excited strips. I rushed the first cast back to the boat to see if any aggressive feeders were on the upside of the bar, and made another quick cast into the same water to work the back side of the drop-off. I worked the second cast back slower to give it time to sink, and within two short, jerky strips, my rod was bent with another strong but modest fish.

The back side of the bar accounted for a handful of fish that day, a working-class grade of fish that was mostly just shy of eighteen inches. The fish were young and strong, and sometimes I wonder if there's some kind of Darwinism at play here that keeps the fish under eighteen inches to ensure that they're released.

I worked inside of the main point and after a few drifts without fish, I headed just upriver to the second point. This bar was a shorter, more concentrated point into deep water and just staying inside the green can that marked it kept me on top of the shallow water. Before I'd even made a cast I knew that the spot was going to be good—my fish finder showed a school of fish stacked on the downside edge of the point.

The current was really moving by then, so it took me a few attempts to get the drift right. I motored well above the current rip, kept the throttle in gear, and cast up towards the shore and paying out a little line so the fly would sink and swing below me just as I began to drift over the bar. This spot yielded the best class of fish of that morning, a nice school of healthy stripers averaging in the mid twenties. A few came unbuttoned deep, but struck the fly with incredible force. I kept one fish for the cooler, a stout twenty-inch fish, and released another fish in the high twenties that I'd had to put on the reel and net.

After I released the last fish, it occurred to me that this was exactly what I had been daydreaming about in February: a simple, consistent day on local waters where the drive had been short, the fish had been willing, and the waters were small and mostly empty of other fishermen. I'd fished two flies all day, both bushy tan over white clousers with copper flash. If the first hadn't been mangled past confident use, I'd have finished the day with it.

* * * * *

The Wye is one of the few rivers where I can say that I've fished about every inch of its reach. It's not a big river like the Choptank or the Potomac, but it's one that I've spent a considerable amount of time on. And after living near it and fishing it consistently for close to twenty years, it's emerged as one of those select bodies of water that I consciously and unconsciously call home water. It's the kind of place that I head to when I'm not looking for huge fish, when I want quiet and pretty scenery as much as I want a consistent bite, and when I don't have the time or gas money for a fully fledged trip to waters that are more exotic.

Spring, summer, or fall, there are times where any part of the Wye holds fish. I've fished the main stem of the Wye all the way north as it nears Route 50 at Queenstown in the spring for perch. I've fished the Wye East River from the mouth and on upriver to where it turns into Skipton Creek in the fall when the shorelines and docks hold good numbers of fish. And in the summers, I've fished the Wye and the Wye Narrows where they stretch across the back of Wye Island until they join with the Wye East River.

Fishing the entire system was never really a clearly set goal and didn't happen in consecutive trips. It was more a summation of summer trips in the lower sections, spring trips in the upper reaches, and fall trips through the whole thing where I fished the shorelines and dock lights at night. One winter I was tying flies and looking at a marked up chart of Eastern Bay when I thought, "Shit, I've just about fished the whole damn thing. When did that happen?" Maybe I hadn't hit every, every little side creek and every little cove, but I'd made a good enough dent to know what was where, and to have a mild sense of ownership that comes with knowing a piece of water pretty well.

I guess that the idea of fishing an entire river had always been a goal of mine, in the way that seeing and conquering can be goals of twenty-something year old men. And as masculine goals go, I guess it's worthwhile, up there with climbing a mountain and building a house—both of which I've done, for the record. But along the way, I do remember thinking that knowing one small river well, was better than spreading my knowledge around a larger body of water without ever really putting the pieces together.

But once I realized that I'd fished nearly all of the Wye, I found myself pretty underwhelmed. I guess I thought that upon knowing a piece of water like that I would feel a little different—hell, a lot different—and that I'd have more wisdom and secrets to show for the effort. In the end I felt noticeably average; like I probably knew what everyone else knew about the Wye, although having fished it with flies was probably a distinction that most anglers didn't have.

I wasn't expecting a merit badge or the heavens to open up in proclamation, but did expect something. Much later it struck me: even small water can remain as inscrutable as the open water of the bay, that even the humblest piece of water, when compared to the big water mystery, can keep you guessing after so much time.

* * * * *

After my last fish off the second bar inside the Wye, I reeled up and stowed my rods. It wasn't quite lunchtime, but I had risen early, my morning coffee was wearing off, and I was getting hungry. By then the sun was high in the sky and the day was a carbon copy of the June days that had preceded it—a warm, clear, gift of a summer day without a hint of the humid heat that would bear down on us later that season.

Just before eleven o'clock that morning, the tide was low and slack, and I headed up river to look for a nice spot on Wye Island to eat my lunch: a few pieces of cold fried chicken and an Italian coldcut sub that I'd picked up earlier that morning.

I veered off into a smaller creek to get off the main stem and away from the growing boat traffic and motored my johnboat into Grapevine Cove to find a spot where I could beach my boat, eat my lunch on solid ground, and wait out the slack water. Although it was a weekday, there was already a good amount of boat traffic on the water: pleasure boaters heading down to St. Michaels for lunch and drinks, a few other fishermen in center consoles heading out to the big water, and off in the distance there was a line of kayaks paddling off along the western shore of the Wye.

Just within the small cove where I was eating lunch I could see a crabber running a trotline from his johnboat. He was a heavy man in a straw hat, in what looked to be a fairly small boat, probably around ten to twelve feet, that looked a bit overloaded with coolers, bushels, and crabbing gear. By crabbing standards, it was late in the morning, but the crabber looked busy as his net moved from the water to his bushel with efficient regularity, and his other hand guided the tiller of his small outboard.

Each fishing season has its happy slow moments: winter with its warming coffee breaks beside empty, quiet water; springtime shore lunches on early perch trips as the sun warms a chilly day; and summer with a boat beached on a quiet stretch of land with a sub for lunch, a cold drink, and a bag of Old Bay chips.

As I ate my lunch a pair of ducks muddled about close to shore, but these were not the domestic, lunch seeking ducks of parks that hassled and begged; these birds were wild and wary, and perfectly fed within this tidal river. Off across Grapevine Cove, the crabber's luck was a joy to watch as I finished my lunch and I wondered at his bounty. Had he filled a full bushel? I pictured the crabs beneath the thin wooden lid—piled and backing against the edges each time the bushel lid lifted, claws raised to the sun with their impossible blue hues and deep orange tips from the simple olive of their shells.

For a moment I considered chicken-necking with the remaining bones of my fried chicken. I had one keeper rockfish in the cooler—just a few crabs would be all I'd need to improvise a simple stuffed rockfish dinner. But in the end I decided to head back. Sedentary fishing has never had much draw for me, but perhaps next time I'd bring a book to give it a shot.

* * * * *

Fly fishing on the Chesapeake Bay is a choice. In a sporting culture dominated by bait, trolling, and light tackle, fly fishing is the clear minority in angling methods, but for me it's the most satisfying. It's not always easy, and often it can be a choice born of habit rather than effectiveness, but it's the way that I prefer fishing these waters. The waters aren't always clear and easy for anyone fishing artificials, but the fish themselves are aggressive to a fault, so the playing field is thankfully level, no matter how you look at it, or how bad of a fisherman you are.

On a deeper level, fly fishing on the small tidal rivers and creeks of the Chesapeake Bay is what defines me most as an angler. It's not the meat and muscle of the spring trophy striper season, or the fast-paced and nautical framework of breaking fish and open-water fishing. The rivers are where I'm most comfortable, and at some point each winter, when the world is cold and bare and the fantasy of warmer weather visits suggestively, it's the thought of fishing a small Chesapeake tributary in early summer that burns me with impatience.

I'll picture a river like the Wye in June, before the shallow waters have warmed to the unproductive bath water exhaustion that comes with midsummer. I'll imagine the fish stacked on submerged points, drifting above them in the tide as I strip bushy bodied clousers through where they're holding. My outboard is idling quietly and my casts never foul with tailing loops. By then the marsh grass will have fully lost the dry brittle yellows of winter and dressed the river edges in a lush, wavy green. The herons will be back and they move through the shallows with still patience, and terrapins will poke their heads from the water with curiosity. I'll be there in my boat in the 70° perfection, casting to willing, eager fish, and occasionally, my rod will bend and pulse with life.

When I come to, I'm usually back at my desk in my office, or in the kitchen looking out over a snow-covered yard with months of winter in store and another three months of spring left before the early summer striper pattern emerges in June. So when June finally comes, it's a relief when the rivers open up for striped bass fishing, and the rush to enjoy the local small water fishery sets in before the heat of midsummer changes the pattern and pushes the fish off into deeper water.

I was conscious of that on the beach on Wye Island, of having made it through winter, even though the last of the snow had melted months before. The spring had been a good one between the perch and the stripers up on the Susquehanna Flats, but here on the summer rivers, I was home.

Eastern Shore Gazpacho

I have a soft spot for Andalusian gazpacho because I once lived in the south of Spain. Summers there can be hot and dry, and gazpacho, a cool tomato-based soup, is commonly served to fight the heat. Maryland gardens certainly have their share of tomatoes, and this recipe combines the two cultures nicely. Most Spanish recipes include stale bread, but this ingredient is often omitted in American recipes. That's a shame because I think it makes a big difference in the final consistency of the soup. And in the tradition of all great soups, using stale bread gives us a frugal way to string kitchen leftovers into a refreshing lunch.

Ingredients:

Gazpacho base:
· Tomatoes
· Olive oil
· Sherry vinegar
· Water
· Stale white bread
· Salt and pepper
  to taste

Garnish:
· Fresh-cut sweet
  corn, off cob
· Cucumber, peeled,
  deseeded, and diced
· Crab claw meat
· Onions, diced
· Green peppers,
  diced
· Salt and pepper
  to taste
· Old Bay Seasoning,
  dash

Directions:
Deseed tomatoes and place in food processor with garlic, olive oil, and vinegar. Add chilled water if the consistency of the base is not liquid enough.

Soak stale bread in ice water until softened. Cut into cubes and add to blender. Pulse until smooth and consistency of the soup base is to liking. I like mine fairly thin and tend to add a bit of water. Taste at this point and add salt and pepper to sharpen the taste.

Cut corn directly off the cob and place in bowl. Peel, deseed, and dice cucumbers and add to bowl. Finally, add crabmeat, diced green pepper, and onion. Mix ingredients and season with salt and pepper.

At this point you can put the soup base and the garnish into the refrigerator to chill.

Once ready to serve, place a heaping spoonful of the corn and crab mixture into the center of a shallow bowl. Ladle the soup base around it until half of the garnish is submerged. Add a dash of Old Bay before serving.

JULY
HEAT LIGHTNING AND WHAT THE THUNDER SAID

Blacktop shimmers in the distance as corn towers above straight country roads. Back in town, crepe myrtles bloom with impossible freshness in the July heat and tiger lilies reach for the sun from the shade. Mars remains hidden through most of the month, listening for the thunder and wishing upon the meteoric tears of St. Lawrence for peace and bountiful gardens.

Eating ice cream before bed
leads to nightmares.

By early July we were moving out of the temperate pleasantries of early summer and it was that difficult time between sleeping with the windows open and pulling the air conditioners out from the coat closets to mount into the windows. Some nights were still comfortable with the cool, evening air coming in through the bedroom windows with the new sounds of crickets and katydids chanting from the trees.

But then there were the hot nights where it was nearly impossible to fall asleep in the still 90° heat, even after a cool shower and a fan oscillating from a bedroom corner. While the tomatoes were overflowing from the gardens and the corn seemed impossibly tall along the roads, I was ten pounds lighter from sweating so much and an overall lack of appetite.

After a few days the heat would break, the cool nights would return, and I'd go back to sleeping with the windows open, holding on to the hope that a mild summer would last just a bit longer before July bore down on us with a heavy weight of harsh, muggy sunshine cast from a hazy sky.

After three straight nights of sweating over my sheets, I decided that it was time to accept that summer was here to stay and that it could only be survived with air conditioning. I pulled out the two old air conditioners I had from the bottom of the big coat closet and noticed that there were still a few dry leaves from the previous fall poking from the vents and that the filters were dry and dirty. The unit I mounted in my bedroom was a near perfect fit for the window there, but the one in the living room had a significant gap that I had to fill with some cardboard, duct tape and a hard back book. It was a temporary solution, but one that would last a few rains while still keeping the bugs out.

Even with the back and forth of the temperatures, the fishing was settling into a nice summer pattern. The stripers had invaded the bay in force, the bluefish were slashing at baitfish through the choppy surface, and there were reports of seatrout and red drum being caught with fair consistency just a bit south. The bay temperatures weren't quite at that mid-summer bath water exhaustion that puts the fishing off completely, but they were getting there. The shallow water pattern seemed to lose its consistency every day, the days grew hotter, and a few times while fishing shallow water around Eastern Neck Island, I'd chosen to just get out of my boat and wet wade in the shallow water, just to cool off.

Back then I was working for *The Star Democrat*, in Easton, Maryland, an old and established daily newspaper that was still very much read on the Eastern Shore. I wrote the outdoor column there and worked within their composition department in the evenings.

Of all the jobs I've ever had, this one was the most conducive to a fishing life. Not having the typical nine to five schedule meant that I could fish in the mornings as much as I wanted during my work week, often having most of the water to myself. I was on the water so much that summer that I had the luxury of actually choosing the best days to fish—usually mid-week days with moving tides just before sunrise. If it didn't look ideal, I wouldn't go. Things like empty boat ramps and uncrowded water became normal to me. I didn't fish very often during the weekends because I didn't have to, and I could afford to snub the crowds on the water.

Most days I'd get up and fish and then I'd come home for lunch and I'd try to write for a few hours, hiding from the hottest part of the day inside before I headed in to the office as the sun began to weaken and slant. I usually started work around four o'clock and I'd work until midnight.

The quality of my time on the water had increased significantly, and from a predatory angler sportsman standpoint, I think I was about as sharp as I've ever been—completely in tune with the fishing and the tides, newly single with tons of fishing time on my hands, and casting a fly line far and efficiently. All of this was mainly due to a four-to-midnight job, and a professional requirement of being on the water.

Although the fishing that summer had been good, there was a monastic solitude that came with it and with working those hours. I was usually heading to work when just about everyone I knew was getting off or meeting for dinner or a happy hour. And even though I had the water to myself in the mornings, it wasn't often that my friends could come with me. Socially, I had working relationships with clerks and coworkers, but nothing much deeper than that.

So I was alone for much of that summer. I'd head out to fish in the mornings, or sometimes at night after work. I'd write in the afternoons and then I'd head into the office to do my work at the paper as dusk was peeking at the edges and the hottest part of the day began to fade. That was the routine, and there was rarely much variance from it.

Looking back, it was the loneliest and most boring summer I'd ever spent in Maryland, and somehow it ranks as one of my favorites. It was one of the only times in my life when I truly knew the comfort and purity that comes with sustained ritual, and when the things that mattered most to me—writing and fishing—were central fixtures to that ritual.

Along with the production aspect of putting out a daily newspaper—page layout, setting advertisements, and the final creation of huge pieces of film that were used to create the metal plates for the press itself—I needed to write and finalize my biweekly column submissions with my editor, Billman.

Billman was a Vietnam veteran and he had the kind of authority and confidence that only comes from military men. There was a natural grumpiness about him that made you want to get on his good side, but there were unexpected, sensitive aspects to him, too. He had a cat that he doted on who he'd talk about with some of the older ladies in the office. He loved ice cream and would make the occasional run to Tastee Freez for sundaes for the office. He was a widower and had a sick son who he sometimes had to miss work for to take care of.

At a local level, he was incredibly connected. He knew about secret items on the Hardee's menu in town, he knew about public boat ramps that weren't printed on maps, and he had a network of important interpersonal relationships that spanned a number of industries: he knew which mechanics to go to, where to buy the best cheap produce and crabs, and who to talk to when you needed a loan from a bank.

With fly shops opening up along the Chesapeake and light tackle fishing gaining popularity, Billman (a fisherman himself) was open to freshening things up with the outdoor column. A few weeks later, he gave me some of the best guidance on writing I've ever gotten in his direct, succinct style, "I'm okay with you doing your thing, but just don't forget who most of these readers are."

We agreed to keep a mix of traditional fishing pieces, a straightforward fishing report along with commentary on Maryland DNR news and regulations or the occasional conservation piece. I could fit in the fly fishing pieces I wanted to write a few times a month, which he asked to review to make sure they were, in his words, "mainstream and readable enough for everyone." The aim, he said, was to introduce, not replace.

This arrangement suited me fine. I could write about subjects other than fly fishing pretty quickly because I wasn't so emotionally attached to them; it was more a job of clarity, and less about personal expression, more actual reporting than what I saw as writing. So each month, I worked on two to three fly fishing articles that I cared about, while still keeping my editor and the readers happy with five to six more accessible pieces about crabbing, chumming, trolling, and DNR regulations.

Our offices at *The Star Democrat* were next to the Easton airport and sometimes around eight or nine o'clock, as the editors were still working on their stories for the next day's paper, I'd head outside with some of the pressmen to smoke cigarettes as the sun set in a rosey-orange flourish above the corn and air fields. We'd stand in the cooling parking lot, kicking gravel and talking about the heat or the fishing. Greedily, I wanted so much during those times to be on the water then, floating in a calm, windless dusk, even though I had seen the sun rise over the lower Chester River in similar fashion that very morning.

I was a few years out of college and fairly clean-cut at the time, and the pressmen were more like the laborers I knew when I worked construction one summer between semesters. They were hardworking, loud-laughing, working-class guys, driving old trucks that they themselves kept running. I think the only visible difference between these guys and the masons and carpenters that I'd known before were the professional daily remains that settled over men like that: much how the construction guys had the sunglass tan, sawdust and cement roughness that comes with working long hours outside every day, the pressmen had similar weathering, but their hands and forearms were always covered with the ink and grease from the press machinery, and their clothes carried similar stains.

Although I liked Billman, or wanted to like him, he wasn't the kind of guy who encouraged casual conversation at his desk, so I didn't spend too much time up in the Editorial Department with him or the other editors. Fairly often, that was about as much talking as I'd get in on an average day—about one and a half cigarette's worth of conversation with the pressmen outside in the parking lot as we took a break before heading back in to the frantic, second half of the night where we'd scramble to put out the next day's newspaper.

Because of the pace of the newspaper and my mid-shift cup of coffee around nine o'clock, most nights I was still awake after I got home from work, rarely tired and ready for bed. Some nights I'd get home after midnight and Centreville would be quiet and still. The traffic lights would be flashing yellow above the streets and the houses were dark and quiet except for the occasional glow of a bedroom television through a window.

Often, in July, I'd see heat lightning up in the sky through the crepe myrtle branches outside my bedroom window as I read and tried to fall asleep: impatient flashes of light in the clouds followed by the occasional rumble of thunder. Between all the light in town and consistent muggy clouds, I rarely saw a clear sky full of stars. Most nights that summer, it seemed like there was this restless, pouty sky above me, grumbling like an empty stomach and always threatening rain.

Other times, especially on those nights early in July when I slept with my windows open, when I could hear the thunder and see the flashes of heat lightning, I'd get out of bed, fueled by restless boredom and unhindered by a drowsy naked woman asking what I was doing, and I dressed in the dark. I would load up my truck as quietly as possible and then I'd make the short drive to Kent Narrows.

Just fifteen miles south of Centreville, between the mouth of the Chester River and Eastern Bay, is a small stretch of water called Kent Narrows. The tidal movement between two relatively large bodies of water through this small channel is significant, and with two bridges crossing over it, along with the remnants of an older bridge, it's an environment that striped bass love. There's also a public boat ramp there, so when you put in, you only have to motor about 100 yards to get into the fish.

The current and the structure create the environment, but it's the light line there that really differentiates it from other mid-bay fisheries. Late at night, once the boat traffic died down from the busy harbor and throughway, stripers held along the edges of the light line as the current rose and fell.

Fishing at night took some getting used to, but between the lights from the highway above and the stern light on my boat I never really felt blind. My eyes got used to the darkness pretty quickly and it was fairly easy to tie knots and unhook fish without having to dig for a flashlight.

The swift current through Kent Narrows, which initially felt so intimidating, eventually became commonplace, and after a few weeks, I could anchor my small boat into position above the light line on my first try, finally fluent in the delicate play of drift, depth, and anchor line. I also quickly learned the unwritten etiquette of the place: of steering clear of the water between the shore and the first bridge piling so that bank anglers could fish there. I had a few sinkers thrown at my boat the first night as I drifted through.

Although most of the stripers were on the small side, I fished an 8 weight most often there after connecting with a stout eighteen-inch that used the current to its advantage and bore off down-current towards the bridge pilings. It didn't break off but it had me worried for a second, and even had me reach for the net I kept at the back of the boat just to be sure.

The fishing was fairly easy. I'd cast down and across-stream, altering my angle depending on how deep I wanted to let my fly sink before I'd tighten up on the line, swinging the fly into and through the light line where most of the fish held. Sometimes I'd add a brisk strip in with the swing to see if that triggered a strike, but for the most part, fishing flies on the swing accounted for most of the fish. It was a nice way to fish, in the dark, in full contact with the fly, and then suddenly feeling the hit and that pulsing connection to a fish.

The fishing there in the Narrows that month was fairly consistent, but not the constant activity you'd find there in the fall where fish would be breaking and feeding throughout the Narrows—in the channel, along the edges, even in the boat ramps themselves—anywhere that had lights to attract baitfish. Still though, in terms of numbers and ease of access, the place was tough to beat. And most nights I almost had the place to myself, with just a few other nocturnal Narrows anglers working the waters for the chance to connect with a striped bass.

Regardless of the pace of the fishing, whether the action was slow or consistent, there was always a point where I'd feel the day catch up with me. I'd feel the tension of the day sweep down current with the falling tide, anchored in the current with the bridge lights above reflecting in the water and the occasional sound of a freight truck's air brakes rumbling above from the highway. The caffeine and hectic pace of the newspaper would have worn off, and the fishing there would have accomplished its labored, ritualistic release.

Often to the northeast, above the horizon glow of Baltimore, there was still the restless flash of heat lightning in the high clouds, but as the night approached early morning, it had an exhaustion about it, like a cat's tail before it drifted off to sleep.

* * * * *

One of the ironies of summertime is that you spend all winter shivering inside, longing for the warm weather and sunburns. But once summer finally arrives, you spend all your time fighting the sun and the heat. The initial, comfortable warmth of summer is nice in June, but once July comes, it's just necessary to fish on either sides of dawn or dusk, or in the dead of night altogether.

For me, getting up early isn't the real hardship. The night before an early trip, I'll pack up my truck, hook up my boat trailer, and get to bed early. The next morning, my alarm will go off at 3:45 a.m., and I'll get out of bed without much struggle, honestly excited for the morning ahead of me. But there's a toll to pay later for this kind of fishing, after the fishing and the caffeine and adrenaline wear off, when the reality of missing out on a full night's sleep starts to settle in before the drive home. The rest of the day has a hollow staleness to it. I'm present, but not really worth much, just counting the hours until I can finish my day and go back to bed.

Most often I'd go when the tides looked right, or on those nights when I was just awake and bored and restless. That was the summer that gas prices started to rise and I felt the pinch on my bank account. I was still in my mid-twenties and my idea of a budget back then meant that I knew I was going to overdraw my checking account before payday instead of just being surprised by it.

Although it was relatively close, the thirty-mile drive to and from Kent Narrows still ate up a good chunk of the three full tanks of gas that had to last between each pay check, so with all the fishing I was doing, I needed to start staying close to home. The reality was that I had heaps of time to fish, but only so much gas and money per week, so staying close to home could pay off in the short term as well as in the long term.

Because I was new to Centreville, I was interested in learning more about the Corsica River, a small tidal creek feeding into the lower Chester River. One thing I've found to be true of Chesapeake Bay tributaries in general is that some rivers simply fish better than others, and this is especially true for fly fishing. I didn't have high expectations for the Corsica, but I was willing to put in some time to see how the immediate area looked and fished.

So some mornings if the tides were right, I'd get up early, tow my boat just a few blocks down to the public boat ramp, and start exploring. I had fished the Lower Chester for years and had even made a few casts along some of the beaches and shorelines down near the mouth of the Corsica, but I hadn't ventured too far up the creek itself.

On initial examination, the Corsica looked like a normal lower river tributary, a small, shallow tidal creek that leaned more to the saltwater marsh side of things than the tidal freshwater creeks in the upper reaches of main tributaries where bass and bluegill can reside. After a few trips I saw that it was thick with perch, small stripers, and taylor bluefish down near the mouth. The shorelines of the Corsica weren't too built up with houses, with most of it being natural marsh and forest. One bank on its southwestern shore had a number of laydowns that looked promising and I imagined yellow perch holding in the submerged branches in the spring before their spawn.

Those first couple weeks of exploring the Corsica were more boating than fishing. I had rods with me, I made casts and occasionally hooked a fish, but for the most part, it was an exercise in studying charts in the evenings, checking out the water itself in the morning to see how the two compared, and running down any rumors I'd heard throughout the whole process.

I discovered what I already knew: small crazy charlies fished on a sinking line for perch worked well, and that much of the best fishing could be found down-river where the water was deeper and some good current rips set up. Falling tides there seemed to fish better than rising tides. If I could find a current rip and water at least nine to ten feet deep, most times I'd find perch and river stripers willing to hit a fly.

After a few weeks, I had a nice morning circuit set up: I'd start out fishing some points and current rips at the mouth of the Corsica, and then I'd head out into the bigger water of the mouth of the Chester River to fool around with the breaking schools bluefish, working my way north to the Love Point rock pile where I usually found stripers and big white perch holding tight to the rocks.

Just before lunchtime I'd start to head home, sometimes diving off my boat into the water to cool off before the ride back to Centreville. If the tide was low enough and my boat could fit under the bridge I'd cut through the tiny inlet that separated Eastern Neck Island from Kent County, and from there it was a short run back to the Corsica River.

I can't think of a single time when I was heading home after fishing the lower Chester that I wasn't absolutely thankful to live where I lived and working where I worked—even if I had gotten skunked that morning, broken a rod, or dropped something important overboard. There was almost a drunk exuberance to the trip home: my boat running open throttle, the water flat calm, buoys and crab pot markers passing by, and the wind in my face until, finally, I entered the main stem of the Corsica River and the sprint home was done. Once I got up river, I'd pull the throttle back and slowly motor the rest of the way to the boat ramp. By then I was completely dry from my quick swim with that chalky feeling on my skin from sweat and bay water.

* * * * *

For a few weeks that July, I added another step to my Corsica River morning ritual that was about as close to an affair that I got that summer. Just across from the public boat ramp and wharf were four small and nearly identical houses. Each had one room on each floor, steeply pitched roofs, and a generous porch overlooking the water. I learned later that they were called the Captains Houses and that they were built for the schooner captains of Captain John H. Ozmon's fleet, which sailed the Chesapeake during the years immediately following the Civil War.

One of the four houses was for sale and I had noticed the real estate sign as I drove between my apartment and the boat ramp. Sometimes on my way home from the Corsica I'd drive by to get a closer look, but eventually I parked out front and grabbed a flyer from the plastic tube attached to the real estate sign. Later at home, as I looked at the pictures and read the details, I saw that the price was shockingly fair. The house itself had character, its description and history were charming, and I began to admit to myself that I was smitten.

The Captains Houses make a pretty picture on the small hill that rises over the Corsica River and they hint of a time when steamboats and carriages were as commonplace as eighteen-wheel trucks and F-150s. And although they're nothing more than tall cottages, they have the dignity that comes with old houses that have sheltered people for nearly 150 years. There's also a modesty about them that I've always appreciated; a restrained tastefulness where the focussed effort is placed upon location and simple amenities, rather than gilding and ostentation.

Although I made very little money at the time, with meager savings that I dipped into regularly and most of my money tied up in fishing tackle and a sixteen-foot johnboat, I eventually called the realtor's number and said I might be interested. She got right back to me and met me there the following day to show the property and answer any questions I had.

The house itself was less than 600 square feet. The main floor had an open living room with hardwood floors and a small kitchen tucked off to the side. Another door from the living room opened to the porch overlooking the marsh and the water. A steep set of stairs led up to a small bedroom and bathroom, while another set of stairs led down to a brick-floored basement with a small wood-burning stove and half bathroom. From the basement, another door opened to a small landing that was partially covered by the porch above and faced the lawn and marsh. At the back of the house was a small fenced-in patio with privacy shrubs and driveway.

The little house was modestly priced and it suited my lifestyle perfectly. To be honest, I'm not sure who else could have lived there, other than a younger bachelor. It's small size excluded most married couples and the steep stairs might put off an older couple looking to retire on the Eastern Shore. A younger woman might appreciate them, but she might be forward thinking, possibly wanting a house that a small family could grow into, not a glorified cabin. And a taller man might not be completely comfortable in the upstairs bedroom with its low, pitched ceilings. That left me, a short, single fisherman.

On top of the historic waterfront charm of the house itself, I was beginning to see that Corsica River was a very nice river to fish and that it had some solid year-round potential. I had heard that the perch fishing could be good early in the year with some good runs into the creek and up some of the smaller streams that fed into it. I'd found that the creek fished reasonably well through the summer with good numbers of perch and small stripers in the rips that formed where the creek drained into the Chester, and there were also few sandy beaches near the mouth of the river that dropped off into deeper water that held stripers in the fall.

Most people tend to expect less from their home water. There's an understanding that what we exchange for ease of access, we lose in overall quality of fishing. And that's okay. I don't think anyone expects to live and experience world-class fishing every day. For most, it's enough to just get out for a few hours with a fair chance of hooking a fish, and if the water is within a fifteen minute drive, so much the better. Because the Corsica was so close to home, I didn't expect it to fish especially well, and I was pleased to see that it was fairly above average. And after fishing it for a while and getting to know its character, I was building the knowledge base where it was starting to feel like a home water. I knew that falling tides here fished better than rising tides, where the heron and osprey nests were, and all those little details that separate locals from tourists.

Along with the fishing, the Corsica was also a fair launching point for the lower portion of the Chester River and the main stem of the bay around the Bay Bridge and Love Point. As an angling base of operations, it was tough to beat, and even slightly off the radar, so parking at the boat ramp was rarely much of an issue.

Along with a connection to the waters, within Centreville and that part of the Eastern Shore I was starting to feel like a part of the community. I liked writing for the paper and feeling an honest, professional need to be out on the water. I liked knowing my banker, the cashiers at the ACME grocery store, and the waitresses at the Hillside Inn. I liked driving down country roads hemmed in by tall corn and the polite waves from other guys driving trucks and towing boats, and feeling the familiarity that came with living in a small town.

My apartment in the bottom floor of the stout Victorian house was starting to feel like home, too, but there was still a monastic emptiness to that summer. Although there was a purity and satisfaction to having dedicated myself completely to fly fishing and writing, the simplicity of that life was smothering. And while I felt myself becoming a part of the Eastern Shore with my roots settling in, most of my days were spent alone, my evenings were spent in a blurred rush at the paper, and my nights were restless with thunder and heat lightning.

What happens with that kind of isolation is that every action and moment becomes pregnant with awareness and meaning. Because so much of what I saw and did went undiscussed, I'd dwell on every moment. I would cast into the wind, let my fly sink through the river waters until it was twelve feet deep, and retrieve it back to me, conscious of each strip of the line through my fingers, praying for connection. I would stop at a gas station at night, watching the numbers at the pump circle and rise, and looking up at a streetlight where moths and beetles flew and bounced mindlessly into the burning bulb until the handle jumped in my hand. I'd rise from bed in the middle of the night with thirst, walk naked to the kitchen to fill a glass with water, waiting at the sink for the tap to run cold. If you can live through a moment, it's possible to live through a day and eventually see a season change before you.

When I mentioned the Captain's House to Billman, he approved of the idea saying, "So many of you young people look to leave the shore so readily. It'd be nice to have someone younger and public facing making a go of it here. Maybe there's a story there, how you chose to be here, committed to it."

Later he told me about a lender that had worked with other folks at the paper, who might be able to process a reasonable loan for me. I was considering making an offer, but not fully committed yet and more curious about the process than anything, so I went and spoke to him to see if my income would even qualify me for a loan. If anything, maybe the decision to move forward would be made for me.

So I met with Billman's mortgage guy and gave him all the info he needed. Over the next few weeks, I cleaned up a few random credit issues that I didn't even know I had and got some more details from my parents on how much they could help with the down payment.

I eventually learned that although my credit wasn't ideal, or my income very high, through some kind of backwards math, my mortgage payments looked to be even lower than the rent I was paying for my apartment in Centreville. Freeing up a few hundred dollars a month would be a difference that I would feel, so the decision to buy hung in the air, heavy like July clouds pregnant with rain.

In one of our last meetings the mortgage guy asked, "You sure you don't want a newer townhouse? We could probably get you in something twice as big down in Trappe or Cambridge for this price." For a broker, the guy was asking some pretty pointed questions.

"I know a townhouse makes more sense in the long run. I'm just not interested though. There's something about this little place in Centreville."

The mortgage guy smiled and nodded as if to say, "I understand. Plenty of time down the road for good decisions and practicality."

He reordered and stacked some of the papers in my folder and then closed it. "Well, we should be all set with the formal approval next week. I'll call you then to finalize everything."

There are four stages to having an affair: curiosity, infatuation, withdrawal, and confrontation. I had reached the third stage of withdrawal and suddenly I felt a distinct need to get out of town.

I walked out of the office to my truck in the harsh afternoon heat and muggy sunshine. It wasn't relief I felt upon hearing the status of my loan, it was a mix of nervousness and minor doom. I had set things in motion the day I called the realtor. Or perhaps it began even before that, when I stopped to take a look at the house.

Sitting down with the lender had added a level of reality to this affair that I was suddenly uncomfortable with: it wasn't casual fun or lustful curiosity anymore. I looked at myself in the rear-view mirror. I was mostly invested with the idea of settling down and committing to my life there in Centreville. It was a good life, and one where I put the things that mattered most to me at the forefront of my priorities. Sport and art were first, everything else was a secondary consideration. But there was a sliver of me that was reserved and undecided, unsure and watching from the sidelines, and waiting for the right moment to speak up.

* * * * *

July progressed, the opportunity to buy the Captains House drew closer, and near the end of the month I was down to running just the bedroom air conditioner in my apartment. The living room unit had only ever put out a damp, lukewarm air, and the only real impact it seemed to be making was on my electric bill, so I pulled it. The thick July heat had settled over Talbot County with a suffocating permanence, and the water temperatures of the middle Bay rose, putting off the mid-morning fishing I'd known at the beginning of the month. I could still catch a few fish from current rips and structure in the mornings, but each morning the action seemed to fizzle out earlier and earlier.

The land around me was saturated with life and the ripeness was palatable. The corn was impossibly tall in the fields along the roads and the roadside produce stands were overflowing with tomatoes, sweet corn, and zucchini. The same saturation could be seen in the waters of the bay. The brackish waters were full of crabs, baitfish, and cownose rays. Egrets and herons stepped quietly through algae-rich waters and along the docks and bulkheads, there was the potpourri of dry wood planking, salt marsh, decaying life, baitfish, and gas fumes. Amidst all this, the gamefish sulked in the midday heat. I knew this to be the natural order of things, but it still felt backwards to me that during these summer months when life was so prevalent, the best fishing times would be so fleeting, at dusk and dawn, just moments on either side of darkness.

There had to be another way, another aspect to the fishery that was viable to a fly fisherman. The more I examined it, the more I kept coming back to croaker. Although they certainly weren't ranked among the premier gamefish of the Chesapeake, they were strong, plentiful, and moderately accepted as table food. By midsummer, the waters of the Chesapeake were full of them, and while most people who targeted them were bottom fishing in deeper water, in some places croaker could be found in shallow water and depths from ten to seventeen feet—water still very accessible with flies and a sinking line.

Some of the best journeys begin with equal parts of curiosity, impulse, and vice. One morning, under the guise of researching my column pieces, I broke out my spinning rods with the intent of bottom fishing in Eastern Bay. I felt a little guilty for some reason when I went into the tackle store to buy bait, but once I was on the water, the knowledge and enjoyment came back. I'd done this kind of fishing with my father when I was younger, and once I got started it felt familiar, not illicit.

I had decent success with the croaker in Eastern Bay using squid and bloodworms on top and bottom rigs. Though I wasn't fully converted over from fly fishing, I could appreciate the appeal. Bottom fishing was relaxing. The action was steady, and it was nice change to be a little more passive, drifting with the current with both rods set out at the stern of my boat, enjoying my coffee until one of the rods bent over, pulsing excitedly with life. A few times, I even had fish on both hooks of the rig. I kept a few croaker to fry up later that night and reexamined my stance on bottom fishing as I drove home.

Later I tried bottom fishing in the mouth of the Chester with Fishbites', a packaged, bait-like product that were nothing more than thin strips of fine mesh covered with a scented coating. I had received them as a sample in my mailbox at the paper and they were packaged in Ziplock' bags like candy and looked like a cross between a Twizzler' and beef jerky. As someone who didn't bottom fish very often, I liked that a package of Fishbites' were contained, easily portable, and lasted indefinitely.

One night in a caffeine-induced fit of insomnia and experimentation I trimmed off what was left of the buck tail on a mangled and discarded clouser minnow, and tied on a thin, reddish strip of bloodworm scented Fishbite behind the dumbbell eyes with about an inch and a half trailing behind the bend of the hook. I stacked on a few strands of copper crystal flash on top and then I covered the hook shank with some rust-colored Estaz cactus chenille.

It didn't have the precise realism of other saltwater flies, but it looked vaguely like a clam worm fly, and with the chenille and dumbbell eyes, it had a buggy quality about it that almost excused the presence of the Fishbites strip. As a cheeky tribute to Lefty Kreh's deceiver, I called the fly, bloodworm artifice.

The next morning while I was anchored off Tilghman Point in Eastern Bay, I gave the flies a try to see if they gave me any kind of edge with the croaker I had caught there previously. I had fly fished the same spot with clousers and crazy charlies before, pulling in stout white perch off the oyster bars while I waited with baited rods out to see if there were any croaker in the area. I had only caught a few croaker on flies there before, but nothing very regular.

I made my first cast up current from where I was anchored, stripping out some more line as the fly swept by and counting down until I was sure the fly was along the bottom. I began a slow retrieve back to the boat, trying to stay as deep as possible, and within three slow strips of the fly I was hooked up.

The strength of the fish was jarring, and it did its best to stay on the bottom of Eastern Bay as I began to fight it on my 7 weight. It worked its way up to the bow of the boat and got uncomfortably close to my anchor line. After catching perch and schoolie stripers for much of the summer, most of which I could easily hand-line in to the boat, it was a small shock to feel that I actually needed to put fish on the reel. My rod was completely bent over and I had the butt of my rod planted in my stomach as I fought what I felt must be a decent fish.

Once I got the fish to the surface, I was surprised to see that it was small, even by panfish standards. That ten-inch croaker had put up the fight of an ocean fresh striper that was at least two times its size. It looked like a small red drum without the telltale spot, stout bodied, with a sandy copper tint to it, and a distinctly downturned mouth. I unhooked it and dropped it back into the water, made another cast and was immediately into another strong croaker, this one just a shade bigger.

Anchored off Tilghman Point that morning I caught a mixed bag of croaker, white perch, and even a few jumbo spot, my first on a fly. After I got snagged on the oyster bar I was fishing over, I tied on a pink crazy charlie to see if there was any significant difference from the Fishbites fly. I continued to catch a few more fish, although not with the frequency that I had before, and not as many croaker.

I wasn't about to start tying all my flies with pieces of Fishbites, but if anything, the addition seemed like a good adjustment to the midsummer pattern and the overall nature to some of the more plentiful panfish. But I had caught more croaker in the flies one morning than I had all summer—that couldn't be denied.

That week I thought more about croaker and targeting them seriously with my new flies. While croaker were fairly plentiful in waters as far north as the Bay Bridge, just a short distance south in the Choptank and Honga Rivers there were reported to be greater numbers, averaging at thirteen to fourteen inch with some specimens pushing eighteen inches. Although the fishing in the immediate area wasn't completely off, I felt that a trip south was in order, if only to see if there was anything to the rumors and the easy drive south.

* * * * *

There's a contradiction that comes with outdoor writing, or perhaps with editors in general. It's the idea of balance: of giving readers what they know and want, but also knowing when to break routine with a new topic. My very writing for the paper was a break of routine for Billman, and having me break out of the normal range of striped and largemouth bass was certainly testing his limits. Still, though, I thought it was worth talking about with him, so one Thursday evening I approached him about a story idea I had about fly fishing for croaker on the Honga River in southern Dorchester County.

Right off the bat, I could tell he was a little wary.

"We've got croaker right here. Why do you want to go all the way down to the Honga?"

"I heard that they're bigger down there. And they're catching them in shallow water right before dusk. It's been real consistent. I want to see if I can get them on a fly rod."

"Well, the fish are always bigger when they're 100 miles away." Billman was a fisherman, and a realist.

"I know. But I'm tired of writing about Eastern Bay and the Choptank. And I think you and everyone else might be a little tired of it, too. Think of this as my destination piece for the summer. Except it's a destination that's pretty accessible."

"Okay. But are you thinking that this will be a fly fishing piece, too? I don't want to get too *out there*." He said that last bit a little pointedly.

"It will be kind of a hybrid. I'll start out bottom fishing with Fishbites as kind of a fun, low-tech fish finder for the light tackle guys, but the bait guys might like it, too. And then I'll work in fly fishing for them."

He leaned back in his chair and looked at me, weighing invisible pros and cons that only he understood.

"You can expense some of this if you have to, the rest you have to cover. Outdoors has $150 allocated. That's your entire budget for the year."

We'd never spoken about a budget and I wasn't even aware that I had one. Blowing a good chunk of my annual funds on a saltwater panfish trip felt a little impulsive, so I decided to split the difference.

"I just need enough for gas and a cheap hotel in Cambridge. I won't use all of it—hopefully less than eighty bucks."

"Okay. If you're going to be down near Blackwater, make sure you borrow a camera and try to get a shot of a nutria or a sika deer—something recognizably Dorchester."

At that point in the conversation Billman's phone started to ring and, without a second thought, he answered it and motioned me out of the office. And that was that. With less than a day's notice I was taking a work-funded trip to a city that most people wouldn't think to visit, to fish for fish that most fly fishermen avoided.

I had Fridays and Saturdays off, so the next day I towed my boat south from Centreville, through the slow, maddening beach traffic on Route 50 between Easton and Cambridge. Even before lunchtime it was stop-and-go traffic for at least fifteen miles as families and young people headed down to Ocean City for their annual week of fun and gluttony on the beach and boardwalk. A drive that would have normally taken me forty minutes, took close to two hours.

Although the Honga wasn't especially far from Centreville, I wanted to fish it a few times, so staying at an inexpensive hotel would save me time and gas from running back and forth. Later in the afternoon I checked into a cheap, rundown, one-story motel just south of Cambridge set immediately off the highway called the Wagon Wheel Motel.

The accommodations there looked uncomfortably permanent for some of the guests, a mixed bag of quiet druggies, migrant workers, and poultry truckers. Some children were playing in the parking lot, a few of the rooms had grills and potted plants outside the sheet-covered windows, and some of the doors were wide open with cats slinking in and out. The Wagon Wheel didn't have much going for it, but it was close to the road down to Hoopersville, it was the right price, and the clerk didn't really care that I had a boat in his parking lot.

My room had air conditioning, the furniture and decorations were an expected Polaroid brown accented by cheap wood, and a few of the previous guests had been smokers—there was a faint smell of cigarettes and some depressing burn stains along the edge of the tub. For some reason, there was a full-sized refrigerator in my room and its compressor had an irregular clank when it kicked on.

Everything about the place was ugly: it had an unfortunate history, it's current state was bleak, and its future did not look at all promising. Nothing about the room or accommodations were at all meant for relaxation or extended stays, so I got back on the road after checking in, and headed south for my evening on the Honga River. I took my time heading south through the farmland that bordered the lower Dorchester County marshes as the afternoon light began to weaken and the evening tide approached. Some of the land I drove through was working but much of it was wild, and there was the feeling that if left unattended, the marshes and tide would reclaim the roads just a few feet above the high water mark.

That first evening I put in by the upper bridge on Fishing Creek, motoring out past the moored work boats and into the middle portion of the Honga River. Once I got past the bridge and through the small inlet separating the upper river from the open bay, I pulled down on the throttle, opening the engine up and for the short run to Wroten Point.

As promised, I had two spinning rods with me set up with bottom fishing rigs. I baited them with some small strips of Fishbites and dropped both off the stern as I drifted with the current. My first drift didn't result in much activity, so I motored closer to shore, surprised to see that a channel ran relatively close to a shoreline point. Before I set out my spinning rods, I tied on one of my Fishbites flies and made a cast up against the marsh shoreline.

As soon as I began my retrieve, I felt that I was connected to a fish, though I could tell that it wasn't very large, and it came to the boat with a slender willingness that felt alien and surprising. Once I had the fish at the surface, I saw that it was a spike seatrout, less than eleven inches long and skinny.

I made a few more casts and caught another small seatrout before I drifted off the point. Although I had come to the Honga for croaker, I was reluctant to leave a pod of biting seatrout because I caught them so infrequently back north. So I motored quietly back to the point and anchored about forty feet off of it, respectfully off the marsh shoreline point, but still within casting range with the wind at my back.

Anchored there as the tide rose and evening settled in, I caught seatrout consistently off the same fly. There was a point when I considered switching over to a clouser or shrimp pattern, but it seemed like a pointless change. I was catching fish, that was what mattered. From inside the marsh grass I could hear nutria rustling and barking at me, a strange combination of a goat and a goose that was mildly unnerving.

I tried a few other spots, but the fish seemed to be schooled up within the channel that ran alongside the point and into the cove. As it got darker and the tide continued to rise, the bite there slowed down, so I pulled anchor and followed the water into the cove and began working the shallow, protected water.

Inside the northern hook of Wheatley Point Cove, I put my trolling motor down and started casting to shorelines, trying to cover as much new water as possible and make the most of my final moments before it was fully dark and I'd begin my ride back to Fishing Creek. The tide was still rising, flooding the marsh, and I could see swirls and action up along the grass edges as fish moved in with the tide to feed on crabs, shrimp, and baitfish.

My first few casts fell short of the immediate shoreline and didn't result in anything, but finally, as I began working the water closest to the marsh grass, I began to connect. My first fish was a stout striper, only sixteen inches, but a thick, healthy fish. My next fish was another seatrout, but much larger than the spikes I had been catching from the main point. I had found the gamefish, but I was just about out of time with little tide and daylight left. Dusk had crept up on me, and looking west over the Honga River the sky was a deep red that hinted of another hot day to follow.

Reluctantly, I decided to end my night after that last seatrout. I could see the lights from the Hoopers Island Bridges and one end of the sky was already dark with the beginning of stars. The way back to the boat ramp was fairly straightforward, but the waters were new to me and I wanted to get back with a little daylight left. On top of any boating safety, I needed to get back to Cambridge for a good night's sleep for an early morning on the lower Honga.

Driving back to Cambridge that night I was pleased with my evening on the river, but there was a notable absence with not having caught any croaker. I tried not to dwell too much on it, fully conscious of how backwards that disappointment was. I had hoped to execute a plan, and this was still a time when I felt that my actual fishing directly affected the story I was going to write, so the trip had a tinge of failure to it.

As I pulled into the hotel parking lot, I saw that there were more people outside the rooms than before. The Hispanic workers were drinking beer and talking quietly around a grill, and some of the younger druggies were smoking cigarettes and pacing between the cars outside their rooms. Nobody was loud or rude, and nobody said a word to me, but I had the feeling that all eyes were on me as I walked back and forth between my room and boat while I unloaded my rods and tackle. Although there was a seedy quality to the place, it seemed like most of the people were just trying to get by and stay under the radar as much as possible, and that nobody was drunk or high enough yet to look for any trouble.

Sitting in the hotel that night, with my tackle and fish finder safely inside, my door locked and dead-bolted, and a fast-food dinner on the table, I realized that I was just like the rest of the guests at the Wagon Wheel. Although I was employed and educated, I was still a man stinking of sweat and fish, eating a cheap dinner alone, in a small room that smelled of damp carpet and cigarettes.

At that moment, I didn't feel so different than the trucker soaking in a tub, dosed with painkillers and bourbon in the hot water until he fell asleep with a cigarette burning on the edge of the tub. Regardless of my reasons for being at the Wagon Wheel, I was there nonetheless; sleeping in the same place as the quiet druggies, the migrant workers, and the poultry truckers, and to question whether they felt disappointment about where they'd ended up was to ask the same of myself.

In the face of a great evening of fishing on the waters of the Honga, I felt unsettled. And the overall gloom of the slatternly hotel room seemed to be a part of the same unsettled pressure that I'd felt after I'd left the mortgage office; the boiled-down reality of wanting a home, but simply wanting more. Perhaps it was all of that, or the newness of the surroundings and the voices I heard out in the parking lot late into the night, but I had trouble falling asleep.

* * * * *

It was still dark the next morning when I left the Wagon Wheel to head back to the Honga River. The moon was so high and bright in the sky that it cast shadows on the rutted gravel parking lot as the birds sang loudly in the trees. The hood of my truck was covered in birdshit.

I left my room key in a rusty box outside the front office and pulled out of the hotel parking lot with lifted spirits. The darkness that had settled over the trip had lifted, and I felt like a young, fortunate guy again. I was on the road, driving a working truck with a boat in tow, and I had a morning of fishing a new river ahead of me. I didn't dwell too much on my change in perspective or the reasons behind it: there are moments in life when you're a guest at the Wagon Wheel Motel, that's inevitable. But often much of your outlook is determined by whether you're checking in or checking out.

Before leaving Cambridge completely I stopped at a convenience store for coffee and breakfast and was soon heading south into the rough marsh country. In southern Dorchester County, the working fields had the well-worn look of an old shovel handle and lacked the fenced neatness of some of the gentleman farms of Talbot County. About ten miles into my drive and getting near the small town of Fishing Creek, I saw a sika deer trotting off into the forest from a field edge—short tailed, shaggy, and low to the ground, like an Australian shepherd.

I had made it through the land around Blackwater Wildlife refuge and was crossing over onto Hoopers Island when the sun began to rise. Dawn in this open country is spectacular, since there's open water to the east and west of the sliver-thin island, so the sky opens up over the water in a grand scale. Most of the trees are fairly short, and the thin strip of land that basically defines the Honga River is just a shade higher than the ever-encroaching tidewater, so there's not much to obstruct a view of the sky, and on this early July morning, the sky was colored in a hazy, still dawn that can only be seen in the mid-Atlantic.

I drove south for another fifteen minutes through Fishing Creek and over the second bridge to Hoopers Island. When I got out of my truck in Hoopersville I saw that it was a windless morning that promised to be another hot day. The boat ramp was already bustling, but the two boats in front of me were fairly competent and efficient, so I was unloaded and launched by 5:45 a.m., and heading towards the mouth of the Honga with the best part of the morning in front of me.

The evening trip before had been an odd combination of fruitful and disappointing, but it had also cleared my head from the initial excitement that comes with fishing new waters. The Honga was only a short distance from my home waters, but even here, around a hundred miles south of where I typically fished on the Chesapeake, the waters felt mildly exotic. The fishery was recognizable, but had mild differences to it, and this newness could lead to impulsive decisions.

But because I had fished and caught fish the evening before, I felt sated and focussed, able to address the task at hand with a plan that I felt held merit. Just a short run across the river to Windmill Point was a shelf that dropped quickly into the river channel with a marked oyster bed that would probably hold fish as well. Drifting between the two red cans off Windmill Point would keep me on the ledge where, hopefully, schools of decent croaker were set up. That was the plan I came up with in the fifteen minutes I waited at the boat ramp with a chart open in front of me as the two boats ahead of me launched their boats. I was open to deviating, but for whatever reason that morning, I wanted to focus my efforts on the relatively open water.

It was just a short run over to Windmill Point from the Hoopersville launch on flat, calm water. Time has taught me that there are subtle differences between striper water, croaker water, and seatrout water. Verbalizing these differences is difficult, much like trying to explain the difference between a ruby and a garnet to someone who's never seen a gemstone. I was in the relative area of where I wanted to fish pretty quickly and I began that microscopic comparison of reading the bottom depth on my fish finder and comparing the findings with the broad strokes of the chart until I was confident with a spot that marked enough fish to stop motoring around. It looked like croakier water.

Well off the northern red can I found the oyster bar on my fish finder and tried to commit the spot to memory. I decided that this would mark the northernmost part of my drift with the rising tide. From there I motored south, watching the depth, trying to see if there were any significant humps or ridges that weren't marked on the chart as I headed south to the second marker.

The tide was beginning to rise, there was no wind whatsoever, and my drift was as slow and smooth as honey. So often when I had tried to fish a channel edge on the Choptank or Chester, the wind and chop had made my attempts to work the lower water column an absolute mess. Here on the Honga, with a mild tide beginning to rise and barely any breeze to speak of, I could actually feel my fly making contact with the bottom.

I didn't set my bottom rigs out. I was dead set on catching a quality croaker on a fly and didn't want to divide my attention. As I strung up my 8 weight, I thought about tying on a grass shrimp fly or crab-colored clouser, thinking that there'd be more sport in catching them on traditional flies, but in the end I decided to use my bloodworm artifice fly again, willing to use any edge I had for the sake of accomplishing a goal.

My first drift was slow and fishless. I was using my 8 weight with a fast sinking line and fishing in about fourteen feet of water. I was marking good numbers of fish on my fish finder, but with the tide only just beginning to rise, I wasn't too worried about the slow action. At the end of the drift I motored around the red can looking for the oyster bed on my fish finder and noticed the thick school of fish that was schooled around it. It's always been a guessing game with me on where exactly to cast, once structure and fish have been identified on the small screen of my fish finder. With the mild current and slow drift, I cast out over my stern, counted down until I was sure I was hitting bottom, and began my retrieve. Still nothing.

The morning was starting off slow, so there was no sense of rushing into it. I still had about half a cup of coffee left over from my drive down. It had cooled down before I had even gotten to Hoopers Island, but I sat down on the front seat of the console to finish it and looked out over the river.

There were worse things to do than waiting for the tide to pick up with a cup of coffee on a boat. I looked out over the Honga and took in the marsh and open water. So much of the fishing I'd been doing near home had been suburban in nature, tame and accessible by comparison. The land down here was rougher at the edges, the marshes wilder with wind-pruned scrappy pines and ospreys nesting among the power lines.

Even the island town of Hoopersville had a tough minimalism to it; a small town with a handful of houses and businesses just a few feet above the high tide mark on a thin strip of land between the Honga River and the open water of the Chesapeake Bay. It felt like the last working town on the Chesapeake Bay and that at any moment it could be claimed by the waters.

The sun wasn't bearing down on me with authority yet, but it would soon. It was still early in the morning, but there wasn't at all a fresh chill to it, and the day promised to be still and hot. I took my shirt off and washed my face in the warm brackish water, and dunked my hat in the river to soak it before I put it back on my head. Although I wasn't at all working, I felt like I was clocking in.

I motored back to the southern red marker and lined my drift up with the norther red can. I waited until I felt any momentum from the engine had died and that my drift was equal to the tide. There was a noticeable difference to the current, where it felt like it was just a hint before, now it felt substantial.

I cast out and counted down, trying not to misjudge the depth, and working to keep my retrieve slow and deliberate. I felt a nibble, much like how I had felt initial exploratory bites when I had been bottom fishing, and eventually felt the fish commit to the fly. The weight of the fish was substantial, played up in part by the depth and the previous night of small seatrout.

Many writers have used the word "dogged" to describe the way a fish can fight, but there's no better word for how a croaker fights. They have a muscular strength to them, and rather than bolting or leaping, they exert everything they have to stay on the bottom. The fights don't last too long, but they're substantial.

Once I got the fish to the surface, I could see that it was certainly an above-average croaker by my standards, around fifteen inches and fairly stout. The fly was neatly hooked in the corner of the fish's mouth.

My next three casts yielded fish hooked nearly exactly the same size, and hooked nearly exactly in the same place. By then I had reached the northern marker, so I headed back to drift along the ledge again. Within no time I was hooked up with another croaker and the scene repeated itself.

Drifting off Windmill Point I'd caught five stout bodied croakers in as many casts and I still had a good piece of the rising tide before me. I fished through my drift, and the action remained consistent with the croaker on the feed. Other than the visible current seams where the channels of the flats emptied into the deeper water, there wasn't much visible activity other than the occasional light splash of a perch or baby striper. The fish were there, but they were feeding deep in the water column. I pictured a school of croaker coming up from the deeper water of the channel to feed on crabs and baitfish as the current washed over the ledges and oyster bars.

After another drift and a few more croaker, my fly was fairly mangled, and I was open to fishing standard, unscented flies. I tied on one of my large perch flies, a size 6 Joe's Grass Shrimp tied with a small glass rattle hidden in the mylar tube body. My first cast came back to the boat untouched, but the second connected with another croaker, this one just a shade larger than the ones I'd been catching, around sixteen inches. My following cast resulted in an unexpected flounder.

I had proven what I had set out to prove at that point. I had caught good numbers of croaker on flies, with some seatrout and flounder thrown in for good measure. Part of me considered calling it a day, but I decided to keep going and finish the tide before I began heading back to Centreville. I motored up to the oyster bar in an effort to end the day on a different note, really just fishing out the tide to see what else was possible.

I had a fair idea of where the bar was, and with the moving tide, now I could see a very minor current seam in the calm water. But there was no mistaking the structure on the fish finder though: it was absolutely covered with a school of fish.

I backtracked a bit and set out anchor in about fifteen feet of water. The current was still coming in strong, and my anchor line was taught within moments of drift. Once my position was stable, I found that I was just above the oyster bar, with the subtle current seam about twenty feet off my stern.

I made a cast up-current, trying to judge the current and sink rate of the fly as it washed down to the oyster bar. I overestimated my first drift, and after two strips of line, I was snagged on the bottom structure. I broke the line as quickly as I could, anxious about spooking the school of fish I knew to be there. I tied on a crab-colored clouser, a fairly intricate clouser tied with olive and tan bucktail with an assortment of crystal flash and tinsel that don't at all mimic a crab itself, rather the complicated color scheme of something that could be a crab.

"Not quite so much drift," I said to myself as I cast out.

After counting down and watching the line play out, I began my retrieve, and within a few strips I felt another dull connection and assumed that I was hung up again on the oyster bar, until I noticed that the snag was moving ponderously away from structure and towards the boat. It only took a few moments for the fish to wake up, but once it did, it started zigzagging around the bottom, bending my 8 weight near to the cork.

There's a point when you're fighting a large fish where you know that losing it is a strong possibility. You start bargaining. "I just want to see it, I don't need to land it." As if lowered expectations could somehow keep the fish connected.

I thought that it might be a heavy seatrout, since I had heard reports of large ones being caught in the area, and it didn't fight like a striper with muscular, running violence. It was a heavy, strong weight that had me fairly intrigued and intimidated.

I started gaining line on the fish and it began grudgingly coming to the surface. I began that blind, one-armed reach for the seldom-used net at the stern of my boat and finally saw signs of the fish in the surface as my hand found the aluminum handle. I netted the fish and looked at it gasping ponderously on the deck of my boat. It was an enormous sandy copper pig of a croaker with the down-turned mouth of its family and the bearing of a tired milk cow. It was, hands down, the biggest croaker I'd ever seen: long and stout enough for me to measure against the handle of the net out of obligation and curiosity. It was just a shade under twenty-four inches.

I took a good look at the fish and released it back into the water. In all the years I've fished the Chesapeake and out of all the memorable fish I've caught, that croaker ranks as one of the strongest fish I'd ever experienced. Up until that morning, I had hidden from the heat of midday by fishing in the mornings and at night, but I had avoided facing the summer heat head on. There on the deck of my johnboat with my shirt off and the beginnings of a fair sunburn beginning to take root, I felt for the first time that summer that I was fishing in July.

Ending that day on a good note wasn't difficult. In celebration I dove off the bow of my boat and swam for a second in the murky slackening tide. Pulling myself back into the boat took some kicking and pulling, but once I had suffered through the scalding green aluminum burns of the sun-baked deck, I stowed my rods, drank the last of my water, and enjoyed the breeze as I raced back to Hoopersville on flat, calm water.

A few hours later, in the clarity that only comes after extended silence in a pickup truck, I thought about my trip to the Honga River and the Wagon Wheel Motel. My time in Dorchester County had set something adrift, dislodging the concept of home and home waters that I'd been trying so hard to define that summer. The legitimacy of the small water town, the wild nature of the marshland, and the quality of the fish themselves made the town and waters I'd know in Centreville feel tame and suburban by comparison. I had grown fond of and familiar with the small waters of the Corsica River, but even home waters do not demand monogamy. For the first time I grasped the scale of the Chesapeake Bay, how it could differ and range in detail from water to water, and that it was all there for exploration. As much as I had the impulse to stake my claim in one small piece of it, it wasn't a necessary step. And although I was rooted in the Eastern Shore, I was still fundamentally dislodged.

It was around lunchtime when I reached Route 50 in Cambridge and the beach traffic was starting to thicken in town, but it wasn't the maddening stop-and-go congestion that would develop later in the day, after half the population of Ocean City checked out of their beach hotels, took one last swim in the ocean, and got something to eat for the ride home. With no other catalyst than catching a fair share of croaker and seatrout from the Honga River, I knew that Centreville could never be the home I'd been trying to make it. An hour later when I turned onto Route 213, I was decided on my stance in things, although I didn't have a concrete plan formed. I was not going to buy the Captains House. And although I liked the idea of working at the newspaper, I didn't want to work at *The Star Democrat* anymore. These two principal decisions would eventually lead to action.

Ten years later, my life doesn't have the restlessness of thunder and heat lightning, or the monastic silence of a one-bedroom apartment, but I still feel that I left something behind that summer, and that my decision to leave can be traced back as I drove to Centreville from Hoopers Island that day. More than that, I see, or imagine, that this was a point in my life when I chose a working life over a life-based on sport and art on the Eastern Shore, and in many ways, this story is a way of paying homage to that time and that decision, and putting those regrets to rest.

When I drive back through Centreville now, sometimes I drive down towards the Corsica River to look at the Captains Houses and I wonder what my days and nights would have been like there if I had decided to stay. I picture fall and harvest time in the surrounding farmland of Queen Anne's County, winters with small fires going in the fireplace downstairs, and springs on the Corsica chasing perch. And summers alone, smoking cigarettes at night on the small porch as I look over the water, while heat lightning flashes impatiently in the clouds, and thunder warns of time and rain.

Traditional Stuffed Flounder

Every region has a signature dish: clam chowder in New England, shrimp and grits in the Southeast, and conch fritters in Florida. Maryland-style stuffed flounder is one of those dishes for the mid-Atlantic. The crab imperial, the Old Bay, and the delicate meat of freshly caught flounder all create a dinner that tastes as good as a summer sunset on the Chesapeake Bay.

There are some minor differences in traditional crab imperial stuffing, and a common tactic in modern restaurants is to simply use the mixture from their crab cakes as the stuffing for stuffed flounder. Depending on the quality of their crab cake this is usually a fine substitute, but a traditional stuffed flounder recipe uses crab imperial, a richly flavored crab dish without filler that's topped with a creamy sauce that's browned and finished under a broiler.

Ingredients:
- 2-3 flounder fillets from keeper fish.
  (Rockfish can easily be substituted here.)

Crab Imperial:
- Lump crabmeat
- Flat leaf parsley, chopped
- Lemon
- Egg
- Old Bay Seasoning
- Worcestershire Sauce
- Mayonnaise
- Mustard

Imperial Topping:
- Mayonnaise
- Heavy cream
- Old Bay Seasoning
- Juice from 1/2 lemon
- Worcestershire Sauce
- Lemon juice

Directions:
Preheat the oven to 450°.

In a large bowl mix all crab imperial ingredients except lump crabmeat. Once blended evenly, fold lump crabmeat into mixture being careful not to break apart the lumps of crab.

Place one fillet down on a buttered casserole or baking dish. Top with a generous heap of crab imperial. Place two smaller fillets on top of the crab imperial that angle down to meet the bottom fillet. Leave the top portion of the crab imperial open so that it can brown while the dish broils.

Bake for fifteen minutes and then switch oven to high broil.

While oven heats, mix all ingredients for imperial topping and spread on top of the stuffed flounder. Place back in the oven and broil until topping browns and the edges of the fish and crabmeat are crispy.

Finish with squeezed lemon juice before serving and dust with Old Bay.

AUGUST

PRETTY WEEDS

Just before full darkness, there's the pale blue of antique mason jars on the western horizon, where Venus rises with tangled hair and the night sky fills with the Moon. When All Things Ripen. Canning season begins as corn and tomatoes near the end of their growing season in the failing summer heat. Sagittarius takes aim amidst the ripening sky, poised to loose an arrow tipped with steel and old wives tales.

Snakes go blind during the
dog days of summer.

I t was late August and I had been driving east for just over an hour, initially rushing out of Washington, DC, on US Route 50, slowing down some on Route 301, and eventually easing into a 50 mph 4th-gear amble on Route 213 that my old truck seemed to appreciate.

The sun was coming up, and along with the red barns and tall green corn fields of Kent and Queen Anne's Counties, there were tiger lilies, Queen Anne's lace, and black-eyed susans blooming beside the road. Some of these flowers grew naturally, while others were courtesy plants of the Maryland State Highway Administration. Seeing them reminded me of an ex-girlfriend who came fishing with me years before one August, a beautiful, good-hearted, and patient woman who walked and sat on a lake dock while I paddled a borrowed canoe on a public millpond.

Much how a dollar can burn a hole in your pocket, at the time I had a new 6 weight fly rod that I was dying to fish. Technically speaking, I think I had actually owned the rod for about a month, but back then I was working as a marine mechanic's assistant making minimum wage and it had taken me a few paychecks to save up enough money to buy the matching fly reel and line. I finally had all three pieces assembled and was just about out the door when Maria called to see what I was doing for dinner.

"I'm about to head out to Unicorn Lake. The reel and line I ordered finally came in the mail and I wanted to see how my new rod fishes."

"Oh, okay. I can come if you want," she said tentatively, more a question than an offer.

Time and experience had taught me that the addition of a girlfriend to a fishing trip could be problematic. The two worlds of women and fly fishing were simply too big to co-mingle easily, and I was too heavy-handed to manage them simultaneously with finesse. Some trips had ended badly because of things like mosquito swarms and oars banged against canoe hulls, while others had worked out just fine. But even then, at best bringing Maria along meant an abbreviated trip: a chaperone is still a chaperone, regardless of their intentions.

It felt like she and I had been hot, tense, and fighting for most of the summer. We had both recently graduated from college, me one year late. I was looking for work in Washington, DC, or Baltimore, while Maria had begun teaching in a local elementary school. Between broken air conditioners, meager bank accounts, and the emerging reality of our lives taking us in different directions, it felt like we were always on the edge of a fight. My pause after her offer was all she needed to start getting worked up.

"I've got to work late tomorrow, and then you work early on Wednesday. I just wanted to see you. It's fine. Just call me when you're done. Or come over later. Whatever."

I could tell that she was trying to be reasonable and understanding, but the disappointment was there, along with a fair piece of politely disguised frustration.

"No, come with me. I shouldn't be too long and we can grab dinner afterwards. I really just want to see how the rod casts; it's not a real fishing trip."

So we went. We drove out to Unicorn Lake together, east out of Chestertown, through the green cornfields and dry wheat fields waiting patiently for harvest, as the sunlight began to weaken and the air began to cool.

I don't remember catching much that evening, but I do remember liking the rod a lot. I had been fishing the local millponds like Unicorn quite a bit that summer because they were close by, full of fish, and offered easy shore and stream access to guys like me who didn't own a boat. I had put a lot of thought into the outfit, wanting something stout enough to handle a decent largemouth and cast a mid-sized foam popper with ease, but still light enough not to over-muscle a decent bluegill.

Even casting from a seated position in the canoe I could tell that the rod and line were well matched. I was making big casts with accuracy after just a few practice casts, and the rod was light enough to let even some of the smaller bluegill show off. I was looking forward to years of fish and happiness with my new 6 weight as I started working my way back to the boat ramp, casting against shore lines and hooking the occasional fish as they hit the popper with slow, deliberate takes.

As I paddled closer, I saw Maria at the dock by the boat ramp. She was smiling with a big bouquet of tiger lilies, Queen Anne's lace, and black-eyed susans in her hands. It was hard not to smile at the sight of her.

"One of the park guys said that I could pick all I want. He said that they're basically just pretty weeds," she said, real excitement in her voice.

Maria was a young music teacher, blonde and full-bodied, a lover of dogs and deadbeats, and a secret and surprising knockout. She was shy with a mild, easy-going personality and tended to play down her looks rather than play them up. She wore glasses, read Wally Lamb novels, and preferred staying in to going out.

As I landed the canoe, I could see that Maria had done a very professional job with the bouquet. The flowers had been picked and arranged proportionally, with the pointed, deep-red and orange tiger lilies acting as the focal points while the rounded yellows of the black-eyed susans provided a fullness to the grouping. Even the intricate white circles of the Queen Anne's lace offered a nice accent of color and texture.

Consistent with her personality, she had even been forward-thinking and inventive: I saw that she had dug through my truck and found a newspaper and wrapped it around the bouquet stem and even used two plastic grocery bags filled with a little lake water to keep the flowers fresh. All of this was tied up neatly with some old twenty-pound monofilament line that she must've found behind my seat.

We drove home to Chestertown that night with the windows down, the full bouquet of pretty weeds resting on Maria's lap. Each time we stopped before we got into town, we could hear the crickets and katydids singing in the fields and trees. It was one of the last times that I remember both of us being relaxed together, where the inescapable summer heat, our diverging life paths, and my mid-twenties male idiocy hadn't pushed us into a constant state of tension, disappointment, and argument.

That night when we got to my apartment, she put the flowers in a plastic pitcher that I used for iced tea since I didn't have a vase. My air conditioner had broken and my apartment was so hot that we weren't hungry. We drank two cold bottles of Corona from my fridge, skipped dinner, and took a cool shower together to wash the sweat and lake water off ourselves.

I remember taking her clothes off that night and thinking that the lacy edges of her white bra seemed to echo the light pattern and texture of the Queen Anne's lace. I remember unhooking it, sliding the straps off her shoulders, and wondering if she saw the semantic connections of our evening at Unicorn Lake: Queen Anne's County and Queen Anne's lace, Maryland and Maria, summer ending and a bouquet of pretty weeds that wouldn't last until September. I remember almost asking her or saying something. There was a fan pointed at the bed to cool us, and even after our shower, there was still the mild and piney smell of bug repellent on her skin, oddly comforting proof that she had chosen to spend an evening on the water, on my terms.

Maria's bouquet sat on my kitchen table for about a week after that trip to Unicorn Lake, a feminine reminder of her that felt out of place in my bare apartment. Once the tiger lilies wilted, I threw the whole thing out even though the other flowers were still strong and vibrant. The bouquet looked nice in my kitchen, but I missed having iced tea easily available.

Maria and I had driven together on many roads through Kent and Queen Anne's Counties, and years later driving on them again caused these memories to bloom. There were the visual reminders of her along the road, but as I drove through a familiar part of the Eastern Shore, I also felt like I was back in a similar position, back in the same directionless and uncertain August of my mid-twenties.

I was unemployed and heading back to Kent and Queen Anne's Counties for an easy day of fishing. I wasn't looking for a challenge. I wasn't looking for sport. I wanted the mindless simplicity of fishing on familiar waters, driving on familiar roads, and fish. Easy, willing fish.

* * * * *

By mid-August of most years, I start to get tired of the night fishing and crack-of-dawn necessities of summer fishing of the Chesapeake, and by the end of July, the appeal of catching stripers from the darkness on either side of dawn and dusk starts to wear thin. By late summer, I end up feeling like I'm putting more in than I'm getting back, with the early mornings, long drives, and middle-of-the-night tide changes. So, by August, I tend to take a breather from the saltwater until the heat starts to break and the beginnings of a fall pattern begin to emerge on the bay.

Kent and Queen Anne's Counties have a few millponds that are special to me: small lakes like Urieville, Tuckahoe, Wye Mills, and Unicorn. They're larger than your average pond, but smaller than most lakes, with warm, shallow water and exceedingly healthy populations of bass and bluegill. The edges of these millponds are lined with cat tails and pickerelweed and lily pads and some of them even have bunches of sunken Christmas trees set off banks to provide cover for baitfish and fishy looking structure to cast at. The water is incredibly full of life.

The good news is that these millponds aren't fished too hard since most locals fish the tidal rivers for serious bass fishing, or the bay itself for what most would call real fishing. The bad news is that sometimes by midsummer much of the water on these lakes can be nearly completely covered in a stringy algae. It doesn't always happen, but it can make paddling difficult and leave only a few open areas for casting.

But either way, once a popper or other dry fly hits a piece of open water, the fish won't be shy about it, and they'll make an aggressive strike at it as soon as the fly lands in the water. Once hooked, the fish will plane off on its side and sometimes between the algae and the overall size of the bluegill, it's tough to tell exactly what's on the end of the line until you have the fish in hand. You spend the first few seconds fighting the fish wondering, "Is this a big bluegill or a small bass?"

What makes these waters unique from other ponds and lakes I've fished are the dammed ends with small waterfalls and spillways, and the beginnings of a moderately paced freshwater stream leading downstream to a tidal river.

Some of these spillway streams flow through thick forests where roll casts are necessary in most places, and even casual casting standing in the stream itself is difficult because of all the tree branches. Other millpond streams are within well-maintained, parklike settings, where there's a mown lawn, open areas for casting, and even picnic tables and public bathrooms nearby. Either way, the shade from the trees, the oxygen from the spillway, and the moving water help keep the fish happy and active when other waters and lakes are bathwater warm.

From the millponds and their spillways, these streams spread out and work their way downstream to the Chesapeake where they eventually begin to taste the saltwater as they connect with the tidal freshwater rivers like the Chester and Choptank.

The streams themselves can fish very well, down from the principal spillway pool, through the thick forests until the creek starts to take on that marshy feel that comes with small tidal creeks, where you're more likely to catch a perch or small bluefish than a bluegill. In these upper reaches of tidal creeks, you can catch bluegill and crappie, largemouth bass, and chain pickerel, even carp or catfish at times. There can be the standard eddies and boulders that most streams have to hold fish, along with a healthy amount of "bassy" structure like tree branches and shady undercut banks.

The lakes themselves can fish especially well, and I've always caught my largest bluegill in them. Just launching a canoe or kayak and working shorelines with a light rod and a small popper can lead to fish, with the best fishing being away from the banks most easily accessed by foot.

If I sound sentimental about millponds and their spillway streams, it's because I am. I learned how to fly fish on water like this casting a 3 weight rod one spring, until I finally felt what it meant to throw a loop. Years later, I proposed to my wife Hannah next to waters like this, I spread a good dog's ashes in its stream waters, and I brought my son here after he was born. Somehow through time and experience, you connect with a piece of water and begin to call it your own. Owning it isn't important, knowing it is. These Eastern Shore millponds are mine in that way.

* * * * *

Route 213 is a two-lane road that takes its time passing through small historic towns and the surrounding farmland of Kent and Queen Anne's Counties. Somewhere between Centreville and Chestertown, my eyes drawn to the linear perspective play of the tall corn field rows, I began noticing redwing blackbirds. A few of the birds were mid-flight with that signature flash of red at their shoulders, while others were watching the traffic drive by from their power line balconies.

Redwing blackbirds are a symbol of the country here to me, the open farmland that borders tidal rivers and marshes, the kind of places that, as it happens, are some of my favorite places on earth. Much like pumpkinseed sunfish with their bright yellow and turquoise sides, there's that same unexpected bravado of color in a redwing blackbird that's always a surprise, and it's impossible not to notice that flash of perfect red at their shoulders. Sometimes, if you're close enough, you might notice the subtle edge of pale yellow against the red and black as well.

I didn't have a real formal plan driving over to Kent County, really just a target destination followed by some options that I'd choose from once I was settled. I mainly just wanted to fish some of the millponds that I knew of—starting at one, working my way over to another, and eventually ending at some farther south as I fished my way back home. Between them there'd be a good bit of driving, but I'd have my share of three to four lightly fished warmwater lakes full of bass and bluegill. And if I timed things right, driving between lakes and taking a long lunch in town, I'd be off the water during the hottest parts of the day.

It was just about 6:30 a.m. on a Wednesday in August when I pulled into the Urieville Lake parking area and I felt some selfish relief to see there were no other cars parked there. Most people were at work, and anyone else who did have the day off to fish had around twenty other better places to choose from. The lake itself was covered with a thick mat of algae, so I headed straight to the spillway stream.

Urieville has a concrete dam at its southern end where lake water spills over into a concrete spillway that runs underneath Route 213. You can barely tell that it's there from a moving car, but once you park, cross over the road, and walk down a little hill, there's a nice spillway pool bordered by large oaks and maples and well-worn paths down each side of the stream. A few larger trees have fallen across the stream making for some interesting structure and current seams at the tail of the main pool.

This stream running from Urieville is one of the branches of Morgan Creek, which empties into the Chester River, one of the main tributaries of the middle Chesapeake Bay. The spillway stream is freshwater, but the dividing line for tidal waters is less than a mile away where Mills Road crosses over it. Because this water is so close to the main stem of a tidal creek and river, there are seasonal visitors and holdovers like white and yellow perch, pods of big carp, and the occasional baby striper.

I picked one side of the stream and began working line out with a series of roll casts until my fly landed along the far edge of the spillway where the water rolled off the lip of the concrete and there was an edge tucked under where some of the larger fish liked to hold.

I was fishing a lightly weighted white crystal bugger that I could see in the clear water, its marabou tail waving and its long body hackles pulsing seductively. I retrieved my first cast back to me with quick aggressive strips and an occasional pause, working it right along the spillway edge with no takes. On my next cast I gave the fly a few twitches once it landed across the stream, but I mended a little line and let the current wash it downstream to swing above where a bush jutted out into the pool.

I watched the fly drift down in the shaded water when, all of a sudden, I couldn't see it anymore, and my line was tight and my rod was arced downstream. I knew immediately that it was a bass—nothing else fought with that muscular, dogged determination. The fish bolted for the shelter of one of the logs crossing the stream, zigzagged back and forth across the pool, and used the current at its back to fight until I finally had it near my feet. I could tell that it still had a little spirit left, so I netted it with the small wooden net hanging at my back. The fish might've been two-and-a-half pounds long with a healthy gut on it. It wasn't a trophy, or even one of the larger fish I had ever caught there, but I was impressed with it— not sure if it was pride or surprise that had fueled the fish to such strength.

The largemouth bass in these spillway streams are different than pond or lake bass. It's not so much that they're bigger or stronger, but rather they're more conditioned. Maybe it was the shade and cool moving water, or maybe the salinity downstream helped charge them. Either way, the incredible pull of this Urieville bass, when compared to a lake or pond fish of the same size, was simply remarkable. I released the bass and made a few more casts, but the feisty fish had thoroughly made a mess of the pool and spooked everything there with any sense.

I could wait the pool out, or move on to leverage what was left of the morning on fresh, un-fished water. It wasn't even eight o'clock yet and Unicorn was just twenty minutes away. If I left then, I'd still have the second half of the morning bite in front of me, and the coffee still left in my truck would still be drinkable. So I called it, walked back to my truck, and took off my wet wading shoes to let my feet dry off in flip flops as I drove to Unicorn Lake.

I looked out at the lake before I drove off. I'd driven an extra twenty minutes for two casts and one fish. Urieville Lake was nearly completely covered with a thick, green mat of algae and lily pads with dragonflies buzzing over them. I had hoped to explore more of it by kayak, paddling up into the northern end where stream water flowed into it, but the algae looked too thick to be passable. Maybe there were open pockets where bass could be targeted, where they'd lived and swam unmolested for most of the summer. I made a note to try to come back in early fall when some of the algae and vegetation had died down.

* * * * *

I'm not sure if there are any small fly shops left on the Eastern Shore anymore. I've seen two nice ones close over the past ten years, and I remember when they started popping up: Winchester Creek Outfitters in Queenstown and the Salisbury Fly shop in Salisbury. Frequenting places like these essentially threw gasoline on the fire of my growing obsession with fly fishing. I learned a lot, and enjoyed the long talks there with guys like Brandon White, John Baker, Joe Cap, and Mason Huffman. Through years of fishing and talking and casting rods outside these shops, I came to feel like I was a part of something, a growing movement of outdoorsmen who were looking at the Chesapeake Bay with new eyes.

I also remember hearing firsthand how hard these businesses were to make profitable, the markup, the amount of goods they needed to sell each month, and the incredible competition of online commerce.

These shops were certainly great spots to hang out, but I'm sad to say that I didn't spend all that much money in them because I was fairly poor at the time. Years later, when I finally had the income to give significant business to them, they started closing, and I had the bittersweet opportunity to buy flies and tackle at substantial discounts. Most of the good rods and reels went pretty quickly, but I remember buying dozens and dozens of dry flies for next to nothing.

Because of where each of these shops were located on the Eastern Shore of Maryland, the lion's share of the shop's fly selection was saltwater based and those had sold pretty quickly, but there were still plenty of what I thought of as western trout flies—dry flies like humpies and royal coachmen, big ant patterns with calf tail parachutes, elaborate hoppers, and turk's tarantulas—all of which didn't have much practical use on Chesapeake Bay tidewaters. With most of the shop picked through, I decided to buy a good bit of the leftover trout flies, probably around three to four dozen of the bushier dry flies and the smaller terrestrials.

When I walked up the register, the guy behind the counter asked, "Taking a trip out west?"

"No, not really. I just take my bluegill fishing very seriously," I said.

The guy seemed to get it and smiled, and without a hint of sarcasm he said, "Well, bluegill fishing is serious business." He emphasized the last two words and I like to think he approved of the flies' intended use.

* * * * *

I took my time driving back through Chestertown, past the cherry and elm trees lining Washington Avenue, and I saw the town where I had lived for six years. I drove past Washington College and the dorms and academic buildings where I had studied, where the students are forever young and beautiful. I drove past the houses and apartments where I had lived with friends and teammates, and past the dining hall where I had eaten countless meals.

Downtown I saw the cast-iron fountain in Fountain Park where Hebe stands at the top pouring water from an endless vase, surrounded on all sides by geese. I turned on High Street and drove past Stam's Drugstore, a small store smelling of mint and aspirin and medicated shampoo, where they still made milkshakes along the back counter soda fountain. I drove past the Imperial Hotel and the well-worn brick sidewalks bumpy with old age and tree roots, until I reached the end of the road, facing the Chester River with the schooner *Sultana* docked within sight of the beautiful colonial houses lining Queen Street.

I drove back through Chestertown trying to find a reason to stop, but I kept driving. I had checked on a town and a piece of water that I cared about and I saw that both were much as I remembered. I was suddenly very content to be driving on familiar roads in a truck full of fly fishing gear, with a kayak strapped to the top of my truck and a day of fishing ahead of me. The morning in Kent County was suddenly full of possibility and the ghosts of old girlfriends and unemployment had vanished with the headlights of passing cars.

This feeling of hope and well-being propelled me out of town and over the Chester River Bridge for the second time that day. Looking to the eastern bank of the river, I saw the marsh grass and the docked boats in the water with the spindly stakes of gillnets anchored in the soft river mud. I worked my way east out of Chestertown, back on Route 213, past the gas stations and convenience stores on the outskirts of town and into the working fields and farm country. I could see that it was that time of year when the growing season was advancing into harvest. On one side of the road the corn was tall and lush green, while on the other, the spring wheat was the dry golden brown of pie crust. I passed through Crumpton and Dudley's Corner until I was just outside of Millington and near the headwaters of the Chester River.

The parking area at Unicorn Lake was empty, except for a few cars of the park and maintenance guys who work there. I had another lake to myself, but I could feel the morning slipping away from me and the sun was getting higher in the sky. It was getting close to 9 a.m. by the time I had unloaded my kayak at the launch, organized my gear, and parked my truck in a parking space.

Unlike Urieville, Unicorn was mostly clear of algae and had the fresh, manicured look of arranged produce. The grass along the banks was freshly cut, there were tall stands of cattails tucked back into some corners with pickerelweed growing along the shore edges topped with purple flowers. Out on the water, the yellow pond lilies were blooming among the lily pad fields. Occasionally, a barn swallow skimmed over the surface of the lake, and here and there, bluegill popped at the surface. Farther back in the lake there were the violent splashes of bass.

I paddled away from the boat ramp across the lake to where a small island dense with trees stood out in the open water beside a stand of pickerelweed poking from the water of a shallow flat. I began casting my 3 weight first, a light rod that could serviceably handle small poppers, but really let the bluegill show off once hooked. I tied on a bright yellow size 6 Betts slider and worked it along the pickerelweed edges to begin my morning. And that was that. The fishing was consistent and, for a while, there was almost a formulaic regularity to it: cast, fish on; cast, twitch fly, fish on; cast, retrieve, pause, fish on.

Most of the fish would hit the fly as soon as it hit the water, but these tended to be smaller bluegill. The bigger ones would wait, finning under the fly as its legs stopped wiggling, watching it until they were sure it was passively edible. Then they'd take the fly with a surprising delicacy. Once the fish was hooked and in hand, it felt like their take didn't quite match up with their size and fight.

I worked the flat and the edges along the small pickerelweed field with consistent bites. Many of the bluegill were decent, but a few were the darkly colored bruisers Unicorn Lake was known for, each of them pushing a pound and filing my hand nicely. After a while, I paddled over to the small island, more for a change of scenery than because the action had died down. The island itself was packed full of trees and bushes, and their branches stretched out over the water, reaching for the sun. The southern side of the island always seemed to be out of the wind, and in this lee portion of the island, I could sidearm cast into the water beneath these overhanging branches where fish held, safe from predators, and waiting for some kind of insect to fall into the water.

By then I had switched to a hopper pattern in an effort to discourage some of the smaller bluegill. I made my first cast, slightly misjudging the distance and the hopper, hit one of the branches before falling into the water. As soon as it landed, the water boiled with the clear take of a largemouth. The fish darted and even jumped a few times before I could lip it from the water. It was a nice fish, maybe a little bigger than the Urieville bass from that morning, and an incredible fight on my light 3 weight. I was grateful for the stouter hook of the hopper and heavy tippet I used for turning a fly this big over. I might not have been able to land it twenty minutes earlier on the small popper.

I stayed along that bank for a while, protected in the lee portion of the island, working back and forth along the seldom-touched shoreline. I didn't pull in any more bass, but as the morning warmed to afternoon, the bluegill got more and more timid, losing their competitive and thoughtless gusto. I'd cast the hopper just against the shore, or right out in front of the overhanging branches, and we'd all wait. I'd wait for the fish and for the rings in the surface of the water to disappear, the fish would wait for something between courage and certainty.

The action became less and less frequent and I could see even the smaller bluegill waiting and watching, tentative and suspicious, watching the fly as it floated on the surface of the water, indecisive. The fish would start to rise, change their minds, and eventually take a half-hearted nibble and then swim away. I don't know if it was the drowsiness that comes with midday and waking at 4 a.m. or just the 1,000-yard stare that comes after a full morning of fishing, but it felt like the more I stared and waited, the less likely it was for a strike to come.

I think it was at that point that I reached behind me to the small cooler I had with me for a cold drink. The morning bite was over, and it was time to start thinking about next moves, lunch, and eventually heading back home. I stowed my rod in the rod holder, leaned back in my seat, and just floated on the lake for a moment with a cool bottle of iced tea in my hand and my paddle resting across my knees. I looked out at the water, south towards where a nice point jutted out, and remembered a time when I saw a doe swimming across the lake one summer, and the embarrassed look it gave me as it swam clumsily by.

It was getting close to noon by the time I started working my way back to the boat ramp. The sun was high and strong and the temperature had risen from the comfortable seventies in the morning shade to the low nineties of mid-afternoon. Sometime that morning, without even knowing it, I had put on my sunglasses and rubbed some sunblock on the back of my neck and arms. I dipped my hat into the water to soak it before putting it back on my head to cool me down for the paddle back.

I considered heading back to Chestertown for lunch and an old-fashioned vanilla milkshake from Stam's, but the pragmatist in me looked at the dashboard of my truck and saw less than half a tank of gas—just about enough to get me back to DC. Although the mid-afternoon lull in fishing certainly granted me the time for a cool indulgence like that, I decided to save a little gas and stick within the direct route home.

* * * * *

The concept and design of most flies not only match the forage and characteristics of the fish they target, but also the tone of the fishing itself. Fly boxes stocked with eastern trout flies have a subtle, understated traditionalism with their natural color palette, neat rows of small, perfectly sized nymphs and dry flies, and tasteful shine from a brass bead or peacock herl. Saltwater fly boxes lean more towards a gaudy utilitarianism with their brightly colored streamers, ample flash, and large stainless steel hooks. Even their size sets them apart, and these fly boxes tend to look more like toolboxes carried by emergency first responders when compared to a slim Wheatley fly box full of muddler minnows, royal coachmen, and hare's ear nymphs.

Warmwater fly boxes, on the other hand, exude the casual ease of summertime with their bright Latin American colors, the wiggly rubber legs and goggly eyes, and the soft foam bodies reminiscent of flip-flops and pool noodles. If there's a realism to them, it's a cartoon realism.

Over the years, I've spent a lot of time apologizing for an over-appreciation of bluegill, to myself and others, feeling insecure about how high it ranks in my list of angling priorities. Initially, I wrote it all off to just-getting-started goofiness, and that once I was a more experienced fly fisherman, I'd lose interest in bluegill and move on to the more glamorous species like bonefish and trout. My infatuation with bluegill never really faded though, and if this was part of an introductory phase, it's lasted quite a while. Lately I've come to accept that I'm old enough to like the things I like without feeling guilty about them.

When I first started fly fishing, I think I initially enjoyed fishing for bluegill with a fly rod because it was easy, but also effective. Once I got my casting down and had a fair understanding of what I needed to do on the water, it was nice to actually be rewarded with fish. At the same time, most of the public places that I fished hadn't seen many fly fishermen, so as a result, the fish were pretty unused to the subtlety of small poppers and other flies, so I did pretty well. I'll admit that there's a juvenile aesthetic associated with bluegill fishing, a simple pleasure like hot dogs or action movies.

Aside from the fish themselves, half of the joy of fly fishing is in the type of waters that you like to frequent. Some people need the cool, flowing waters of a mountain trout stream, others need the warm turquoise waters of a tropical flat. Fishermen who love these kinds of waters can look at them and immediately understand them.

These Kent and Queen Anne's Counties' millponds are like that for me. I like their purpose-born history along with the straightforward pleasure of their still and moving water fisheries. I like the idea of someone long ago using the waters here to power their livelihood: a simple miller or carpenter with a vision to expand, going about his day and making a nice pond in the process.

When these lands were just being colonized, in the town of Millington, known previously as Head of Chester, the Old Forge Mill was constructed before the Revolutionary War. It was later named Unicorn Mill from which Unicorn Lake gets its name. Unicorn Mill had a few uses as grist mill and a tan bark mill, but was most notably a textile mill that processed local wool. Just a bit to the east, in the early 1700s, Daniel Perkins acquired the water rights and built the grist mill at Urieville, which resulted in Urieville Lake.

Over 200 years later, on another level, I draw much of the same professional sustenance from the potential energy of these waters. When I fish the tidewaters of the Chesapeake Bay, I feel connected to an important body of water, and all the history and culture that comes with it. Millponds, with their agrarian history and blue collar fish, link me in the same way to the land and people of the Eastern Shore—the farms and fields, the roads and roadside produce stands, and the small towns connected by bridges and tidal rivers. All of the depth and reach of the Chesapeake Bay begins on a small level with these millponds.

* * * * *

The clouds forming in the late afternoon seemed like a welcome development after the harsh midday sunny skies, but soon the clouds thickened, darkened, and the breeze died down to an ominous silence. The afternoon sky had the greenish tint of a summer thunderstorm. What had looked initially like relief from the heat had turned mildly threatening. After a quick gas station lunch in Millington, I headed back to Unicorn Lake to focus on the shaded portions of the spillway stream, which tended to fish better in the midday when most of the other water was taking a siesta.

I had been fishing the head of the main spillway pool, casting an olive nymph with a bead head and gold ribbing up into where the water tumbled over rocks and entered the pool. I wasn't using a strike indicator, just maintaining contact with the fly as it drifted downstream and watching the tip of the fly line for any pause.

I was mostly catching smaller bluegill, along with one tiny crappie—certainly nothing noteworthy, but not bad considering it was getting close to 3 p.m. in August when most fish were drowsing in the deep water. After about half an hour of fishing I noticed that there was a gray, muggy stillness; then came a sharp warning shot of thunder off in the distance, and a few moments later, a hard, drenching rain began.

These late summer storms can wear themselves quickly, so I tried to wait it out underneath one of the covered picnic areas. At first I was comfortable and dry underneath the simple roof, as the temperature dropped and the growing breeze cooled me. I watched the rain and storm grow stronger and without the mindless monotony of casting and unhooking bluegill, my mind wandered back to my bank account and potential job leads that I needed to follow up on.

Soon the wind began shifting directions. The trees swayed back and forth and the leaves showed their pale backs as they shook in the wind, trying to keep their grip on the branches. The rain began falling at an angle, and the roof over me lost its value. I ran to my truck, pulled a bottle of cold water out of the cooler, and listened to the rain on the truck's tinny roof. I had the mid-afternoon lazies, and if I hadn't been damp with sweat and rainwater in a steamy truck, I might've dosed off. After about half an hour, the rain didn't seem to be letting up, so I decided to start heading south. If it was still raining by the time I got to Centreville, I'd stop for a snack and a drink to kill more time before heading home.

With my windshield wipers on their highest setting, I got one last look at the Unicorn Branch as I drove out of the park and I remembered an August years before when a pod of big carp had forged upstream from the Chester River and set up residence in one of the deeper pools there.

I had been casting small poppers up along each side of the stream and getting the occasional hit, when a pod of around six or eight fish—large fish—came into focus. They were holding in a deep channel of the stream, too big to be largemouth bass, and impossibly large for the small stream. They were so big in comparison to the rest of the stream that it took some time for me to actually notice them finning against the bottom. Within less than a second I went from happily casting poppers and noisily stripping them through the water to suddenly being afraid to move because I didn't want to spook these impossibly huge fish.

I knew that carp weren't real aggressive, that I had seen other fishermen use dough balls and corn to catch them, and that they weren't especially handsome fish. But there they were in plain view, noses in the current, with the biggest one at the front of the pod well over fifteen pounds. With no better plan, I tied on the biggest bead head nymph I had and started casting.

It was a little trickier than I'd anticipated. These were wary, intelligent fish in an incredibly healthy stream and they weren't going to waste any energy with an abundance of food drifting by in the current. Because they were ugly, I assumed that they'd be stupid and easy to catch. But after a few casts, I saw that they weren't the voraciously opportunistic feeders that bluegill were, or aggressive predators like bass. These carp were cautious, subdued, and spectacularly huge—and I wanted desperately to catch one.

I was about thirty feet downstream and my first few casts drifted well over them and they made no move to rise to take the fly drifting above them. Others drifted behind or alongside them. They ignored drift after drift in the clear, slow moving water and, eventually, they put off that spooked and annoyed feeling that heavily pressured fish exude after a while.

I walked away from the pool to rest it for a while and when I came back thirty minutes later, I could still see them. I knew my first cast would be my best shot at hooking one of these fish. I had finally guessed at the correct distance for an upstream cast, along with the drift and sink rate of my fly to essentially feed my fly to one of the carp's down-turned mouths.

I remember that initially there was no visible sign to tell that the fish had taken the fly. I could see them open their mouths occasionally but it wasn't what you'd call aggressive feeding behavior. It wasn't until the fish turned its head ever so slightly and it felt the resistance of the leader and fly line that the fish reacted and started running up and down the pool. The rest of the pod scattered.

It was the first time that I'd fought a sizable fish on a fly rod. It raced up and down the pool, well below a bend and right above a swift riffle, back and forth, and charging upstream with the drag from my reel screeching. Each time I played the fish close to me, it would take off on another run upstream to pout and shake its head in annoyance as it held steady in the channel. I knew that I couldn't control the fish at all, that it was still strong, and after a few minutes of back and forth, it was clear that the fish and I were at an impasse. Maybe I could've played the fish longer and tired it out, but out of desperation I tried horsing the fish into a slow eddy right above where the big riffle started, hoping that it would settle down some if I could beach it.

I was fishing a 6 weight at the time, with the ends of a warmwater leader ending with a few inches of 8-pound tippet. It wasn't ideal, but it wasn't too flimsy. Once the fish sensed the shallow water, only inches deep with its shoulders well exposed, it made one last surge and into the beginnings of the riffle. From there the current caught it, it gained momentum, and headed off downstream into swifter water and another bend in the stream. I tried one last time to turn it, but the current and the strength of the fish were too much and the line broke.

Part of me knew that landing the fish would be difficult, but fooling a smart fish into taking the fly had been the principal goal. I was disappointed, but not shattered. Hooking a fish like that was enough. I drove home that night feeling confident that I could hook another one the next time I was back.

A few weeks later, Hurricane Floyd began its angry journey from the Florida coast and tore through the mid-Atlantic states. It dumped so much rain on us in Maryland that even after it dissipated, it took a few weeks for the tidal rivers to clear up and the bay to get back to normal. Less than a hundred miles inland from the coast, Unicorn Lake grew dangerously full and the stream nearly crested its banks. One side of the stream eroded significantly and eventually had to be replaced with large granite boulders and the small steel bridge crossing it was closed for quite some time. Trees were uprooted and dislodged, creek channels were redefined, and the pod of giant carp was washed downstream to live the rest of their lives unmolested by young men with fly rods.

* * * * *

As I drove south in the rain, I stopped in Centreville for a cold coke and a slice of pizza, something between a snack and an early dinner since I hoped to be on the water through the early evening if the rain let up. Colosseum Pizza had its front door open to the street. The sound of the steady rain falling and the hiss of cars driving by came unimpeded into the restaurant, so the dining room had the cool dampness of a screened porch during a storm.

I was mainly just trying to kill time and wait out the strongest part of the rain, and after a second slice of pizza and a few minutes of cable news on the television, I headed back into the slackening rain. Fifteen minutes later I was at Wye Mills, looking at the bare space where the Wye Oak once stood beside the old mill house.

There was a gray, dripping stillness in the early evening as I got out of my truck. The storm had moved through but left the cooling temperatures behind it. Outside town and on the water, it actually felt refreshing to be outside. Although there was a break in the clouds to the east, the cloud cover and coolness brought the feeling of an early dusk as the light seeped in from the edges of the cloud cover.

The swallows were out in force, diving and gliding gracefully over the water as I began the slow paddle away from the boat ramp. My first few casts were ignored, although at one point, I saw a young bass following my fly with a wary curiosity.

During times like this, when even the subtle movement of a small slider with it's wiggly legs and cup-less face fail to work, sometimes I'll switch over to a bushy dry fly. This is a luxurious departure from warmwater standards because you have to treat these dries with floatant to stay buoyant, and they seem to get bogged down by the string's algae a little more than a standard popper or foam beetle would. It's a little more work with the cleaning and the casting, but it's an exercise in subtlety that can work when nothing else does.

I'd fished two of my favorite millponds on the Eastern Shore, and the last part of my trip at Wye Mills had a feeling of seasonal conclusion to it. In the damp coolness of a beginning dusk on the water, I had the feeling that the heat had broken, and that within the space of a few weeks, the beginnings of harvest season would be upon us. There was no denying that the storm was a summertime storm, but it had the edges of fall, with the steely gray skies that hinted at the upcoming season. Many of the cattails still had the perfect cigar brown of summer, but a few were starting to tatter and fray like cotton. For now though, it was still undeniably summer, and red-eared sliders poked their heads from the lake waters, and watched from downed timber at the pond edges.

This last pond was a waiting game. I imagined the pond before the storm, of the fish having that electric aggression of striking a popper as soon as it landed, charged by the growing storm. Now that the storm had passed, the fish seemed to be coming out from their cover, hesitant to feed until they felt comfortable with the water that had been stirred and doused with heavy rain.

My casts against the flooded timber and cattails waited. I'd twitch the fly mildly and eventually they'd sink just beneath the surface, and I'd twitch the fly again. A few bluegill committed to the sunken dry flies, brave, dark, deep-bodied fish that fought even after I had them in hand. After I released the last one, I switched to a large hares ear nymph, and worked the same water with better results. The fish came more frequently from the deeper water near the timber and cattails, mostly medium- to large-sized bluegill, with one heavy crappie thrown in for good measure. Off in the reeds, the redwing blackbirds called and sang in a language that I could easily recognize but not quite understand.

I fished through dark, hoping for one good largemouth that didn't come. I ended the night with my 8 weight and a furry foam wooly bugger, but the bass couldn't be tempted, so I paddled my way back to the boat ramp and loaded my truck for the ride home, thinking in the dark of bass, the "Help Wanted" section of the newspaper, and job applications.

* * * * *

Throughout every moment of that millpond trip through Kent County I felt an unavoidable and hyper-conscious tension between being worried about unemployment and trying to enjoy the present. Years before there was that delicious moment when that pod of huge carp came into focus directly in front of me where I was caught between being paralyzed with surprise and an intense desire to take action. And I guess on a literal level that there's the clearly defined boundary between tidal waters and freshwater that's drawn on the upper reaches of these millpond streams, and on a larger scale, Maryland itself, a small humble state situated between the North and the South. And even August, a pensive month full of pretty weeds and bluegill, brooding at the end of the summer and the beginning of fall.

All of this maintains the idea of living, and sometimes struggling between two separate realities, whether they're economic, mental, physical, or temporal. It's not a study in right or wrong, or choosing one side over another, it's just August in the middle of a fishing life, and a moment of thought before another cast.

Panfish
BLT Sliders

My sisters always avoided eating fish that my father brought home after a day of fishing.

"We want fish sticks," they'd say.

He always looked a little wounded as the food sat untouched on their plates saying, "But this is better than fish sticks! It's fresher!"

Along with being a fisherman, he was a surgeon, so knife work came naturally to him and he was proud of the amount of meat he could get from a small panfish. But my sisters were adamant and avoided any fish he brought home.

"It's weird," they'd say in unison, and the fish would sit on their plates untouched and my mom would start to boil spaghetti.

Conversely, I think I had the boyish fascination with gross things that older brothers develop alongside sisters, and I loved the fact that we could eat something we caught from a pond, something that minutes before he cooked it was a bloody, scaly mess in the kitchen sink. The fact that it grossed my sisters out was just icing on the cake.

One day after he came home from fishing, he cleaned his fish (a mixed bag of bluegill, catfish, and small largemouth bass, if I remember right), and instead of his usual approach of frying the fish in vegetable oil, he used a cast iron skillet that had the ample leftovers of bacon grease from the morning's breakfast. This simple adjustment, unsurprisingly, changed everything. My mother raved, I ate three servings, and my sisters begrudgingly admitted that although his fish still wasn't better than fish sticks, it wasn't quite as weird.

Ingredients

- Bacon
- Panfish fillets
- Milk
- Salt and pepper
- Masa flour
- Cornmeal
- Garlic powder
- Black pepper
- Soft dinner rolls
- Mayonnaise
- Lettuce
- Roma tomatoes

Directions:

Cook bacon in a seasoned cast iron skillet or non-stick pan until crispy and set aside to dry. Save pan and bacon grease. Ideally, you will have a decent layer after cooking three-quarters of a pound of bacon, enough to pan fry a few batches of fish fillets.

After panfish have been cleaned and filleted, check for bones and soak in milk for 1 hour. Remove from milk, pat dry, and lightly season with salt and pepper.

On a dinner plate, add masa flour, cornmeal, garlic powder, and black pepper. Mix ingredients thoroughly and coat fillets evenly.

Bring the bacon grease back up to medium heat.

Fry fillets in bacon grease until a deep golden brown, around two to three minutes per side. Set aside with bacon to dry. If bacon grease is nearly all soaked up, add butter to the pan.

Serving Suggestion:

Use dinner rolls and small fish fillets to make small sandwiches. Top with lettuce, thinly sliced Roma tomatoes, and bacon.

ACKNOWLEDGMENTS

Writing is a fundamentally solitary profession but the process of publishing a book takes far more than one person. That saying about about it taking a village to raise a child, well, the same holds true for writing a book. There truly was a village of friends and family behind me as I wrote this book so I wanted to take a moment to formally thank everyone involved.

Before everyone, I want to thank my wife, Hannah. In the years that it took me to write the proposal, win the business, and author the book, Hannah held down the fort with our two kids while I was off writing in cafes and fishing for "research and rejuvenation." Thank you, Hannah, for never making my writing (or fishing) an uphill battle and for letting me go when I needed to go. I know that I'm not easy, but at least you can say that you're married to a man who deeply loves the things that he loves, and strives to finish the things that he starts. Also on the family side, I'd like to thank my dad for always taking me fishing, and my mom for buying me my first fly rod.

Next, I'd like to thank Danielle Spradley. Danielle is the talented St Louis based artist who carved and printed the chapter header images and cover art for the book. She was the first to partner with me on the project—before we even had a publisher interested—but even more important than providing the visual depth that gives the book such a distinct and rural character, she made me accountable. Art oozes out of Danielle naturally. Writing for me comes begrudgingly. So often over the course of the writing this book I'd slacken and dawdle, struggling to finish a sentence or complete a scene. The thought of keeping pace with Danielle was what usually pushed me into writing again. Thank you, Danielle, for being such a professional, for your genuine excitement in creating gnarly shit, and for being a true partner though all of this.

I'd also like to thank Jennifer Bodine for the use of her father's beautiful images within this book. As I looked for inspiration early in the my writing I came across two books of A. Aubrey Bodine's images, *My Maryland* and *Chesapeake Bay and Tidewater*. These books had been gifts from my mother that I'd enjoyed years before, but seeing how Bodine divided Maryland and Virginia into two bodies of work helped me break down the Chesapeake Bay into my own workable pieces. I didn't have high expectations when I reached out and asked if there'd be any interest in licensing the images for my book, so I was completely surprised and humbled when Jennifer agreed. Before that point I was a bum with an idea and a laptop—after that, I felt legitimate. If Bodine could take me and my book seriously, I could take myself seriously.

To add further that debt of legitimacy, I'd like to formally thank John Gierach and Merle Haggard. I mentioned their influence on me earlier in the book so I won't belabor the points, but I actually reached out to each of these men while writing this. Although both declined my request to use their likenesses in one of Danielle's wood carvings, the very fact that they were polite enough to write back and consider my offer further added to that sense of legitimacy. Despite having heard two polite "No's," within the space of a few weeks, I felt like I was gaining momentum. The project was real enough for two very well-known and respected men to consider it, and this gave me confidence to finish.

Special thanks goes to Kathy Wagner and other members of the Washington College community. I've been fortunate to have a number of professors over the years (John Wenke and Michael Waters from my time at Salisbury University come to mind specifically) but Kathy was has always been one who did more than teach or guide me: she made me feel like a writer and that I could be successful at this if I put in the work. That belief had a big impact on me. Knowing how to write was one thing, believing that I could actually do it was something else entirely. Special thanks also goes to Josh Young at the Chesapeake Bay Foundation.

Along with Kathy, I'd like to thank Sarah Ensor and Michelle Strunge for their collaboration and first-rate editing. I'd also like to thank Michael Buccino for always having time to talk about ideas, and Chef Chuck Reeser for reviewing my recipes and showing me upscale Chesapeake Bay cooking during our time working together at the Imperial Hotel.

My career in advertising creative has blessed me with an army of designers and art directors who've helped me with this book over the years. Structurally the book has a number of elements to each chapter and visually tying them together took some finesse. I'd like to thank Keith Fleck, Alison Medland, Carrie Seaver, and Molly Allen for all of their help, feedback, advice, and support.

On the other side of the business, I'd like to thank my mangers and mentors here at Skype and Microsoft for enabling me to see this book through to the end. Many companies pose behind a work/life balance, but I've never known true balance until my role here. Special thanks goes to Charlotte Ospici and Joe Nick.

Lastly, and in many ways, most importantly, I'd like to thank my editor, Dinah Roseberry, and all the great people at Schiffer who believed in this book and made it a tangible reality. Thanks for letting me write the book I wanted to write and for all of the support you've given me. It's been great working with you all.